ON THE AIR

THE KING BROADCASTING STORY

THE KING
BROADCASTING
STORY

DANIEL JACK CHASAN

ISLAND PUBLISHERS
ANACORTES, WASHINGTON

Copyright © 1996 by Daniel Jack Chasan.
All rights reserved. No portion of this book may be reproduced in any form, or by
any electronic, mechanical, or other means, without the prior written permission of
the publisher.

Printed in the United States of America.
Published by Island Publishers, Anacortes, Washington.
Distributed by Sasquatch Books, 615 Second Avenue, Seattle, Washington; (206) 467-4300.

Cover and interior design, graphics, and composition: Rohani Design,
    Edmonds, Washington
All photographs are from the archives of Dorothy Stimson Bullitt.

Library of Congress Cataloging in Publication Data
Chasan, Daniel Jack.
On the air: the King Broadcasting story / Daniel Jack Chasan.
    p. cm.
    ISBN 0-9615580-6-7. — ISBN 0-9615580-7-5 (pbk.)
    1. King Broadcasting Company—History. 2. Bullitt, Dorothy
Stimson, 1892–1989. I. Title.
PN1992.92.K56C53   1996
384.54'06'573—dc20

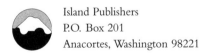

Island Publishers
P.O. Box 201
Anacortes, Washington 98221

CONTENTS

CHAPTER ONE

ROOTS OF AN EMPIRE
1892–1946

ONE COOL SUMMER DAY in 1990, the Seattle media converged on the turn-of-the-century Stimson-Green mansion on First Hill. The half-timbered structure at Minor and Seneca Streets, with diamond-shaped leaded glass in its upper windows, had been built when First Hill was a genteel neighborhood of single-family houses and unpaved streets. The brick first story reflected the third-little-pig prudence of a pioneer generation that had lived through the Great Seattle Fire of 1889. Its elegant but dim interior, muted by Persian rugs and runners, darkened by exposed oak beams and wainscotting, also reflected the tastes of its time.

A century later more than tastes had changed. Seattle boomed in the mid- and late 1980s, its economy propelled by Boeing's rapid growth, becoming a fashionable city with a high-rise skyline, the world center of computer software, the national mecca for espresso and grunge rock. The rapid growth of the 1980s petered out by 1990, but Seattle was certainly not the place it had been when the First Hill mansion was built. At that time, the city was the lone metropolis

As a symbol of Seattle's history and the people who shaped it, the Stimson-Green mansion—Dorothy Stimson Bullitt's childhood home on First Hill—was the appropriate site to announce the sale of the company she had built.

in the old-growth timber economy of Western Washington, a rowdy seaport with a booming red-light district, the supply center for gold-rush Alaska.

On this August afternoon in 1990, the Seattle media had been called to a press conference by Priscilla "Patsy" Collins, sixty-nine, and her sister, Harriet Bullitt, sixty-five, who were chairman of the board and chairman of the executive committee, respectively, and the main individual stockholders of the King Broadcasting Company, a six-state broadcasting and cable television empire founded by their mother, Dorothy Stimson Bullitt. Their grandfather, a one-armed pioneer lumber baron named C. D. Stimson, had built the mansion in 1900.

The King Broadcasting Company owned television stations in Seattle, Portland, Spokane, Boise, Twin Falls, and Honolulu; radio stations in Seattle, Portland, and San Francisco; and cable television systems in Washington, Oregon, California, and Minnesota. Analysts believed the company was worth up to $650 million. Before Dorothy Bullitt died in 1989 at age ninety-seven, *Forbes* had embarrassed her by listing her—inaccurately—as one of the 400 richest people in the United States.

Sitting at a table by the windows in the mansion's expansive living room, with its stone fireplace and grand piano, Patsy Collins and Harriet Bullitt announced that they were going to sell the King Broadcasting Company. Although the sisters carefully avoided mentioning a price, the press reported that they would ask more than half a billion dollars for the company and were in no hurry to sell. Bullitt was quoted saying, "There are certain people that we would *not* want to sell it to."

Earlier that day, the sisters had told shocked employees of the company's flagship Seattle station, KING-TV, that they had decided to sell. Word had gotten out, so the press people assembled in the mansion knew what was coming. Still, the announcement that the Northwest's largest broadcasting company would soon change hands was treated as big news. King Broadcasting Company had been in the Bullitt family since 1946. KING-TV had been the first television station in the Northwest, the first local station in the United States to bounce signals off a satellite, the first American TV station to editorialize against the Vietnam War. For five years, KING-TV had been the only television station in Seattle, and it had been one of the city's three network affiliates ever since. During most of that time, King Broadcasting had stood for something: it had often spent money on high-quality, public-minded documentaries and programs, rather than on shows designed to make the largest possible profit. It had earned a reputation for displaying political courage during a time when most broadcasters avoided controversy and for its frank political liberalism during a time in which most of its Northwestern competitors were blandly conservative.

The sale was "sort of an end to a wonderful period in broadcasting," said former KING-TV commentator Charles Royer, who had just finished his third term as mayor of Seattle. "King Broadcasting has been the standard against which anybody else [has] been measured," recalled retired executive vice-president of NBC Bud Rukeyser. "It was certainly the sense that KING was the premiere affiliate in the network." And for a lot of employees, the station was more than just another place to work. "I'm feeling a little sad," said KING-TV anchor Mike James, who had worked for the company since 1966. "It's the end of the family in a way." Jim Compton, who had worked for the company in the 1960s and 1970s, then had been a network correspondent in Washington, D.C., and London before returning to do commentary and features, recalled that "when I told people in London that I was going to work at KING, everybody was envious. They said, 'That's the greatest place in the world to work.'"

Patsy Collins and Harriet Bullitt had called their press conference at the mansion largely because it was owned by Collins and had more free space than anyplace else at their disposal. But they also knew it was an appropriate spot to announce the end of an era.

Their mother, Dorothy Bullitt, had lived there as a girl. Dorothy's father, C. D. Stimson, whose family had owned mills and timber in the Midwest, had come to Seattle in 1889, just in time for the fire that destroyed most of downtown, only months before Washington became a state. He built a mill on Shilshole Bay in Ballard, then a separate community north of Seattle. With his wife, Harriet Overton Stimson, and his son, Thomas Douglas, C. D. settled his family at what is now the corner of First Avenue North and Ward Street, on the south side of Queen Anne Hill. Every day, C. D. would tie his lunch to his saddle and ride his horse to Ballard, crossing a creek on a shaky wooden bridge.

Stimson's missing arm, which he lost in a childhood accident, never seemed much of a handicap. It didn't keep him from driving the first automobile in Seattle or even from smoking a cigar and tipping his hat to the ladies as he drove. It didn't keep him from playing golf, either. In 1909, when President William Howard Taft visited Seattle for the Alaska-Yukon-Pacific Exposition, he and C. D. played a round of golf.

Dorothy Stimson was born in the house on Queen Anne in 1892. Eight years later, her family moved to the mansion C. D. had built on First Hill. The neighborhood was "a peaceful, quiet enclave of unpaved, tree-lined streets, where lily ponds flourished, rose gardens bloomed, and children could safely ride their ponies at full gallop," described *Seattle Weekly* writer John Robinson. "Here, in vast, drafty wooden houses, which they had begun to build after the fire leveled most of the town below, lived the city's ascendancy. . . . Families knew each other almost too well. . . . It was a slow-moving life of tennis parties and Sunday night buffet suppers."

The Stimson family lived on First Hill until 1914, when C. D. built a Spanish-style mansion in The Highlands, an exclusive private residential neighborhood that he and several friends founded

A shrewd businessman, outgoing and athletic, C. D. Stimson was destined to become one of Washington State's wealthiest men.

north of the city. (Pioneer banker Joshua Green later bought the house on First Hill and lived there with his wife until 1975, when they died at ages 105 and 100. Green never made any substantial changes to the building, so that later, when Patsy Collins acquired it, she was able to restore it to authentic turn-of-the-century form.)

Dorothy Stimson was known in the neighborhood as a tomboy, but she also took piano and singing lessons and clearly absorbed some of her mother's desire to elevate the cultural level of her provincial metropolis. Harriet Overton Stimson, who had taught piano lessons before her marriage at nineteen, helped start the Seattle Symphony Orchestra Society in 1907. She brought her former music teacher from Michigan to be the orchestra's first conductor. Nellie Cornish, the founder and for many years director of the Cornish School for the Arts, remembered Harriet Overton Stimson as "tall, stately, with lovely white hair. She could look straight in the eye of anyone in Seattle, man or woman, and make him enjoy giving money to her causes." Harriet Stimson helped keep the Cornish School afloat financially; when she died in 1936, she was chairman of the Cornish board of directors, spending much of her time working on the struggling school's affairs. She also helped found what is now Children's Hospital and Medical Center.

Harriet Overton Stimson was active in civic and artistic causes in early Seattle. Daughter Dorothy's cultural pursuits were influenced by her mother's passionate interest in classical music.

At age sixteen Dorothy Stimson was sent East for three years of finishing school at Briarcliff Manor, north of New York City. She returned to Seattle and then, when she was twenty-one, moved to New York, where she studied singing, piano, and composition with private teachers and attended concerts and operas. She wrote some music reviews under a pseudonym. In 1914 she moved back to Seattle, where she lived with her parents in their new home in The Highlands and worked as volunteer for the Red Cross during World War I. In September 1917, she served as maid of honor at her best friend's wedding, and met the best man, a gregarious, highly political, Princeton-educated Louisville lawyer named Scott Bullitt, who was then serving his second term as prosecuting attorney of Jefferson County, Kentucky. The son of a Confederate cavalry officer, Scott Bullitt came from a long line of Southern lawyers and Kentucky pioneers who traced their roots back to a brother of Chief Justice John Marshall and a sister of Patrick Henry. He was a boxer and played football at Princeton—then the Ivy League school of choice for genteel Southerners—where he had taken history courses from the future president of the United States, Woodrow Wilson.

Although there was a fifteen-year difference in their ages, Dorothy Stimson and Scott Bullitt experienced love at first sight. They were married in May 1918, at the chapel in The Highlands. The couple moved to Louisville, Kentucky, and to Washington, D.C., while Scott, who had enlisted in the Army soon after their marriage, worked as a lawyer for the military. Dorothy Bullitt returned to her parents' home in Seattle for the birth of a son, Stimson, in 1919, and a daughter, Patsy, in 1920. After Patsy's birth, Dorothy Bullitt refused

Dorothy and Scott Bullitt with their children, Patsy, Harriet, and Stimson.

to leave her home town. Scott eventually joined her in Seattle. Their third and last child, Harriet, was born there in 1924.

By that time, Scott had made himself well known in downtown Seattle. His son, Stimson Bullitt, recalled that "When [C. D.] Stimson or his son-in-law, Scott . . . would walk down Second or Third Avenue, greetings were exchanged with about one of three passersby. This owed to the community being small, to [C. D.] having lived here for close to forty years, and to Scott's gift for friendship."

During the 1920s, Scott became a leader in the Democratic Party of the then strongly Republican state. He opposed Prohibition and the Ku Klux Klan; he favored free trade. In 1926, he ran for the U.S.

Senate against incumbent Senator Wesley Jones. Speaking from a platform between signs that proclaimed "Our Bullitt Is a Straight Shooter" and "Scott Bullitt Is Not a Double-Crosser," Bullitt drew the largest Seattle crowd that had turned out to see any Democratic candidate in recent memory. He lost to Jones, but only by 14,000 votes; Jones's last opponent had lost by 100,000. Bullitt then ran unsuccessfully for governor in 1928. Dorothy Bullitt evidently tolerated but never liked her husband's political activity. Although Scott Bullitt practiced law in Seattle, helped his father-in-law run the real estate business, and finally ran some of the original business himself, his heart wasn't in law or business. Politics were his real love. As head of the state Democratic Party, he became an early supporter of Franklin Delano Roosevelt's 1932 presidential candidacy.

Years before, Scott had become estranged from Dorothy's brother, Thomas, who had been helping his father run the C. D. Stimson Company. So in 1928, C. D. split his holdings between his son and daughter, giving Thomas the C. D. Stimson Company, which owned the Ballard mill and some of the real estate, and Dorothy the new Stimson Realty Company, which owned property in downtown Seattle.

C. D. Stimson had started buying downtown property in the 1890s. He built the ornate, Italian Renaissance–style Coliseum Theatre at Fifth Avenue and Pike Street in 1916, the first theater in the world designed explicitly for movies, as well as the Fifth Avenue Theatre up the street. He owned property on First Avenue and at Westlake Square and stock in the Metropolitan Tract. He built a fifteen-story, sandstone-faced art deco office tower at 1411 Fourth Avenue, which was completed in 1929. There is no evidence that Dorothy Bullitt ever took part in her father's business activities, any more than she took part in her husband's politics. But she was close to her father, and she seems to have learned a lot about business just by being around him—which turned out to be a very good thing. When Dorothy Bullitt was forty years old, in the depths of the Great Depression, she was plunged suddenly, traumatically, into the world of business.

In Dorothy Bullitt's time and social circle, women simply didn't run businesses, and she probably wouldn't have either if fate hadn't given her the chance. Her father had a stroke and died in 1929, before many tenants had moved into the 1411 Fourth Avenue Building, leaving Scott in charge of the Stimson Realty Company. Two years later, her brother Thomas was killed when a small plane he was flying crashed near Nespelem in Eastern Washington. Then, tragically, Scott died in 1932 after a short battle with liver cancer. Suddenly, responsibility for running the Stimson Realty Company fell in her lap—in the middle of an economic crisis. She had never really worked at anything for money.

In Dorothy Bullitt's time and social circle, women simply didn't run businesses, and she probably wouldn't have either if fate hadn't given her the chance.

Her plight should not be exaggerated. On one hand, she had lost her husband, her father, and her brother; she had three young children to raise; and she had to make a business survive during the worst economic conditions of the century. On the other hand, she wasn't exactly poor—at the end of 1932, Stimson Realty had a book value of over $2 million—and living in The Highlands trying to rent commercial real estate wasn't quite the same as living in a Hooverville shantytown and trying to make ends meet without a job.

Emotionally, it must have been a devastating time. Dorothy Bullitt recalled years later that she and the Stimson Realty Company's bookkeeper closed the door to the office, hugged each other, and cried. The tenant of her Coliseum Theatre had broken his lease. Bankrupt tenants of her 1411 Fourth Avenue Building left without even taking their furniture. But things could have been a lot worse. Seattle was a small community, the middle-aged and older men who ran banks and real estate companies had certain ideas of chivalry, and she got some breaks that a man in a similar position wouldn't have gotten, along with some practical advice. She "was handicapped not only by ignorance but by the difficulty of dealing with other business executives, all of whom were men," her son, Stimson Bullitt, has written. "Some refused to deal with her because they felt inhibited from shouting and pounding on the table, and others she could not deal with because they insisted on shouting and pounding on the table. On the other hand, some went out of their way to help her, in part because they did not regard her as a competitor. Her friend and neighbor, Bill Boeing [founder of The Boeing Company, who had left the aircraft business in 1934], whose business judgment was good, sometimes would give her advice when they saw each other in the office building elevator. [As well as a neighbor and friend, he was a tenant.] Whether they treated her well or ill, none of these men ever forgot she was a woman."

Dorothy Bullitt didn't rely exclusively on the kindness of strangers, or even of the people she had known socially all her life; she learned the business in a hurry. She went to New York and answered newspaper ads for commercial office space, just to see how other people went about selling it. She learned the details of the Stimson Realty Company's finances and of her buildings. Figuring in depreciation, the 1411 Fourth Avenue Building lost money in 1932, 1933, and 1934, but after that, the company started running on an even keel.

Before the decade was over, Dorothy Bullitt was looking around for new things to do. It is unclear just how she found her way into broadcasting. Years later, she told people that after World War II her son, Stimson, who had been wounded in the war, would sit around with his friends and talk about finding something worthwhile to do with their lives. They got interested in broadcasting, so Dorothy Stimson Bullitt went into the broadcasting business to provide an opportunity for these fine, idealistic young veterans. This was a nice story, and in the patriotic years of the late 1940s and 1950s it may have helped her gain the goodwill of federal regulators, but it was simply fantasy. She had been interested in radio before the Japanese bombed Pearl Harbor. (In fact, the war delayed her first step into broadcasting by about five years.) Whatever her real reasons may have been, they had nothing to do with helping veterans.

Broadcasting was certainly more glamorous than commercial real estate. It dovetailed with her lifelong interest in classical music. And it interested her cousin Fred. Fred Stimson had inherited what for the time was a considerable fortune, but he drank too much, he liked fast cars and grand gestures—lavishing huge tips, buying silk shirts for his friends—and by the late 1930s, he had run through all his money. He got enough cash to live on from Dorothy Bullitt, whose bookkeeper doled out to the one-time playboy the less-than-princely sum of five dollars a week.

The one thing that appealed to Fred—besides fast living—was radio. From 1938 to 1940, he worked at the Swanson Radio Shop as a repairman. He urged Dorothy Bullitt to get involved in radio. There is a good chance that she chose broadcasting at least partly because it would give her cousin Fred something to do.

She had certainly acquired an interest in radio by 1940, when she met Gloria Chandler, who became one of her closest friends. A short, heavyset, energetic woman with a huge collection of flowered hats, Chandler had been a children's theater director and had done radio broadcasts since around 1924. For years, she had worked for the Association of Junior Leagues of America, traveling around the country consulting with children's theater groups. In 1940, she started working on children's radio programs, as well as theater, for the Junior League. That year, the association held its international convention in Seattle, and Gloria Chandler wound up staying at Dorothy Bullitt's home. As Chandler remembered in 1953, "Mrs. Bullitt and I found that we had one interest particularly in common . . . an interest in radio. From that time on we kept in touch with each other. I saw her when she came east to New York and each time I visited Seattle after that I spent time with her. We had discussions particularly on the subject of radio."

By the time she met Gloria Chandler in 1940, Dorothy Bullitt may have already developed an interest in television. She saw television demonstrated in New York as early as the 1939 World's Fair. Television cameras covered the fair's opening ceremonies, caught the arrival of President Franklin D. Roosevelt's motorcade on opening day, and showed a close-up of New York's mayor, Fiorello LaGuardia. Perhaps a couple hundred people watched the programming on home television sets in the New York area. More watched a bank of monitors at RCA's Manhattan headquarters. Hundreds more watched the programming at an RCA exhibit set up at the fair. Spectators stood behind a steel railing and looked at a bank of big television console sets with screens on top pointing at angled mirrors in which one could see the images. NBC followed its initial coverage with regular broadcasts from the fair on weekday afternoons and broadcasts from its Radio City studio on Wednesday, Friday, and Sunday evenings.

Dorothy Bullitt not only saw television at the time of the World's Fair; either then or within the next two years, she recalled, she also "got some letters [of introduction] and was taken into some laboratories where these things were being developed. It was like going back in history to Edison or the telephone in the early [years], and these men were manufacturing great clumsy things that turned out to be electric light bulbs eventually."

During the mid-1940s, the Dumont Company, which manufactured television sets and also ran an early network, set up in Wanamaker's department store in lower Manhattan a television studio that the company claimed was the largest in the world. When Dorothy Bullitt saw a show being produced there, the studio was evidently more modest. "On the main floor of the store there was a little corner curtained off, and that was the television station. They were doing a drama with live actors and actresses . . . and to do this scene they borrowed a coffee table from the furniture department. . . . When the half hour was over and I was talking with the director and others, I heard him give an order to send the coffee table out to be [refinished], as the surface of the table had been blistered [by] the lights."

Dorothy Bullitt later claimed that she had been keeping an eye on television ever since that visit to the World's Fair in New York. "Everyone knew there was such an invention as a box you could have in your house that you could see as well as hear," she said. "I thought it would be quite a thing if we could get television in our homes."

After she had seen the laboratories and the broadcast from Wanamaker's, "I couldn't help thinking that if it was financially feasible, it would be a great thing that was coming. . . . From 1939 on, I learned all I could and talked and listened and read so that when the station in Seattle was offered for sale, I was ready."

––––––

Whatever thoughts Dorothy Bullitt may have harbored about television, her real focus as the 1940s began was FM (frequency modulation) radio. Radio was the main broadcast medium and it was very popular and lucrative, but it was virtually all AM. The AM (amplitude modulation) transmissions of the time didn't reproduce sound accurately though, and many moments were filled with static.

FM promised better sound reproduction and no static. It must have seemed a natural for someone who was interested in broadcasting classical music. Its inventor, Major Edwin H. Armstrong, had already made a fortune and a national reputation as an AM radio inventor. He had, among other things, created the superheterodyne, which made it possible to use a radio without an outside antenna. He sold his inventions to RCA for $200,000 and 80,000 shares of RCA stock, and became a personal friend of RCA's president, David Sarnoff. Sarnoff and RCA offered to buy FM from Armstrong for $1 million. But RCA saw FM as an adjunct, not an alternative, to AM broadcasting, and Armstrong, who saw it as a whole new medium, refused to sell. Armstrong was forced out of RCA's broadcasting studios in the Empire State Building, where he had been experimenting with FM, and his relationship with Sarnoff turned sour.

(Armstrong spent his last years and most of his money in patent fights with Sarnoff and RCA. Discouraged and embittered, he opened the window of his elegant East Side apartment and jumped to his death.)

Armstrong had a 400-foot FM broadcasting tower on the New Jersey Palisades, across the Hudson River from the city. He had another transmitter on Mount Washington, in New Hampshire, and other FM transmitters were broadcasting in Albany, New York, and at Connecticut State College. General Electric had started manufacturing

From the time she first heard music on the radio, Dorothy Bullitt was fascinated by the medium's possibilities.

FM radios. But FM was still a relatively exotic medium. Dorothy Bullitt herself had never heard a radio program broadcast in FM.

In April 1941, she made an appointment to see Major Armstrong. One evening at five o'clock, she left her room at the Roosevelt Hotel and went up to the inventor's thirteenth-floor Manhattan apartment, overlooking the East River. She found him a "very modest" man with "a great deal of charm." Presumably over cocktails ("over a cocktail," *New York Times* radio and television columnist Jack Gould wrote thirteen years later, "the Major could be cordiality itself . . ."), Armstrong told her about FM broadcasting, then turned on his FM radio to let her hear the Boston Symphony. The sound lived up to its reputation, clearer than any broadcast Dorothy Bullitt had ever heard. There was no static. The demonstration may have been much like the one a *New York Times* reporter described in 1939: "With a five-foot wire dangling from a Venetian blind in his home . . . [Armstrong] now reveals through a radio receiver resembling a standard console . . . that radio can be pure; that static can be kept out." Armstrong's demonstration impressed Dorothy Bullitt. But she had evidently been determined to start an FM station before she ever met him because she came to New York prepared to discuss transmitter sites with Major Armstrong.

Despite its clarity of sound, FM wouldn't take off for another two generations. World War II put FM's commercial development on hold for four years. By the end of the war, AM radio had improved its sound and lost its annoying static, reducing any competitive advantage FM may have had. Maneuvering by RCA's Sarnoff and others—who wanted FM's frequencies for television sound—pushed FM to a different spot on the radio frequency band, so it could no longer be found where its few listeners had grown to expect it. In addition, the rise of television made it obvious that FM would not be the medium of the future; radio in general was going to take a back seat.

In Dorothy Bullitt's opinion, FM also had something of an image problem. It had two things working against it, she told an interviewer in the 1960s. "One was the term 'FM.' If it had been given a name of any kind, 'Fine Music' or anything, [it might have succeeded]; but when people said, 'What's FM?' [and the answer was] 'Well, it's frequency modulation,' then they wished they hadn't asked. This was against it, and the fact that people didn't know the difference [between AM and FM]. I would sometimes be at a friend's house and say, 'Do you have FM? Do you receive it?' 'No, we don't have it.' Well, the set [was there] and FM [was] on it, only [they] never knew what that button [was] for."

But in 1941, FM struck Dorothy Bullitt as something new and promising, and she wanted in. The first step was finding a lawyer who knew his way through the labyrinth of federal regulations within which radio operated.

Somehow, she was introduced to a thirty-six-year-old Washington, D.C., lawyer named Andrew G. Haley. Haley knew everyone; he was, in fact, the person who set up her evening in New York with Major Armstrong. Notes for what may have been her first meeting with Haley, not long before she met Armstrong, observe that he was a "Tacoma boy"—no doubt a big plus with her, a Northwest chauvinist—and that he had been "put on law staff of the FCC by [Washington Senator Homer T.] Bone." Actually, Haley had worked for a different senator from Washington, Clarence Dill, and then, in 1933, had been placed on the staff of the Federal Radio Commission, the government agency that preceded the Federal Communications Commission (FCC). He helped write the Federal Communications Act of 1934, which established the FCC, the government agency that still oversees the broadcasting industry. Haley then worked for the FCC's law department, heading several of its sections, including those that handled complaints and investigations, decisions, and appeals. In 1939, he had gone into private practice, leading other people through the pitfalls of the legislation he had written and interceding with bureaucrats he had worked with or hired. Haley's expertise was just what Dorothy Bullitt needed. He would be perhaps her closest adviser for the next twenty years.

They made an unlikely pair. Haley was a big, loud, flamboyant man who wore expensive suits and drank a lot. When he left for the airport, he would sometimes pour a tall glass of whiskey and stick it in his breast pocket so he'd have something to drink on the way. At the Democratic Party's annual Jefferson-Jackson Day fundraising dinner, where people paid the then-astronomical sum of $100 a plate, Haley would reserve a table for twelve and sit right in front with his guests. But he was not simply a glad-hander. He knew the law, knew the broadcasting industry, knew how to carve up his opponents in a formal hearing, and knew how to negotiate. Deeply interested in technology, he started the Aerojet Engineering Company for the Army, to develop solid rocket fuels during World War II. He later became president of the American Rocket Society.

Dorothy Bullitt could not have succeeded—or even started—in broadcasting without Andrew Haley. The first thing she tried to do with his help was get a license for an FM station in Seattle. She was starting from scratch. In April 1941, she asked him for a copy of a General Electric booklet entitled "How to Plan an FM Station." The booklet proved sobering, suggesting that a new station might take two years to break even. That "seems a long time," she wrote Haley. "If other stations have had better experiences than that, I would be very glad to hear about them."

But she wasn't discouraged. By the end of April, she was already complaining to him that "our progress seems to be very slow." In early May, she sent him a check for $250, "signifying our intention to go ahead with the application." She told him that papers for a new corporation were prepared, but she didn't want to file them in Olympia until she had filed a license application with the FCC, "to reduce the gossip and conversation and carry out the matter as quietly as possible."

Dorothy Bullitt could not have succeeded—or even started—in broadcasting without Andrew Haley.

First, the new station would need a transmitter site. She had been thinking about putting the transmitter on a downtown building, possibly on top of the 1411 Fourth Avenue Building, but Major Armstrong had suggested that she set her transmitter up on one of Seattle's hills, preferably at the edge of a hill with a steep face. She thought the largely unused broadcasting studio at the Cornish School for the Arts near the western slope of Capitol Hill might be just the place. She figured they could erect a transmitter on the studio roof and rent the studio itself from Cornish. But she wasn't sure it would work. "Please tell me how we can get some technical advice as to whether or not this location would really give us good reception," she wrote Haley. "Since it may be the first FM station, I feel very strongly that the reception should not be faulty, as the receiving sets will have to be sold on the strength of the quality of the reception."

Haley put her in touch with an experienced East Coast radio engineer named William L. Foss. (Five years later, she wrote that "Foss alarms me sometimes with his quick, unconsidered answers and cost estimates, but I still think his engineering is good and careful.") Foss may have discouraged her about the Cornish School site; for some reason, Cornish dropped out of her correspondence, and a month and a half later she wrote to Haley about another Capitol Hill site, the brick water tower in Volunteer Park. She hoped he would get engineers to come up with specifications for an antenna and sketches showing how it could be fastened to the tower "with special consideration for its appearance because of its being beside a public place. There is a lily pond nearby that might serve as a ground." Two weeks later, Haley sent her Foss's blueprints of the Volunteer Park location.

In mid-September Foss went to Seattle, where he and Fred Stimson spent hours in government offices trying to run down topographic maps that would enable him to figure out how much of the city could be covered by a transmitter in Volunteer Park. Foss evidently looked at a number of transmitter sites and didn't care much for the ones Dorothy Bullitt had been contemplating; he preferred the forty-two-story Smith Tower, then the tallest building in Seattle.

Even before Foss's visit, she must have had her own doubts about Volunteer Park. At the beginning of September, she had told Haley she was thinking again of putting the antenna on the roof of 1411 Fourth Avenue and broadcasting from a studio in the basement.

Finding a site for the transmitter wasn't Dorothy Bullitt's only worry. One of FM's many handicaps was the shortage of people who owned FM radios, and she didn't know how fast manufacturers could produce enough hardware to create an audience. When Haley visited her office in September, they discussed the problem, and Haley wrote letters to a dozen radio manufacturers, asking if they could satisfy the anticipated demand for FM sets. On September 29, she telegraphed him, asking anxiously, "Have you received any answers from manufacturers of receiving sets as to their anticipated ability to fill orders? Please wire answer and forward whatever letters you may have, as soon as possible." He sent several manufacturers' letters to her the next day, and in mid-October he wrote, "I was wondering if your reaction to the letters from the FM manufacturers was as optimistic as mine . . . these manufacturers committing themselves to an optimistic outlook to me carries a conviction of dependability on which we might well rely." He told her that he had most of the details in place for a formal application to the FCC. She sent the completed application to him at the end of October. In November, Haley had Foss finish the necessary engineering work. They were ready to go.

At the beginning of December, Japan bombed Pearl Harbor, the United States entered World War II, and the FCC stopped processing license applications. Dorothy Bullitt's dream of broadcasting would have to wait.

Economically, for her city, as for the rest of the Depression-bound country, the war was a godsend. Seattle's port and shipyards boomed, and the Boeing Company employed up to 44,000 people to produce military planes. Profits at the 1411 Fourth Avenue Building soared, and Dorothy Bullitt started buying property in other parts of the city. But the war was not an easy time for Dorothy Bullitt or her family. Early in the war, she fought unsuccessfully to keep her longtime Japanese-American household employees, the Ohatas, from being shipped to inland internment camps. Her son, Stimson, enlisted in the Navy and was wounded in 1944. Her daughter Patsy's fiancé, an Army Air Corps bombardier, disappeared with his B-24 over Europe in 1944.

The war didn't dampen her enthusiasm for radio, however; she was merely forced to postpone her plans. Less than a year after V-J Day, Dorothy Bullitt formed a corporation to resume her hunt for a broadcasting license.

CHAPTER TWO

NOBODY LISTENING
1946–1949

F IRST, DOROTHY BULLITT HAD to find someone who could run the new venture. "We needed a businessman to head this," she said later. She knew that she herself wasn't the one to do it. Dorothy Bullitt was no administrator; she had a knack for being in the right place at the right time, she combined fiscal conservatism with a willingness to take big risks—and she had a talent for hiring able people. To run the broadcasting company that did not yet exist, she found Henry Owen.

Owen was a talented and experienced manager who had been hired away from Procter & Gamble in 1924 by Donald E. Frederick of Seattle's Frederick & Nelson department store. He had run the store until old Mr. Frederick died, when he left to manage Frederick's rival, the Bon Marché. During the war, he had been assistant regional administrator of the Federal Office of Price Administration for Washington and Idaho and served in the Army, leaving the military as a lieutenant colonel. Like Dorothy Bullitt, Owen tended to approach

Henry Owen was a charming Southern gentleman, as well as an experienced manager and a pragmatist who possessed the business skills Dorothy Bullitt needed to make the new venture work.

a subject indirectly, starting out with small talk and sneaking up on the main point. A smart, charming Southerner, Owen drove fast and recklessly even when sober and had a lifelong tendency to grab women, whom he addressed as "baby." But he was a man with connections. He was close to Senator Warren Magnuson and deeply involved in Democratic politics. He also maintained cordial relations with Teamsters Union leader Dave Beck. Beck started out as a Seattle union official, then ran the Teamsters on the West Coast, and became president of the national union before he was sent to prison for grand larceny in 1957. (In the early 1950s, Owen called a young KING-TV engineer into his office and explained that a friend was having trouble tuning his brand-new television set. Owen gave the young engineer an address and told him to go tune this friend's set for him. He told the engineer to be discreet about it. The young man went to the address and found that the special friend who needed his TV tuned in was Dave Beck.)

Owen's wife, Frances, daughter of the president of Whitman College and a member of the Seattle school board, had served with Dorothy Bullitt on the board of Children's Orthopedic Hospital. The two had become close. Dorothy Bullitt knew that Frances Owen's husband might be available. She also knew, she said later, that once upon a time, "Mr. Frederick had searched the country to find him." John Leffler, dean of St. Mark's Episcopal Cathedral and a close friend of Dorothy Bullitt for many years, observed that "her great ability was in picking the right person for the right job. If she thought someone was the right man, she'd do anything to get him." She had evidently decided that Henry Owen was the right man for this job, and she gave him a call. "He went to the library and took home an armful of books, great big books [about radio], and spent the weekend reading them, and came in and said, 'I'll go.' "

Why did Owen say yes? Dorothy Bullitt explained years later that since the company faced such an uncertain future, "we couldn't look for someone who was doing very well or had a very good job." It is true that Owen hadn't yet found a civilian job, and there were lots of returning veterans looking for work. But exactly why an executive of his experience would commit himself to a nonexistent broadcasting company isn't entirely clear. Possibly he liked the idea of getting close to the Bullitt real estate.

Whatever his motives, Owen did say yes, and on June 18, 1946, when Dorothy Bullitt incorporated her broadcasting company, he was one of the seven board members. The others were Dorothy Bullitt; her cousin, Fred Stimson; her son, Stimson Bullitt; her niece Nona's husband, Charles Clark; her lawyer, Ray Wright; and a younger lawyer, Dick Riddell, who had known Stimson Bullitt as a boy and who was to be the new company's attorney. Dorothy Bullitt, Fred Stimson, and Charles Clark were the three incorporators. The company was christened Western Waves, a name that Dorothy Bullitt said was just "picked out of the air."

She and at least some of her fellow board members had already decided to apply for an AM license at 1540 on the radio dial and an FM license for a transmitter to be built on Squak Mountain, east of Seattle, where Stimson Bullitt had bought property.

With her plans already taking shape, she didn't seem to pay much attention when Charles Clark reported to her in July his conversation with a rather pompous Boston radio expert. Clark, who hadn't yet graduated from Harvard business school, went to a vice president of the First National Bank of Boston and announced, as he described it to Dorothy Bullitt, that he "wanted to meet the top men in radio in that city." The banker introduced him to a Mr. Wright, who had once been program director of the big Boston radio station WBZ and was now in charge of buying radio air time for an advertising firm. Wright said he would introduce Clark to the men who ran Boston's radio stations, but he impressed Clark so much that the young man stayed and talked with him all day. Wright said the new company should just hire an experienced radio man to run the station, then get out of his way. That clearly wasn't what Dorothy Bullitt had in mind. By that time, she was already thinking about starting a 50-kilowatt AM station. Wright thought that building a 50-kilowatt AM station would be a big mistake. At that time, a stronger signal might still give a station a competitive advantage, but within five years, Wright expected FM to take over, greatly increasing the number of stations and forcing those stations to compete on the basis of programming rather than signal strength. (He saw the future clearly, but a generation or so too soon.) Besides, he figured, "some day television is bound to come in."

As for programming, he told Clark to leave his personal taste at home and aim for the lowest common denominator. Although Wright personally hated soap operas, he claimed, "The only thing that competes with the soap opera is music. The reason for this is that women can do what they have to do around the house and still listen to [soap operas] . . . the people who listen to them want escapism and they want to be able to get their work done at the same time. Experience has shown that people have to sit down to listen to a more serious program. Your idea about reading fifteen minutes a day from a good book is no good for many reasons; one is that women would realize they had to sit down to listen."

The better class of people didn't listen to daytime radio anyway. "You must also remember," he told Clark, "that . . . the upper income classes, who have the best taste, . . . are not radio listeners very often during the daytime. [But] the radio station [manager] whose programs offend you does not care. He is catering to the people who buy a suit with two pairs of pants."

Dorothy Bullitt wasn't intimidated by Wright's warnings about the future of AM radio. When FM did take hold, she figured the smaller AM stations would fall by the wayside first and a more powerful 50-kilowatt station would probably be among the survivors. Besides, although Clark didn't seem to have realized it, Dorothy Bullitt had already made her move. At the beginning of July, Western Waves sent Andrew Haley its FCC applications for the AM station at 1540 and the FM transmitter on Squak Mountain. A week later, Haley formally submitted them to the FCC. Western Waves got its construction permit for an FM station at the beginning of November, but an AM station in Waterloo, Iowa, that broadcast at 1540 objected to any competition, however distant, on that frequency. The FCC decided to hold a hearing on all the outstanding applications for 1540 AM, and scheduled a hearing in March 1947.

The resulting delay made Dorothy Bullitt and company think twice about their plans for FM. There were only two FM stations on the entire West Coast, and manufacturers still weren't making enough FM sets to create much of an audience. Because the Squak Mountain site would be expensive—the road up the mountain was bad, the site was all but inaccessible in bad weather, and construction costs would have to include road improvements—and because the AM station had the best chance of making money, they decided to wait on the FM station until they could start AM broadcasting or find a cheaper site. Dorothy Bullitt still thought about using the old brick water tower in Volunteer Park. "If we can get the water tower," she wrote to Henry Owen and Fred Stimson, "we could go on a six-hour-a-day operation—with one person playing records—a bare minimum of overhead and plenty of publicity." Instead, she and her colleagues decided to buy a couple of lots on Capitol Hill and put a transmitter there. Haley asked the FCC for permission to change the FM broadcasting site.

The new company wasn't just shuffling paper. Afraid that the price of transmitter equipment would go up, Western Waves started negotiating at least as early as July with the Western Electric Company for all the hardware it would need. In early September the company put money down on the new equipment, agreeing to buy it if the FCC approved Western Waves' license application. This commitment to buy equipment spooked Clark, who wrote to Dorothy Bullitt that he had "been led to believe" that the company wouldn't decide whether to actually build an AM station until the FCC granted it a construction permit. "Now, by the signing of this option contract . . . it seems we are obligated to go ahead." Clark thought this constituted "a definite reversal of our previous plans." He didn't like it. The next month, the Clarks sold 60 percent of their stock to Dorothy Bullitt.

The AM station would need call letters, as well as hardware, and Dorothy Bullitt had decided that she wanted the letters KING. Haley told her everyone wanted KING—but the call letters already belonged to the S.S. *Watertown*, an old merchant ship in the Atlantic. Legend has Dorothy Bullitt rowing out to the *Watertown* with a case of champagne and bartering with the captain for the call letters. Reality was more prosaic. Bullitt simply insisted that Haley get the call letters for her. Haley tracked down the ship's owner and phoned him in the Bahamas. The owner didn't care about the call letters—as Dorothy Bullitt put it, they were just dots and dashes to him. The *Watertown* would soon be decommissioned, anyway. The ship's owner

Legend has Dorothy Bullitt rowing out to the Watertown *with a case of champagne and bartering with the captain for the call letters.*

simply gave up the letters, with the understanding that Haley would make a donation to his Anglican church. (Haley may have also given him a case of rum.) In November, the Maritime Commission released the letters to Western Waves. "We are keeping this a dark secret for now," Dorothy Bullitt wrote at the end of November, "since so many other stations have tried to get KING and would be so green over our having it that they might send us time bombs in the mail."

As 1946 ended, Western Waves was in limbo, waiting for the FCC to hold its hearing. Dorothy Bullitt had decided against going for 50 kilowatts right away; she wrote Haley that she didn't have the courage to make the extra investment that a 50-kilowatt transmitter would cost. Instead, Western Waves was asking for FCC permission to build a 10-kilowatt station. Even that would be a substantial gamble. Seattle already had eight AM radio stations, and there was no reason to believe the market would welcome one more—particularly one that was located at the end of the dial. In January 1947, Arch Talbot, one of Dorothy Bullitt's tenants at 1411 Fourth Avenue, heard she was about to start a new AM station. Talbot already owned a station, KEVR, 1090 on the AM dial, with a studio and transmitter on the twenty-first floor of the Smith Tower, a tower on Maury Island, and a minuscule listening audience. Why didn't Dorothy Bullitt just buy KEVR from him? "It's on the bottom of the [ratings] list anyway," she recalled him saying, "and if you come in [with a new station] you are going to be below the bottom."

Talbot obviously figured she'd be a sucker: he asked $750,000 for a business that was losing $4,000 a month. She wasn't about to pay three-quarters of a million dollars or anything close to it for a station that she described as "quite definitely the bottom of the heap here in town," but she figured that with decent management, KEVR should be able to do well. In fact, she figured that "there is very little excuse for a station in that position losing money." It was doing badly because by his own admission Talbot didn't pay much attention to the station and because, she thought, its expenses were much too high. Talbot even hired his own orchestra. She wrote that Talbot's orchestra "of course is a third-rate one and cannot compete in any way with the good recorded orchestras." She bargained with Talbot for the next couple of weeks. When his price came down to $190,000—just about what she figured the station's capital equipment was worth—she bought it, borrowing money from bankers who had known her father and knew that her credit was good.

Finally, Dorothy Bullitt was in the broadcasting business—or would be as soon as the FCC approved the sale. She and Henry Owen worked long days getting their FCC application ready: "Henry got some crackers and cheese and I brewed some coffee and got into the Pantry Shelf [a soda fountain and deli on the ground floor of the 1411 Fourth Avenue Building] for cream and sugar," she wrote after one of their sessions. In late April, Haley telegraphed the news that the FCC had approved the sale, and on May 1, 1947, Dorothy Bullitt, Henry Owen, and Fred Stimson moved into KEVR offices in the Smith Tower. Owen took the manager's desk, Dorothy Bullitt a desk in the hall. In June, the call letters were changed to KING, and Western Waves was rechristened the King Broadcasting Company.

She and her colleagues started by learning the details, financial and otherwise, of their new station. "The news," she reported on May 20, "when we really got into it was really even worse than we had expected. . . . We will probably lose $8,000 this month and I don't see that there will be very much change for next month." She thought—optimistically—that "it may be a year before we really get to the point where we are making money."

The new station certainly wasn't a gold mine. "There was no place to go but up," Dorothy Bullitt remembered later. "We had moved into the office only about two weeks when in the mail came a letter from Mr. Hooper, who [did] the ratings. He returned our check because he found no listeners. It was nothing but zeros, so he returned the check. I thought this was very decent of him. We needed it." This story, like so many others about the King Broadcasting Company's early days, may or may not have been entirely true. In late May, she wrote that KING-AM had 2 percent of the Seattle audience. The station may have picked up that 2 percent in the preceding weeks or, more likely, it may not really have been starting from absolute zero; either way, not many people were listening. "As you know," Dorothy Bullitt wrote Haley a couple of months later, "our Hooper is extremely bad. . . . Our big problem is [advertising] sales because we can establish no proof of a listening audience."

Expectations would have to be scaled back. "I believe we should slow down our construction of the FM station to almost the vanishing point," she wrote. She thought they should "only do as much as required by the FCC in order not to lose our license, so that we have adequate financing for KEVR."

In late April, before Western Waves had actually taken over KEVR, Dorothy Bullitt had written: "There have been a great many applications for jobs in the station and we have answered them all that we are assuming the personnel who are down there are doing a good job and that after we get in we will know very much more about it, but we do not contemplate any changes in personnel at the present time. This has found its way back to the station and as [a] result has buoyed up the morale of the personnel down there to some extent."

She was no doubt glad to see morale improve, but once Western Waves took over the station, she wasted little time in getting rid of most of the old KEVR staff. She probably didn't get rid of them herself. She hated firing people, but Owen was a master at it. He would become known as the man who did King Broadcasting's firing—and did it so nicely that people walked away feeling good. He started by firing employees the company had inherited from KEVR. In July Dorothy Bullitt wrote Haley that "we only have about one-third of the old staff of KEVR. The two-thirds replacement has

> *She knew that the station wouldn't attract listeners until it broadcast programs people wanted to hear. This did not mean the kind of culturally or politically uplifting programming with which people later came to associate her company.*

taken time . . . but I can now feel that the morale is beginning to grow and the whole operation is showing signs of going smoothly."

She knew that the station wouldn't attract listeners until it broadcast programs people wanted to hear. This did not mean the kind of culturally or politically uplifting programming with which people later came to associate her company. Only weeks after buying KEVR, she hired Martin Deane Wickett, who had been program manager at WTOP in Washington, D.C. "I think this will take care of our most immediate need," she wrote Haley, explaining that their need was "complete program revision toward the commercial side in order to get out of the red as quickly as possible."

Two months later, she told Haley, "We are doing everything possible to [acquire] programs that we can promote in order to increase our listening audience." On Tuesday evenings, KING-AM was running Tommy Dorsey, three mysteries, and a program of symphonic music. Elizabeth Wright Evans, who worked with Dorothy Bullitt for years, remembered that early on "she started to upgrade the station by insisting that her people buy better programs. I will never forget the representative of the ZIV Corporation, which had such standard [and highly commercial] shows as 'Boston Blackie'. . . . She bought these better shows, and the ZIV man was just furious, because he didn't want his shows on this little station. He said, 'You just wait. That woman will be out of business in no time. She doesn't know what she's doing.' He told me this one time when he was in Seattle. 'She is going to be off the air. She's going to lose her shirt.'"

He was wrong, of course, partly because Dorothy Bullitt could tap the real estate company's resources to keep the broadcasting operation afloat, and partly because she was willing to buy shows with mass market appeal. Nevertheless, her aspirations always went beyond the commercial appeal of "Boston Blackie." In 1946, before Western Waves even had a broadcasting station, Dorothy Bullitt invited Gloria Chandler to have lunch with King Broadcasting's board of directors to talk about community service programs and her experience forming community radio councils. In 1948, KING-AM started running every Saturday morning Chandler's "Books Bring Adventure," radio

Vivacious and creative, Gloria Chandler was Dorothy Bullitt's closest friend and adviser, as well as a nationally recognized expert on children's literature and drama.

adaptations of children's books—for which Chandler had won a Peabody Award the previous year. King brought Chandler to Seattle to promote the show.

The idea of carrying her good friend's award-winning program doesn't *seem* to have occurred spontaneously to Dorothy Bullitt. In the summer of 1948, representatives of the Parent-Teacher Association, the Seattle public schools, and the Seattle Public Library asked her to do it. But there was probably more to this programming decision than met the eye. Dorothy Bullitt always let other people take credit for ideas she wanted to push. That was her executive style. At board meetings, she'd go around the table asking everyone's opinion until she heard the one she wanted, then she'd say, "*That's* a good idea," and do exactly what she had intended to do all along. It is entirely possible that she had dropped a hint to the schools, the library, and the PTA, and they had given her the excuse she had been looking for to run Gloria Chandler's program on KING-AM.

The station subsequently incorporated "Books Bring Adventure" into a children's program it called "KING's Three-Ring Circus." The show brought Chandler's book adaptations and classical music to children every Saturday morning. The star of "Three Ring Circus" was a fictitious dog named Queenie. When Queenie had a litter of puppies, KING-AM asked the children to mail in names for them. The show started without a sponsor, but in 1948, "KING's Three-Ring Circus" won the new station its first national award.

The King Broadcasting Company wasn't making money yet—in May 1948, Dorothy Bullitt told the other shareholders that the company had lost $101,746 during the previous twelve months, and that she had advanced it $75,000—but it had started expanding. Only a couple of months after the company bought KEVR, King Broadcasting applied for permission to build a 50-kilowatt transmitter after all, and it started FM broadcasting in 1948. At first, the FM station broadcast only from 3:00 to 9:30 P.M., barely meeting the FCC minimum of six hours air time a day. And its stock in trade wasn't classical music. Whenever possible, KING-FM broadcast the Seattle Rainiers' minor-league baseball games. When the Rainiers played at night, the station signed off the air before the game was over.

The AM station, which increased its power to 50 kilowatts in March 1949, started broadcasting all night long. "We have been anxious to buy a closing spot on a Seattle station saying that they were going off the air and suggesting the audience turn to [KING-AM's frequency at] 1090 and listen to KING," Dorothy Bullitt wrote to Haley. "We did this with our tongues in our cheeks, because we were pretty sure what the answers would be. We were turned down by every Seattle station but KRSC [which since the previous November had operated the Northwest's first television station]—they did squirm a little, however, in turning us down. We would like to do an exchange deal with KRSC by their running [KING-AM's] spot . . . and we running an equal amount of spots on KING promoting the sale of television sets. . . . We would very much like to see the set sale grow faster."

King Broadcasting wanted to boost the sale of television sets in Seattle because Dorothy Bullitt had already agreed to buy KRSC-

TV. It isn't clear exactly when she decided to get into television. Possibly, she really had been thinking about it ever since 1939. Certainly, she had made her mind up more than a year before KRSC came up for sale. Television "cannot be underestimated in its threat to [radio] broadcasting or in its opportunities," she told King's other shareholders. In 1948, when the FCC was preparing to grant licenses for three television stations in Seattle, King Broadcasting was one of six applicants. The others included three larger Seattle radio stations, KOMO, KIRO, and KJR, plus a movie company, Twentieth Century Fox, and a private investor, Ed Lasker. The FCC planned to hold hearings. King Broadcasting could

> *At first, the FM station wasn't on the air much; broadcasting from 3:00 to 9:30 P.M., the station barely met the FCC minimum of six hours air time a day. And its stock in trade wasn't the classical music for which KING-FM would later become known.*

hardly have been a front-runner in the competition, although Haley's expertise and his personal connections at the FCC would have been a big ace in the hole. But the hearings were never held. The FCC decided it first had to sort out the allocation of television frequencies all over the United States, so on September 30, 1948, it placed a temporary freeze on the granting of new licenses.

That left KRSC, which operated AM and FM radio stations and already had a television license, as the only game in town. It was owned by P. K. Leberman, an Annapolis graduate who started the AM station with KRSC's station manager, Bob Priebe, in 1927. Leberman had lived in New York for years, but he still owned KRSC. Early in 1948, after he and Priebe started Seattle's first FM station, he realized that his AM operation had developed a problem: the station had been sending him a check for a couple thousand dollars every month. Suddenly, the checks stopped coming. Leberman sent a young employee named Lee Schulman to Seattle to find out what was going on.

Schulman had been working for Leberman at a radio station on Wall Street. As Schulman remembered years later, he walked into Leberman's long office with its big table piled high with papers, and without even saying hello, Leberman handed him a plane ticket and told him, "You're going to Seattle at 9:30, and here's what you'll do." Schulman figured later that he had been chosen to represent Leberman in Seattle because he was one of the few people around who had had some experience with TV. He had studied cinematography at the University of Southern California and after the war, he had worked for fledgling television stations in and near New York.

It didn't take Schulman long to find out what was wrong with Leberman's radio station—one of Leberman's managers was, as Schulman put it later, "stealing him blind." A few weeks later, when Schulman and Priebe were cruising on Priebe's motor sailboat in the San Juan Islands, Leberman called them. Did they think Seattle was ready for TV? They both said yes. Leberman got money from his partners in New York; Priebe acquired an old neighborhood grocery store on top of Queen Anne Hill as a studio site and bought a 10-kilowatt military-surplus transmission tower. The station ordered all the necessary hardware from RCA—then the only domestic manufacturer of camera tubes—in Camden, New Jersey. When the cartons full of equipment arrived, the radio broadcast engineers stood around wondering what all the new gadgets were for. RCA sent an engineer to show them how to put it all together.

The Northwest's first television station went on the air on Thanksgiving Day, 1948. The station wanted to go on the air for the first time with a big event. It was decided that the state high school football championship game between Wenatchee and West Seattle would be just the thing. A medium that brought moving pictures into viewers' living rooms cried out for action. Sports were perfect, and sports in Seattle meant high school and minor-league professional games.

The Thanksgiving Day game of 1948 had the additional virtue of being close to the transmitter—no small consideration when remote broadcasts required crude microwave transmissions in a direct line of sight to the tower. The game was to be played in Memorial Stadium at the base of Queen Anne. Signals could be microwaved directly from the stadium to the top of the hill, then broadcast to the estimated 1,500 Seattle residents who owned TVs.

KRSC-TV had run a couple of closed-circuit television demonstrations at the Shrine Auditorium and Frederick & Nelson's to acquaint people with the medium, but the football game would be the first broadcast. The engineers worked twenty-four hours a day to get ready, setting up at Memorial Stadium a day or two in advance. The two big, heavy cameras were placed along the sidelines and connected by Army surplus field wire to the remote broadcasting equipment that had been crammed into an old bread delivery van, which was parked outside the stadium.

When the game started, KRSC-TV became the first television station west of Kansas City and north of Los Angeles. At the time, American television was largely an East Coast phenomenon. The manufacturers were all in New York and New Jersey, and the first broadcasts were still largely limited to the New York metropolitan area and the GE laboratories' hinterland in upstate New York. After television more or less made its American debut at the New York World's Fair in 1939 (the BBC had started limited broadcasting in London two years earlier), David Sarnoff of RCA had expected to sell 20,000 to 40,000 sets in the New York metropolitan area that first year. This prediction turned out to be wildly optimistic. The sets were expensive—$395 to $675 apiece—and not many people figured that watching eight to twelve hours a week of baseball, boxing, old movies, and crudely produced live dramas was worth the money. Three months after the world's fair opened, only 800 sets had been sold. Another 5,000 sat in warehouses. Sarnoff cut the price of RCA sets by one-third, but even price-slashing didn't help. Nearly three years later, when the U.S. government stopped all private production of television sets for the duration of World War II, only a few thousand sets had been sold.

After the war, the new medium took hold very slowly. "By 1949," David Halberstam writes in *The Fifties*, "radio was on the

The field was muddy and the images murky, but the significance of the Northwest's first television broadcast on Thanksgiving Day in 1948 was unmistakable.

verge of being overtaken by television as a commercial vehicle. For more than two decades, radio had virtually been minting money; now it was struggling, changing, and trying to find a new role." Television was obviously about to become the dominant medium, but for all its promise, it wasn't yet profitable. It was not a money-maker in the 1940s. When KRSC-TV went on the air in 1948, most Americans had never seen television.

In Seattle on that Thanksgiving Day in 1948, the few people with access to sets got their first look at the new medium by watching Wenatchee beat West Seattle. The experience must have been a little strange. Rain had fallen earlier in the day, and light reflecting off puddles on the field distorted the picture. The Image Orthicon picture tubes used in television cameras at the time were hypersensitive: if a camera was trained steadily on an object, the image burned into the tube and lingered in the picture after the camera moved on to something else. To avoid that effect, the cameramen, Jack Shawcroft and Tom Priebe, kept the cameras moving, even when the players were in a huddle. But they couldn't avoid the effect altogether; as Dorothy Bullitt remembered, the players looked as if they had tails.

Dorothy Bullitt, who watched the game on a brand-new console television set with a seven-inch screen, suggested later that the choice of subject matter had been "unfortunate." It was certainly a far cry from the classical music she had listened to with Major Armstrong. Unfortunate or not, the high school football game had a lot to recommend it, and in many ways typified the kind of programming that would become the new station's bread and butter, even after Dorothy Bullitt took control.

Still, it was television, and Seattle now had it. On that first day, Dorothy Bullitt sent a big bouquet of red roses to KRSC-TV; later, she and Gloria Chandler drove by the station and saw the flowers in the window.

Television may have represented the latest communication technology, but the process of putting KRSC-TV on the air each day had a makeshift quality. The studio floor slanted on its rotting foundation, so that if a cameraman released his grip on one of the heavy cameras mounted on wheeled dollies, it rolled across the room. The old bread van continued to serve as the remote truck; to load or unload it, someone backed it up to the porch at the rear of the studio. Cables from the studio couldn't be connected directly to the antenna; instead, the connections were made in metal junction boxes. If moisture collected in the junction boxes, the signal would short out. To prevent that, someone had to climb the eighty-foot tower periodically and re-waterproof the boxes.

KRSC-TV had no link to the network studios in the East— there was no satellite transmission, of course, and it wouldn't even be possible to send broadcasts across the country by telephone wire for another four years—so if KRSC-TV wanted to show anything but films of network shows shipped west from New York, it had to generate its own programs. With minimal space, only two cameras, and very little money, producing shows in the KRSC-TV studio was difficult, so the cameras were sent out to capture live events as much as possible.

In the spring of 1949, KRSC started televising the Seattle Rainiers' local baseball games. The station's two cameras were hauled to the roof of the grandstand, and Shawcroft and Priebe, wearing jackets on the chilly April afternoon, caught the first five innings of the game. During the sixth inning, a relay transmitter failed and the picture disappeared, but the announcer, Bill O'Mara, pressed on with the play-by-play.

Erratic though they may have been, those early broadcasts started to attract an audience. By the time KRSC broadcast that first baseball game in 1949, an estimated 5,500 television sets had been sold in the Seattle area, and the *Seattle Post-Intelligencer* figured that the television audience was several times as large as the live crowd of 13,000.

In May 1949, Leberman decided to sell KRSC-TV. He had no more capital to invest in the station, and besides, Fairchild Publications had offered him a job in New York as publisher of its high-circulation *Family Circle* magazine. Leberman couldn't take the *Family Circle* job and continue flying to Seattle every weekend to run a television station. He started looking seriously for a buyer. Actually, he had already been looking at least casually for a buyer, and he had talked with Dorothy Bullitt about selling the station to her. She had already made it clear that she *was* interested—sending roses on opening day certainly indicated that she had noticed—and when she talked with Leberman at the National Association of Broadcasters convention in Chicago earlier that year, she had no doubt let him know she was serious. In April 1949, Dorothy Bullitt, Henry Owen, and her radio station manager, Hugh Feltis, agreed to try buying Leberman's station. She subsequently called Leberman, who told her that someone else was interested in buying, too. "Hope to goodness it's not already

By the time KRSC broadcast that first baseball game in 1949, an estimated 5,500 television sets had been sold in the Seattle area, and the Seattle Post-Intelligencer *figured that the television audience was several times as large as the live crowd of 13,000.*

sold," she wrote in her journal, "as I think we *must* have it." But she hadn't made a real move by May 2, when Leberman called and told her that he was going to sell the station, period. He was flying to Seattle, where he was going to talk with representatives of Marshall Field, which owned Seattle radio station KJR and was interested in buying KRSC; he was willing to talk with her, too.

She jumped at the chance. "Decided we must move fast, as [the Marshall Field people] have come to *buy* and it is *vital for them and vital for us*," she wrote in her journal. "This is the great battle—instead of the hearing before FCC, this is *it*. Didn't sleep." King Broadcasting's lawyer, Dick Riddell, who would work with Dorothy Bullitt for the next thirty-eight years, once said that in all the time he knew her, only once had she taken the initiative to make a major decision without waiting to let someone else come up with the idea: when she decided to buy the television station. Riddell, in fact, tried to talk her out of it. Leberman was asking $500,000, and he thought it was too much. She wouldn't listen. "We gambled," she explained years later, "hoping the [FCC] freeze would last until we got on our feet."

She approached the owners of Seattle's network radio stations about going in with her. Saul Haas, who owned KIRO, turned her down. So did the Fisher family, which owned KOMO. Neither was interested. Television wasn't making money yet. Evidently, the smart guys who owned Seattle's big radio stations wanted to let someone else develop a television audience, then step in and reap the benefits. No one expected the FCC freeze (on granting new licenses for television stations) to last long. Her competitors apparently figured they'd be able to get into television whenever they were good and ready. But they were wrong. The freeze lasted into 1952, and by the time new stations could get FCC licenses and build transmitters, King Broadcasting Company had a five-year head start. The smart guys outsmarted themselves.

The crucial negotiations took place one May night in Dorothy Bullitt's brick house at Federal and Galer on Seattle's Capitol Hill. Dorothy Bullitt wouldn't make a move this significant without Andrew Haley. She had tracked him down in Pasadena, California, got him out of the shower to answer the phone, and told him what was going on. He said he'd fly to Seattle the next day. Leberman had scheduled a meeting with Marshall Field in the morning and a meeting with Dorothy Bullitt in her office at 1411 Fourth Avenue at 2 P.M. Haley called the next day to say he had missed his plane and couldn't get there before evening. She wasn't about to negotiate without Haley, but she was afraid that if she called Leberman to postpone the meeting, he'd spend the rest of the day getting cozy with the people from Marshall Field. So she let Leberman show up at two o'clock, knowing perfectly well that no real negotiating was going to happen until Haley arrived. She just sat and asked Leberman questions, stalling for time. Finally, he said that she had been asking the same questions over and over, and he wanted to know what was going on. She told him Haley had been delayed and suggested they get together at her house that evening. At six o'clock, Leberman showed up with his local lawyer, John Ryan, whom she knew, and a station broker named Ray Hamilton. She and Haley were there, of course, along with Henry Owen and Stimson Bullitt, who had just been admitted to the Washington bar. Leberman and his associates occupied the living room. The King Broadcasting people huddled in the study. The two groups would get together to negotiate, then go back to their separate rooms to confer. King started with a lowball bid of $200,000. The station broker was offended. Haley told him to "shut up."

Very much in his element, Haley dominated the evening. Dorothy Bullitt felt that this was a now-or-never occasion. Other people in the room took it more casually. Stimson Bullitt, present largely as a spectator, did not have any sense that King Broadcasting faced a once-in-a-lifetime opportunity; rather, he was uneasy because Leberman's price seemed like a lot of money and the company's radio stations were still running in the red. If his mother had any such reservations, she kept them to herself.

Dorothy Bullitt and Leberman liked each other, and the negotiations went well. Around midnight, they agreed on terms: she would buy the television and FM stations for $375,000. Everyone was afraid that if they stopped for the night without a signed agreement, one of the participants would have second thoughts in the morning and the deal would fall apart, so the lawyers went downtown to Ryan's office on the fifth floor of the White-Henry-Stuart Building to draw up a contract. They got a secretary out of bed to take down the contractual language and finished around 3:00 A.M. Dorothy Bullitt and Leberman joined them at Ryan's office and signed on the spot. "Too much liquor consumed by lawyers," she noted. "Home about 4:30 A.M."

The next morning, Leberman called. He had forgotten something the night before, an omission that would cost him a lot of money. Could he amend the contract? Dorothy Bullitt let him. That was that. The television station was hers. She took out a $200,000 line of credit from Pacific National Bank, and in August 1949, the FCC approved the sale. At midnight on August 19, King Broadcasting owned the only television station in the Northwest.

Ten days before she actually took over the station, Dorothy Bullitt put on a conservative dress and went up to the transmitter building on Queen Anne Hill to meet her new employees. Henry Owen went with her. No one knew who she was. She introduced herself as the new owner and talked about her goals. "I hemmed and hawed and didn't know what I was saying," she remembered nearly forty years later. Lee Schulman recalled that she had created a good first impression—which was critical. He and the station's engineers had been quietly planning to leave for Los Angeles. But "her hopes and dreams were so positive," and he was so impressed by her straightforwardness and warmth that he and the engineers decided to stay.

CHAPTER THREE

INVENTING TELEVISION
1949–1953

DOROTHY BULLITT HAD HER television station. But she was losing money hand over fist. She would call Frank Yanagimachi, who joined King Broadcasting as a bookkeeper in 1948 (and stayed with the company until 1983), and ask him what big expenses were expected in the next month or two. He realized that she had to transfer money from the real estate operation to pay the broadcasting company's bills.

Henry Owen's wife, Frances, remembered one day when she and Dorothy Bullitt had stopped at the brick house on East Galer. "She said, 'I just wonder how long I can hang on. I've got a TV station but no one to look at it and advertisers who don't see any value in it.' "

"Stayed awake all night in a deep pit of fear and discouragement," Dorothy Bullitt wrote in her journal during that first difficult year. Three days later, she noted, "Couldn't sleep—how did I walk deliberately into such a financial mess?"

Designed by Walt Disney, KING Mike was King Broadcasting's first logo.

No wonder her new television station was losing money. When the King Broadcasting Company bought Leberman's station and re-named it KING-TV, there were only 6,000 television sets in the Seattle area. Lee Schulman would sometimes drive around town and count television antennas on people's roofs; on weekends, he would drive north of the city and count sets. The more people watched, the more KING-TV could charge for advertising time. So King employees called local television dealers every week to see how many sets they had sold. The numbers weren't high—hardly surprising, since a television set with a seven-inch screen cost $180 and a set with a ten-inch screen cost $300, plus $60 to $100 for installation, which was a lot of money at the time. But there were alternatives to owning your own set. People watched television in stores and in bars. The station sold time to some advertisers on the assumption that thousands of people would see their programs in store windows. Nevertheless, advertisers wanted to know how many people watched at home, so the number of sets was crucial, and someone always reported on sales figures at broadcast staff meetings. By fall, the numbers looked mildly encouraging. The minutes of an October 1949 meeting noted that "only about 1,000 sets a month will be sold for the balance of this calendar year because of the limited supply available. Although this is disappointing, it is a complete reversal of the trend to date where the supply has exceeded the demand."

While television was struggling to get off the ground, the AM radio station remained near the bottom of the Seattle ratings. "It is absolutely imperative that our Hooper rating be changed almost overnight," stated the minutes of a May 1949 radio staff meeting. "This necessitates ruthless program changes in the direction of more

Dorothy Bullitt's first cousin, Fred Stimson, was an amateur engineer who encouraged her to to get into broadcasting. He worked as the night manager at the Queen Anne transmitter until 1974, four years before his death.

music and less talk. This formula has been . . . the most successful pattern in other independent operations throughout the United States. Religious and all talking programs [must] be cancelled or changed."

Dorothy Bullitt didn't want KING-AM to remain an independent operation. KING-TV carried the offerings, such as they were, of all three television networks, but KING-AM had no network affiliation. Dorothy Bullitt wanted one badly. She dropped in to see people at all the networks when she was in New York, but she mainly pursued ABC, the weakest of the three, which was affiliated with Marshall Field's Seattle radio station, KJR. She courted ABC at least as early as the beginning of 1949. ABC vice president Otto Brandt visited her in Seattle and explained that there was no chance of switching before the network's contract with KJR expired that fall. "They can negotiate again in September," she noted, "if we can just live that long." She stayed in touch with Brandt over the summer, and at the end of August, she went to see him and ABC president Bob Kintner. She

Flamboyant and sometimes difficult, Lee Schulman (left) "was the genius who really ran the operation, a pioneer in early television," said Dorothy Bullitt.

found Kintner "rude and crass." In November, ABC turned her down. She talked with Saul Haas, owner of Seattle's successful KIRO, about allying her television station with his profitable radio station. "Mr. Haas called and we did some fencing," she wrote. Haas is "mighty difficult to deal with but IF it strikes him right would be wonderful solution for us." She never worked out a deal with Haas. Not long after that, she wrote, "Awfully low in my mind. Headaches."

Her headaches included her cousin, Fred Stimson, who was working as a station engineer. In November she wrote, "Fred called me. Taxes on his house are $310. He has the $10." Around that time, Fred drove Dorothy and her daughter, Patsy Bullitt Collins, to the studios from Capitol Hill, a wild ride during which the car spent time on the sidewalk as on well as the street. Not long afterward, Dorothy

Bullitt issued Fred an ultimatum: quit drinking or stop working at King. The job was evidently the most important thing in Fred Stimson's world. So far as anyone knew, he never drank again—and he kept working at the station until 1975.

Despite the frustrations and anxieties of keeping her new business going, Dorothy Bullitt had already assembled most of the people with whom she would build the company in the next fifteen years. She had already known Andrew Haley, her broadcasting industry guru, for the better part of a decade. She had worked with Henry Owen, her administrator, since 1946.

Her relationship with Lee Schulman, KING-TV's program director, was less personal. Schulman had as much to do as anyone with "inventing television" in Seattle. He was widely considered a genius—and a difficult guy to get along with. "When Henry was late to dinner," Frances Owen recalled, "I knew he was probably calming Lee Schulman down." Schulman would sometimes yell at people— one could hear the sounds coming from his office—but he didn't mind if people yelled back.

Schulman could figure out how to shoot something that television had never covered before and estimate accurately how much the operation would cost. "He was forceful, resourceful, and bold," Stimson Bullitt recalled. "He would have made a good wartime field officer. If his soldiers came to a river, he would figure out how to organize the work, devise tools, build the bridge, and get the troops across." Schulman was primarily responsible for pushing camera crews out of the station to film live news wherever they could find it.

Soon after Dorothy Bullitt bought the station, a tunnel excavation at the University of Washington caved in, trapping several construction workers. Schulman sent a camera crew to cover the rescue operation. It was KING-TV's first live news broadcast.

A tall young man named Ken Hermanson, who was working part-time fixing radio and television sets for a local wholesaler, was so fascinated by broadcasting that he hung around the transmitter just to watch what was going on. He kept pestering people for a job. Finally, in the spring of 1950, he was hired as a summer replacement. In

August, when the station bought another camera and needed a larger staff, he was hired to work full-time. "When I first came," he remembered, "it was the theory of the station that anybody could fix anything," but people soon realized that they had to specialize. Hermanson became responsible for maintenance. He stayed until 1992, retiring as corporate vice-president in charge of engineering.

Hermanson found at the beginning that everyone was "just stumbling" through the technical problems. At best, "the equipment barely worked." Things were always breaking down, so people learned to compensate for technological idiosyncrasies. "Once in a while, a camera [image] would all of a sudden expand on the right-hand side," remembered Al Smith, who became a KING-TV engineer in the late summer of 1950 after servicing TVs for the Herb Zobrist Company on First Avenue. "The way to stop it was to raise the viewfinder and drop it with a crash."

At first, the station broadcast only in the late afternoons and evenings, five hours a day. Even so, finding ways to fill air time was a constant challenge.

Television technology depended entirely on vacuum tubes, and suppliers frequently shipped new kinds of tubes with new characteristics. Even a familiar tube performed differently as its temperature changed, so engineers had to wait for the equipment to warm up and then adjust it constantly. A camera could not even be left alone to record something from film; someone had to sit at a console and watch because, for example, a dark picture would suddenly flame out in a burst of brightness.

Early television stations often used cameras to photograph moving film. The resulting "kinescopes" were the only means of recording shows. In the days before videotape, satellites, or coast-to-coast cables, kinescopes were the only way a television station in Seattle could broadcast a program made in New York. All the network programs arrived by plane on "kinnies." But their quality left a lot to be desired. Al Smith recalled that they looked "like captured war film."

At first, KING broadcast only in the late afternoons and evenings, five hours a day. Even so, finding ways to fill air time was a constant challenge. KING-TV's search for local talent led it to a University of Washington student named Stan Boreson, who studied accounting and personnel management and played the accordion. He had seen television; his family bought a set in 1949, and that summer, he spent a lot of time sitting indoors with the blinds down, watching the tiny screen. In the fall of 1949, Boreson hung around at Club Encore, where people booking performers for Elks Clubs and the like would hire student musicians. Schulman came by, looking for entertainers to perform on television. Boreson and another student, a piano player named Art Barduhn, auditioned for him. Schulman liked what he saw and asked them to perform on

With no network schedule to accommodate and, at first, no sponsor, the show could run as long as anyone wanted it to. Sometimes Boreson and Barduhn would see Schulman signal them to stretch it out, and they'd keep going until he told them to stop.

a half-hour "College Capers" feature, then hired them to play a regular fifteen-minute show, "Two Bs at the Keys." Boreson brought his own accordion, and the station got Barduhn a piano from a downtown music store in exchange for advertising time. The performances were all live. There were no teleprompters. The studio provided a blackboard with a hole in the middle through which a cameraman could stick a lens. Boreson could scrawl a few notes around the hole, but that was it—he had to learn the words to six songs and a monologue before each week's show. He would put the lyrics on the front seat of his car and study them at red lights. (Even after teleprompters were invented, Schulman wouldn't let people use them. "I had a fetish," he explained later. He felt that if people were reading their lines, "there wasn't the eye contact that was so important at that period in television.")

With no network schedule to accommodate and, at first, no sponsor, the show could run as long as anyone wanted it to.

From 1950 through the mid-1960s, kindly Bea Donovan reigned as the popular "KING's Queen," cooking up new recipes and dispensing household tips to her viewers. Here she exchanges pleasantries with KING-TV documentary producer Howard Hall.

Sometimes Boreson and Barduhn would see Schulman signal them to stretch it out, and they'd keep going until he told them to stop. When Gloria Swanson appeared as a guest and started talking about old movies with her interviewer, Tom Dargan, the fifteen minutes stretched to an hour and a half. During one show, Boreson became convinced that Barduhn was playing out of tune, and they argued about it—on the air. When Best Pies agreed to sponsor them, Schulman had them hit each other in the face with the sponsor's products. Best Pies called the next morning to cancel its sponsorship.

Clipper Gas subsequently sponsored Boreson and Barduhn's show. With a sponsor, the station could afford to bring the rest of Barduhn's trio onto the show, which was christened "Clipper Capers." Clipper put the musicians on a flatbed truck and took them to play at one of its gas stations. When they arrived, they were amazed to find hundreds of people waiting for them. It was their first indication that anyone was actually watching the show.

Early in 1950, KING-TV moved into considerably grander studio space at the base of Queen Anne Hill, but the atmosphere stayed improvisational. At first, the studios occupied only the lower floor of a two-story industrial building. A manufacturer of fishing tackle occupied the top floor, and things thumped and clattered overhead. Elizabeth Wright Evans, who soon became involved in community programming for the station, recalled years later that "there were these trucks constantly rolling overhead, and in the middle of a [televised] discussion, you could hear [them]." Once, when Bea Donovan, who in 1950 started a regular cooking show called "KING's Queen," was on the air, a knot fell out of a ceiling board and landed in the food she was preparing. Unfazed, she picked the knot out and kept going.

Nothing that happened outside Seattle could be seen live. When KRSC-TV broadcast the 1949 Rose Bowl between California and Northwestern, the game was filmed in Pasadena, the film was flown to New York for developing, and the developed film was flown to Seattle in time to be shown two days later.

When KING-TV crews took the cameras out of the studio in the spring and summer to cover baseball, the cameras had to be hauled to the roof of Sick's Stadium before every game. Clare Hanawalt, one of the early station engineers, remembered the process more than forty years later: "We had a boom sticking out from the roof at the back side of the bleacher section where it adjoined the parking lot. [A] block and tackle was used to hoist a wooden box containing usually one camera to the roof. . . . The parking lot was usually empty [when] we carried out this little operation. The pulley end of the rope was attached to [a] car bumper and the car would be driven the necessary 75 to 100 feet to hoist the box to the top. Flashlight signals were used to tell the driver to stop."

Nothing that happened outside Seattle could be broadcast live. When KRSC-TV televised the January 1949 Rose Bowl game between California and Northwestern, the game was filmed in Pasadena, the film was flown to New York for developing, and the developed film was flown to Seattle in time to be shown two days later.

That winter, KING-TV broadcast University of Washington basketball games. But the university was afraid that the broadcasts would cut into live attendance and told KING that it could broadcast two upcoming games with Washington State only if the games were sold out. When the *Post-Intelligencer* took a survey, 98.9 percent of the people it asked "demanded return of Washington basketball to the TV screen." Fans were already getting hooked on televised sports.

KING's audience was growing. At the beginning of May 1950, 29,000 sets had been sold in the Seattle area. Sales were slowing down, though, according to television staff meeting notes, "probably because of the weather, the anticipation of a summer slump in programming, and perhaps because of [the] terrific amount of commercials we are putting on."

Even when KING-TV had a good month financially, Owen was reluctant to let anyone know. "The April profit showing is the best yet," he wrote to Dorothy Bullitt in early May, when she was out of town. But he added a note of caution: "It will not be easy to maintain a good profit showing during off-baseball months with network affiliates and other stations fighting for business during the transition period of the radio industry."

He suggested that "it would probably be a good idea for you to drop a note to [station manager] Hugh [Feltis], commenting on the showing for April. Might be even better to telephone him, for then you can say you would like the fact that there was a fair profit in TV for April be kept confidential." Then he wrote—but crossed out, "Union personnel and others start thinking about making greater demands." He concluded, "April is a single month, so let's wait a while and see how our trend goes."

Dorothy Bullitt evidently didn't need much persuasion. She was perfectly willing to see the cloud behind the silver lining. Her company had wallowed in red ink for four years. Her TV station had never shown a profit before. She was pleased by the April numbers, she wrote Feltis, but she expected the company to lose at least $68,000 over the next twelve months. And she couldn't understand why KING-TV was spending so much money on its advertising salesmen. "The TV sales cost is really alarming," she said. The salesmen's healthy salaries and commissions income "do not take into consideration that risked capital has given them something unusually good to sell—there is at present no competition in the TV field, and if any sponsor or product wants the Northwest area through the medium of TV, it is not solely dependent on the skill and energies of our salesmen."

The commissions paid advertising salesmen were a major sore point. She held Feltis at least partly to blame: "Hugh's attitude is all wrong and very disturbing as he has aligned himself as god of the staff against management. We can never hope to satisfy our TV salesmen and cut them back to where they belong." The next spring, Feltis was gone.

Advertisers weren't exactly pounding on the door. Those that did buy time on local television knew that they had KING-TV over a barrel. Minutes of the TV staff meeting for May 24, 1950, note that "some clients are beginning to take advantage of over-limit times such as . . . paying [a] one-minute rate for [a] 77-second spot. Decided nothing we can do about it this summer, because not strong enough yet to refuse the business."

Dorothy Bullitt was still pursuing a network affiliation for her AM radio station. Any network was going to ask how many listeners her station could reach, and she wanted to claim a large potential audience. After KING-AM started broadcasting at 50 kilowatts, she and Gloria Chandler drove around to see how much area the new signal covered. "We got a special receiving set mounted [by Fred Stimson] in the back seat of my Ford, and headed north," Dorothy Bullitt recalled. "Gloria was mostly on her knees in the back seat of the car while I drove. . . . And behind hills we went and made notes. And we laughed a lot."

But their measurements didn't sway the networks. Dorothy Bullitt talked with Robert Kintner and Otto Brandt at ABC: "I said, 'We get letters from all around. You'd be surprised where our mail count comes from.' They said, 'Well, we take our own measurements.' Which they did." ABC also had a tape of a KING-AM broadcaster saying, "I've been told to put on brass band records with all the loud music I can find [so that the signal will be easier to hear]."

Dorothy Bullitt had her mother's desire to elevate the cultural level of the community and a kind of earnestness that made her a strong advocate of educational TV.

However hard up King Broadcasting may have been, it tried to set some standards for its new TV station. In the fall of 1949, staff members at the weekly television meeting discussed a Lucky Strike cigarette commercial that had filled six minutes of air time. Although the company was basically grateful for any advertising it could get, staff members "agreed that even short commercials or programs with bad commercials should be refused if they do not meet our program standards—regardless of the amount of time used."

Although imposing standards of good taste on the television screen carried a price tag—as did trying to inform, rather than simply amuse, potential viewers—KING-TV soon began showing more than local sports and old movies. Early in 1950, it ran an Encyclopedia Britannica film about the atom bomb entitled "No Place to Hide." After talking with community groups, the station decided to follow the film with a panel discussion, and it got in touch with Elizabeth Wright Evans at the University of Washington's adult education division to set up the discussion.

KING and the university were made for each other. Evans was eager to reach a wider audience and KING was eager to fill air time. Dorothy Bullitt had her mother's desire to elevate the cultural level of the community and a kind of earnestness—she saved detailed notes on all kinds of lectures, speeches, obscure facts—that made her a strong advocate of educational TV.

After "No Place to Hide" was aired, Evans recalled, "We simply called the station and said 'so-and-so is coming to the university' or 'we think that it's time to get some people in to talk about the atomic bomb,' and away we would go." Dorothy Bullitt liked it all well enough to want the university on television more often. In the summer of 1951, she called Evans and asked her about putting together a daily half-hour show. The two of them, along with other King Broadcasting executives and representatives of various nonprofit groups, got together in the back yard of the university's president, Raymond Allen, to talk about the idea. "There were doubting Thomases, believe me," Evans said. "There were those who said, 'Oh, you can never get an audience with that kind of show. And you certainly can't get all the high-priced talent'—meaning the professors and the doctors and lawyers and all the busy people—'you can't get them to come down and share their time.' I always laugh now and say that it was the women who said, 'Of course you can do it.'"

Initially, as the doubters had predicted, most of those busy people at the university weren't eager to stand in front of a camera. "Many educators regarded television as a tawdry gadget—a debauched invention dedicated to wrestling and 'Westerns'—totally unworthy of their efforts," Dorothy Bullitt wrote in 1954. She described "a professor at the University of Washington who [at] first flatly refused to go on the air . . . [partly because] he was sure that his associates would look down their noses and he would lose caste for having stooped so low."

The first faculty star was the chairman of the university's music department, Stanley Chapple, a London-born conductor who had helped start the Tanglewood music festival and who had come to the university in 1948. "Let's call him a classical ham," Dorothy Bullitt said some fifteen years later. "He looked well on the screen, he dressed the part, and he was a natural. It didn't bother him at all [that] there was a camera on him. And he does know his music." Elizabeth Wright Evans recalled that "he had been on the air in St. Louis the summer before, so that he was kind of a pro. . . . Chapple was great. He was by far the best show we had done yet. Dorothy Allen rushed up and kissed him on the forehead, and Lee [Schulman] was so excited he could hardly stand it. That is how Lee got acquainted with Stanley and how it happened that the first opera ever televised outside of New York City was one of Stanley's operas offered [in Seattle in 1952]."

Faculty members may have been reluctant at first, but it didn't take them long to get hooked. By 1954, Dorothy Bullitt wrote, the professor who had worried about his friends looking down their noses at him "has had his program on KING for two years. He is stopped in the street, in the barber shop; his mail has gone out of bounds and he would be just as reluctant to go off as he was to go on. And no one looks down his nose—his income has increased and his classes are crowded."

Locally produced programs that occupied the broad middle ground between professional wrestling and lectures by university professors largely established KING-TV's early character and its place in the community.

The bulk of KING-TV's programming was a lot less high-minded and Dorothy Bullitt didn't always like it. At the end of 1954, she wrote in her journal that professional wrestling "was dirtier than ever and I could hardly contain my anger at the lack of attention paid my requests by Otto and Henry." Whether she liked wrestling or not, professional sports were a bread-and-butter part of the weekly schedule. Every Monday night at 9:45, the station set up two cameras next to the ring at the Eagles Auditorium and covered the wrestling matches. Every Wednesday and Thursday evening and Sunday afternoon when the Rainiers were playing at home, KING-TV put the cameras in the press box behind home plate.

Dorothy Bullitt really did want to bring culture and enlightenment to the masses. But, despite her distaste for pro wrestling, she was certainly not above satisfying some of her community's less

"March On" became a popular hour-long weekly show featuring singers and musicians in the military at Fort Lewis.

exalted tastes, doing whatever it took to attract viewers and keep her business afloat.

Locally produced programs that occupied the broad middle ground between professional wrestling and lectures by university professors largely established KING-TV's early character and its place in the community. Perhaps none did more than Stan Boreson, Bea Donovan, and other homegrown acts that were broadcast live from the studios on lower Queen Anne. The live shows were still triumphs of improvisation. During one episode of "KING's Queen," Donovan burned a cake. She went into her dressing room and came back with a handful of face powder, which she sprinkled over the cake to cover the charred spots. Since the picture was black and white, the cake looked fine. In another incident, Boreson and Barduhn were doing a live commercial for a lawn mower. They got the mower started, but they couldn't shut it off. Finally, they pushed it out a door and went on with the show.

Program director Lee Schulman was always looking for things to put on the air. The Korean War was raging, and Fort Lewis, south of Tacoma, was full of troops, some of which were talented performers.

A colonel from Fort Lewis approached Schulman about putting military talent on TV. Schulman leaped at the chance to get real talent that didn't have to be paid. The first half-hour "March On" show appeared on the first Saturday night of February 1951. Originally scheduled for just eight weeks, "March On" became a regular feature. The soldiers wrote their own music and built their own sets. Two thirty-voice choruses appeared on alternate weeks. Once, so many military performers were crammed into the fifty-by-fifty studio that Schulman had to place a camera outside the door in order to get everyone into the shot.

In the fall of 1950, with congressional elections coming up, Representative Hugh Mitchell's administrative assistant, Ancil Payne, who later played a key role in King Broadcasting, bought half an hour of air time for Mitchell on KING-TV. The congressman and his family arrived at the studios on Second Avenue West. Payne wanted to see how the congressman looked on the screen, and since there were no monitors in the station, he watched from a nearby tavern. Mitchell's young daughter kept scratching her backside. Mitchell's wife kept telling her to stop. Finally, the little girl lifted her leg high in the air and announced, "My *bite* itches." This was a slice of reality everyone could empathize with. The people in the tavern loved it. (Mitchell was re-elected.)

————

The number of sets was growing, but King Broadcasting Company continued to struggle. Dorothy Bullitt needed capital. While she wasn't ready to give up, she talked to prospective buyers, and considered the advantages of merging with a larger company. A number of people wanted to buy the AM station, but not at a price she considered adequate. She was getting discouraged. "Don't know what to do," she wrote. "Can't seem to give it away."

She would have been happy to own a radio station that made money. In fact, for its clear signal, she still coveted the AM radio frequency held by KIRO and kept pushing to buy it, just as KIRO's owner, Saul Haas, kept trying to buy at least a share of KING-TV. Neither would give up what he or she already had. On one occasion,

"Saul came and he wanted to talk about TV. I wanted to talk about KIRO." Nothing came of the meeting. The next day, Haas's wife "called to say S was in a terrible humor as our conversation had not worked out as he had planned—Good."

In the spring of 1950, she talked with Howard Lane of Marshall Field about a deal. Lane was interested in buying KING-TV and selling her Marshall Field's Seattle radio station, KJR, which she didn't want. He reserved a room for her at Chicago's Blackstone Hotel for that year's National Association of Broadcasters (NAB) convention, and she sent him information about King Broadcasting's corporate structure. In July, Marshall Field proposed buying both KING-TV and KIRO radio's parent company, Queen City Broadcasting, and forming a new company, of which Dorothy Bullitt and Marshall Field would each own 45 percent. She told Lane that the board refused to go along with less than majority control of the company. It seems likely that the board member who refused to go along with anything less than majority control was Dorothy Bullitt, and she found it convenient to attribute her attitude to the rest of the board. However, she may have been ambivalent about keeping KING-TV. Later in the year she wrote, "Sick to death of this whole business. If it's to be on my shoulders alone would like to sell out completely." But when someone offered her $750,000 for King Broadcasting, she wrote, "Will tell him it is not interesting enough for consideration."

She kept talking with Lane, and when she saw him again in Chicago in the spring of 1951, he said Marshall Field had refused an offer of $1.5 million for its Seattle and Portland radio stations. Maybe, he suggested, King Broadcasting would like to offer more than that. Dorothy Bullitt's notes dismiss this suggestion with a simple "Huh!"

In 1951, she sold some jewelry to raise extra cash for her broadcasting company. It wasn't just a matter of keeping a marginal business afloat; the company needed money in order to grow. She talked to a lot of people about potential deals. She discussed selling King Broadcasting to the Meredith Publishing Company, and other companies offered to buy individual parts of King. She was in New

York when "Henry Owen called to tell me that a representative of William Randolph Hearst, Jr. [whose Hearst Company owned a newspaper publishing empire and a number of radio stations] had come to . . . ask if the company would sell Channel 5 to Mr. Hearst. When I got my breath I asked if he was sure the man was talking [about] the right Mr. Hearst, and Henry was convinced he was. I felt as if someone had suddenly set before me a large tray of diamonds and rubies and told me to help myself. We were still running in the red and getting awfully tired of it—and [we had] no assurance that it would ever get any better. But I didn't want to sell that station. I had high hopes for it. I agreed to talk with him—his name was Mr. Brooks [Tom Brooks, the vice president and general manager of Hearst Radio]—over a few months. I grew to like and respect him as a gentleman of his word. . . .

"I came to the offer of 25 percent of the whole [company] but no more. He said that would be impossible because Hearst had a firm rule never to own more than 10 percent or less than 90 percent. . . . When I planned a New York trip, Mr. Brooks invited me for lunch several days in advance and asked me to bring our figures.

"I found at lunch at the Lotus Club . . . Mr. Berlin, president [and] CEO, and Mr. Huberth, chairman of the board of the Hearst Corporation. After the usual courtesies of conversation, Mr. Berlin suggested I produce the figures. Both men looked at them closely . . . then asked [about] one figure [of $350,000] . . . titled Debt to Stockholders. 'What is that?' And I admitted it was me, which seemed to amuse them. . . . It seemed to have something to do with breaking the ice, and from then on we were friends."

The Hearst Corporation decided to buy 25 percent of King Broadcasting. Dorothy Bullitt was almost sixty at the time, and the Hearst Corporation—which couldn't know that she would live another thirty-seven years—evidently figured that when she died, the corporation would get the rest of King. For the time being, Hearst would become the second-largest stockholder and would be represented on King's board. Dorothy Bullitt's 85 percent ownership would be reduced to 64 percent.

"After the approval of the deal was understood, Mr. Brooks came to Seattle to get an option, which he needed to show the [Hearst] board meeting Monday. He also brought an engineer with him and asked if he might see the [transmitter] installation on Vashon [Island]. I sent one of our engineers to take them both over and that evening when they got back, Brooks drew me aside to say, 'Do you know why our engineer wanted to go? Because the tower [cost] figures were so low he thought we must have tied the wires to the trees.'"

Brooks also brought along Wells Smith, Hearst's acting controller. The two of them, along with Hearst's local lawyer, Paul Ashley, Dorothy Bullitt, and Ray Wright, worked out an agreement that was signed or at least dated on Tuesday, June 12, 1951, although negotiations evidently continued through the week. For $1,000, Hearst took an option to buy 2,500 shares to one-fourth of King stock any time until June 28.

On Friday, Dorothy Bullitt remembered, "Brooks took his plane back with his option in his pocket."

The following Tuesday, June 19, Brooks died of a heart attack at his home in Leonia, New Jersey. "I was really stricken . . . I felt we would be safe in his hands. With him gone I thought we would be adrift. I wished I had that option back. The telephone rang. It was Mr. Berlin. . . . He said, 'If you have any doubts that the understanding you worked out may not be upheld, I'll put your option in the wastebasket.' I could only say, 'Do you want it to stand?' and he said, 'Yes,' so [I responded], 'All right, then, it can stand as his good work for both of us.'"

That conversation took place several days after Brooks died. Despite Berlin's reassuring call, Dorothy Bullitt had to wait well into the next week before she knew Hearst wouldn't back out, and she must have spent some anxious moments. But the next Wednesday, June 27, when the option had only one day left to run, she received a cashier's check for $374,000, and the notoriously conservative Hearst organization owned 25 percent of the King Broadcasting Company.

Dorothy Bullitt didn't expect Hearst to grasp all the subtleties of King's operation. That fall, she sent her company's October financial statement to New York along with a letter that acknowledged, "There are undoubtedly items that puzzle you, one of which may be the live-stock. This is generally a summer item as the radio transmitter site grows deep grass around the three towers and we have bought a few whitefaced cattle to graze and keep the grass down, as otherwise it might be a fire hazard. Last year we sold these at a small profit and think we can probably do the same thing again next year."

Seattle, an athletic backwater at the time, was ready to become enthusiastic about a local sport that most other places didn't have. And hydroplane racing, with its action, speed, and spectacular crashes, was a natural for TV.

Despite the cattle grazing around their radio towers, the people at King Broadcasting weren't hicks. When Hearst sent out an engineer from Baltimore to help make decisions about building a 100,000-watt television transmitter, the engineers in Seattle discovered the East Coast expert didn't know any more than they did.

Dorothy Bullitt viewed the 100,000-watt transmitter as a way to cement KING-TV's control over the Northwestern market after the FCC's freeze on new broadcasting licenses ended. "Since we were the first station to go on the air in this area, there will be no excuse for our losing the dominance," she wrote Helen Hruby at Hearst, "unless we blunder, which I do not propose we shall do."

One way to avoid blundering was to hire experienced talent from the center of the television industry: New York. She wanted a seasoned broadcast executive. Andrew Haley looked for her but found no one. In the spring of 1951, she decided that Otto Brandt, the young ABC vice president in charge of television stations for the network, was her man. Less than two years earlier, Brandt had "told me in no uncertain terms, 'You're not good enough,'" she recalled long afterward. But she wanted him. "I talked to Otto at the broadcasters' convention in Chicago," she remembered. "He was a little *surprised*." As well he might have been; Haley asked her later why she had hired a man who had turned her down. "But he did it so *nicely,*" she replied. The whiz-kid ABC vice president moved to Seattle where he became a corner-stone of King Broadcasting Company's administration.

(After reaching an agreement in Brandt's New York office, Brandt, as Stimson Bullitt has written, "courteously followed her down the elevator . . . and out to the sidewalk. As they parted when she boarded a cab, he assured her that now she could feel free to return to the bridge table and to picking out hats. She did not burst out at him and cancel their deal. She said nothing and continued to employ him for several years. Her humility and restraint in part reflected what women used to be accustomed to endure.")

That summer, fortified with Brandt's experience and Hearst's capital, but still hunting for ways to fill air time, KING-TV decided to cover a relatively obscure sport: unlimited hydroplane racing. Few people in the Northwest had ever paid much attention to it; the national center of hydroplane racing was Detroit. But Seattle, an athletic backwater at the time, was ready to become enthusiastic about a local sport that most other places didn't have. And hydroplane racing, with its action, speed, and spectacular crashes, was a natural for TV. Lee Schulman talked to local hydro drivers to find out how the sport worked and then, when the boats lined up on Lake Washington for the Gold Cup race in the summer of 1951, KING-TV had cameras with rented telephoto lenses set up on the official barge, right at the finish line. There was no electricity on the barge, so KING engineers made a deal with a homeowner and ran four hundred feet of cable from his house. KING's sound booms and cameras caught the roar and spray of hydro racing and also caught their first crash. People in their living rooms could watch, live, as the *Quicksilver,* heading for the turn at the south end of the course, hurtled past the official barge and disappeared in a cloud of spray. The *Quicksilver* disintegrated, killing the driver and the on-board mechanic, and sank in eighty feet of water. KING's sportscaster, Bill O'Mara, dropped to his knees on camera and recited the Lord's Prayer.

Even then, the station tried to examine events well beyond the shores of Lake Washington. KING-TV had been producing an

An old bread truck served as KING-TV's first remote truck, which, with the transmitter on Queen Anne Hill, brought Seattle and the Northwest their first live television broadcasts.

evening news show since 1950. In 1951, it sent its news director, Charles Herring, and a cameraman to Cold-War Europe. The station also put a camera on the first troopship home from Korea as the troops arrived in Seattle.

When General Douglas MacArthur, the hero of World War II in the Pacific, disregarded orders and was relieved of his command by President Harry S. Truman, MacArthur remained a hero, particularly among political conservatives. When he returned to the United States, MacArthur was invited to address a joint session of Congress. His speech became the biggest national television event to date. Although a television cable from the East Coast to California had been completed, it hadn't yet been connected to the only station in the Northwest, so there was no way to broadcast the speech live in Seattle. But when MacArthur spoke at the University of Washington in November 1951, as part of Seattle's centennial celebration, KING-TV had two cameras there. A few weeks later, when Senator Estes Kefauver delivered a speech at a Jefferson-Jackson Day dinner in the Olympic Hotel, KING had cameras covering him, too. Kefauver had become a celebrity earlier that year, when his Senate committee held televised hearings on organized crime. Seattle viewers were unable to watch, but people on the East Coast and in California were glued to their screens.

At the end of November, though, the Northwest got some televised hearings of their own. The hearings focused on vice and official corruption in Tacoma. Seattle's neighbor to the south was still known as a bawdy port city near Fort Lewis, a center of prostitution and illicit drinking and gambling. After Prohibition, "[n]ight life in Tacoma meant bookie joints, slot-machine and pin-ball routes, unlicensed drinking spots, and an abundance of brothels, most of them in Opera Alley, between Broadway and Market Street," Murray Morgan recalls in his book *Puget's Sound*. "They offered all the glamour of a fast-food franchise, but the operators paid high rent." Morgan writes that "the military threatened to put the town off limits. . . . National magazines ran articles deploring 'Seattle's Dirty Back Yard.' "

There were allegations of wide-open prostitution, payoffs to the cops, threats made to honest citizens to keep them from talking. This was potentially juicy stuff, and a legislative committee chaired by state Senator Albert Rosellini decided to take a look at Tacoma vice. Rosellini's committee scheduled hearings at the old Tacoma armory.

KING-TV jumped at the opportunity to cover the hearings, but they presented a major technical challenge. Although Tacoma was only thirty miles away, getting a signal from the armory to the transmitter on Queen Anne required several steps. KING engineers ran 300 feet of cable from the hearing room, out of the building, and across a narrow street to the old bread truck. The signal was microwaved from the truck to the roof of the old Tacoma courthouse, relayed to the top of Squak Mountain, and relayed again to the transmitter on Queen Anne. There was a road to the top of Squak Mountain, but KING-TV needed an employee of the King County sheriff's department to unlock the gate and to stay there while the station's engineers used a sheriff's department's building on top of the mountain. There was no telephone, and the engineers had to keep in touch with the station on Queen Anne, so they drove up Squak Mountain in Dorothy Bullitt's Chrysler, which had a mobile phone.

At least they tried to drive the Chrysler up the mountain. Otto Brandt, still fresh from ABC headquarters in New York (where they probably didn't have to contend with problems like this), described their adventures in a memo the following week: "The first morning of the telecast, [engineers Bob Ferguson and George Freeman] left about 6:00 A.M. in the Jeep and Jim in the Chrysler. At one spot on the road up they could not move the Chrysler even with the county's four-wheel-drive truck and the Jeep both towing . . . so they used the winch on the county truck to drag the Chrysler up over the bad spot.

Some people who didn't have television sets bought them just so that they could watch the hearings, others watched at friends' houses or in taverns, still others stood on sidewalks and watched the sets in store windows.

"The next morning a gravel truck went up to attempt to gravel the road in the bad spot and got stuck. The Jeep and county truck winched him out of trouble—they put a cable on the truck, Jeep, and Chrysler and went up in tandem.

"Thursday, Friday, and Saturday [the remaining days of the hearing] we left the Chrysler on the mountain, taking up gas so we could keep the Chrysler battery charged, since the mobile telephone took a lot of power."

KING-TV managed to give its audience all forty hours of the Tacoma crime hearings. Spectators jammed the Tacoma armory, where KING-TV had set up one camera behind the committee with a frontal view of whoever was testifying and another to cover the witness from the side. The *Tacoma News-Tribune* described the first day's action: "Mrs. Delbert Gundstrom, smartly clad blonde recall leader, highlighted Tuesday morning's Rosellini committee hearings by weeping softly as she told of a threat on her life. Amid the hum of two television cameras, Mrs. Gundstrom . . . said her life had been threatened in a nocturnal phone call. 'The most vicious one,' she sobbed, 'was a night phone call where a man said I would look nice on a lonely road with a hole in my head.'"

The next day, the committee heard a prosecutor say that the police had received payoffs worth $20,000 in April alone. A madam told about giving liquor to patrolmen and paying $1,600 to "Pete," whom a police office had described as "the right man." The Public Safety Commissioner drew laughs when he said, "I was elected on truth and honesty." When the hearing wound up, Rosellini astonished no one by observing, "We definitely know that some people committed perjury this week."

The hearing captivated people in Tacoma and Seattle. It was the biggest local televised spectacle so far, the first local event that large numbers of people felt they *had* to watch. Some people who didn't have television sets bought them just so that they could watch the hearings, others watched at friends' houses or in taverns, still others stood on sidewalks and watched the sets in store windows. Rainy weather didn't keep the sidewalk viewers away. The *Seattle Times* ran a photograph of people in downtown Seattle clustered on a wet sidewalk outside a store window, watching in the rain, and noted that "the scene was a common one throughout the city, wherever television dealers turned on their sets in display windows. . . . Tacoma businessmen complained that 'the big show' was ruining Christmas shopping."

Seattle merchants weren't happy about what the televised hearings did to Christmas shopping, either. When Frederick & Nelson held a Friday night sale, a lot of potential customers stayed home to watch TV, and many of the people who did venture out gathered in the store's television department to watch—not to buy.

"Homes with television sets were occupied in many cases by fifteen to twenty persons," a KING-TV press release said, "and one patient husband remarked, 'I think the hearings are great, but the women looking at home are going through three or four pounds of coffee a day.'"

In Renton, the high school brought in television sets so that the students could watch.

———

The age of television had arrived. In 1949, the nation's television stations earned broadcasting revenues of $34.3 million and lost $25.3 million. In 1950, they earned more than three times as much but still lost $9.2 million. In 1951, though, revenues more than doubled again to $239.5 million, and the industry showed a net income of $43.6 million. Of the nation's 106 television stations, 93 were profitable. KING-TV had turned the corner, too. In the Seattle area, sales of television sets were closing in on 120,000. During the first sixteen months that King Broadcasting owned a television station, the number of sets increased twentyfold. April 1950, when Owen and Dorothy Bullitt were so reluctant to acknowledge that things were going well, marked the watershed. Before that, every month's accounts ended with a loss typed clearly in red ink. After that, except for an August loss of less than $700, every month showed at least a small profit. By the end of 1951, a good month netted KING-TV more than $40,000.

Not that Dorothy Bullitt was feeling flush as 1952 began. Howard Lane went into her office on February 15 and told her that Marshall Field would probably still be willing to sell its Seattle and Portland radio stations if it received an offer above $1.5 million. She noted, "Told him too steep for us."

The new year began unremarkably. KING-TV covered Golden Gloves boxing, the NCAA basketball championships (held in Seattle), and Memorial Day ceremonies at Washelli Cemetery. In March, during a local election, KING-TV kept a camera in the county auditor's office pointed at the blackboard on which people wrote vote totals as they came in. On Easter Sunday, KING-TV covered a sunrise service at Volunteer Park. "A light rain dampened the TV crew and the crowd," a memo noted, "but cameras were protected by canvas stretched over a framework."

While KING-TV's cameras focused on local events, the company went to New York again for big-time talent and hired Jim Middlebrooks, who had been chief facilities engineer at ABC.

Middlebrooks had played a key part in setting up television stations and network television centers in New York, Chicago, San Francisco, Washington, D.C., and Los Angeles. His technical expertise and knowledge of the industry would soon become very important to King Broadcasting Company.

During the summer of 1952, the coaxial cable from New York finally reached Seattle, and KING-TV was no longer isolated from live broadcasts in the rest of the country. The first event east of the Mississippi that KING's viewers saw live was the Republican National Convention, which was the first convention thoroughly dominated by television and a media event that dwarfed the Tacoma crime hearings. The telephone company had been scheduled to complete the cable up the West Coast by December 1952—much too late for KING to broadcast the convention live. Schulman, Dorothy Bullitt, and Otto Brandt talked with the head of the phone company. He said the only crew was in Nebraska. Schulman said he should bring the crew west. The telephone executive said the company didn't have the poles it needed. Schulman told him that King Broadcasting Company would get the poles. Eventually, the phone company strung the coaxial cable from Sacramento to Portland and set up a series of microwave relay stations on hilltops between Portland and Seattle, just in time for the convention. On July 6, Seattle was finally hooked into the rest of the country. "In thousands of Seattle homes," the *Post-Intelligencer* reported, "people turned knobs at 3 P.M. Sunday and were transported to Chicago." On Sunday afternoon, KING-TV brought Seattle viewers images of delegates milling through the corridors of the Chicago Hilton, and on Monday, July 7, KING brought them the convention live. The sound failed from time to time, but the picture came through clearly.

People standing at bus stops would crowd around the television sets in store windows to catch a bit of the action. Sets were purchased in unprecedented numbers. "Television set distributors in Seattle are having a hard time keeping up with the demand for sets since the start of KING-TV's network coverage of the Republican convention," the *Post-Intelligencer* reported. "One distributor reported he delivered

300 sets last week to retailers and has ordered five carloads more. A carload contains about 150 sets."

Watching all those new TVs instead of just reading about the convention in newspapers or listening to the speeches on radio enabled people to see the little human touches that no reporter would have bothered to describe. "Minor mannerisms of the leaders, seen and heard for the first time, evoked comment," reported the *Post-Intelligencer*. When General MacArthur gave the keynote address, viewers "saw [him] lean forward slightly from the hips . . . attacking a battery of microphones. . . . People learned for the first time that the general bounces on his toes when he hits the 'heavy' part of a speech. No news commentator would have told them the general took one drink of water . . . a human act that made the man more real."

MacArthur's heightened reality did not mark a step toward greater political understanding. The camera that focuses on a general sipping water makes it easy to concentrate on personal details, rather than political substance, and makes it hard to see public figures—except sports or entertainment figures—as larger than life. "[I]mages displace ideas, personalities replace policies, and fiction merges with fact," Ronald K. L. Collins and David M. Skover argue in *The Death of Discourse*. "As politicians master the strategies of advertising and entertainment programming, the gulf between important political expression and pure amusement nearly vanishes." Politicians started to master those strategies in the presidential campaign of 1952.

KING-TV broadcast Dwight Eisenhower's nomination at the Republican convention and Adlai Stevenson's nomination a couple of weeks later by the Democrats. It also covered politics closer to home, where Representative Henry M. Jackson, a Democrat, won the nomination to run against Senator Harry Cain, the Republican incumbent who was considered very vulnerable. Ancil Payne's employer, Democratic U.S. Representative Hugh Mitchell, who had lost that nomination to Jackson, was running for governor, against a former Seattle mayor and former governor, Arthur Langlie. Stimson Bullitt was running as a Democrat for Congress.

In October, Senator Joseph McCarthy of Wisconsin scheduled a trip to Seattle to campaign for Cain and other Republican candidates. Around the middle of the month, a Seattle advertising executive called KING-TV to see about buying fifteen minutes of air time for McCarthy, and sent the station a check for $267.75 as payment for the time slot between between 8:45 and 9:00 P.M. on October 23.

At the time, McCarthy was perhaps the most feared public figure in the United States. An otherwise undistinguished junior senator, he stumbled across the issue of Communists in the federal government and rode it for all it was worth, making allegations that were never supported by fact, but making them so brazenly—to such a large, receptive audience—that the nation's leaders were afraid to cross him. "McCarthy . . . held two presidents captive—or as nearly captive as any presidents of the United States have ever been held—in their conduct of the nation's affairs," wrote Richard H. Rovere in a 1959 biography, *Senator Joe McCarthy*. "Harry S. Truman and Dwight D. Eisenhower, from early 1950 through late 1954, could never act without weighing the effect of their plans upon McCarthy and the forces he led."

Some KING-TV people were uneasy about having McCarthy on the air. A KING-TV sales account executive, John Pindell, discussed with the Seattle ad agency KING's policy of reviewing scripts before people went on the air and said that the afternoon of October 21 would be the normal deadline. The ad agency said it had already given information about the policy to Senator Cain's office, which would wire the details to McCarthy. Whether or not McCarthy's camp ever got the message isn't clear, but late on the afternoon of October 22, the advertising executive told Pindell that he hadn't heard anything back.

Worried, Pindell called the ad agency the next morning. He and the agency's Dave Crockett agreed that two o'clock would be the absolute deadline for giving KING-TV a script. When two o'clock rolled around, he called the agency again, and was told that McCarthy was dictating the speech at that very moment; a script would be available by three. Pindell said that if it wasn't there by

3:30, the speech was off. Then he left the office, leaving instructions that if the script arrived, it should be rushed to King's attorney, Dick Riddell. When he returned after 4:30, he was told that the script had finally arrived.

Most of it was routine political rhetoric, but the third and fourth paragraphs caught Riddell's eye. McCarthy planned to accuse two employees of nationally syndicated columnist Drew Pearson, with whom the senator had a bitter running feud, of Communist associations. One was "proven to be a Communist by FBI undercover agents." The other, under an alias, "worked for the official Communist paper, the *Daily Worker*, and then was rewrite man for the Communist Party organization."

Riddell wrote "delete" next to the two paragraphs, but asked Pindell if it would be better to simply delete them or to suggest substitute language. Pindell thought it would be better to have some substitute. He called the ad agency and explained the situation. He and Crockett agreed that the script with substitute language appended would be waiting at the studio when McCarthy arrived. To replace McCarthy's defamatory statements, Riddell wrote out, "Did you know that two of the men who have worked on Pearson's staff are reputed former Communists?" Pindell had typewritten copies of that new language stapled to copies of the speech. He also called Lee Schulman and said that the moment McCarthy deviated from the written speech, he was to be cut off the air.

Riddell, in the meantime, went home to his house on Mercer Island, took off his shoes, put up his feet, and settled down with a Scotch and soda. He was ready for a leisurely evening at home when Henry Owen called and asked him to meet him at the studio right away. Owen and Riddell arrived at lower Queen Anne after 8:00 P.M., just before McCarthy and his entourage walked in. McCarthy had been speaking at a Press Club Gridiron Dinner across the street at the Norway Center, telling local journalists that "you can't fight skunks with kid gloves and lace cuffs."

McCarthy came in grinning, accompanied by a congressional candidate, Al Canwell (who as a Washington State senator had used a legislative committee in McCarthy fashion to run a Communist witch hunt of his own), Senator Cain's wife, and others. Riddell was called over to explain the situation. He told McCarthy that the speech contained some unacceptable language and would have to be changed. McCarthy said he was a candidate for office, so the station couldn't censor his script. Riddell replied that he was a candidate for office in *Wisconsin*. The conversation went back and forth. Pindell "got the impression that McCarthy did not give Riddell a chance to discuss the matter with him but seized upon our request as material out of which he could make an issue and proceeded to do so, stating that he would not permit his speech to be censored. . . . He also referred to our suggested substitution as 'libelous material.' At this point Mrs. Cain became dramatically upset." Riddell told McCarthy that he would have his finger on the button and the moment McCarthy started to say anything unacceptable, he would cut off the sound. McCarthy refused to go on under those circumstances. McCarthy then took the copy that KING had prepared and started to make his own changes.

"The group then moved to the lobby," Pindell recalled, "and at this point Riddell asked to see [a quote about J. Edgar Hoover]. Riddell again tried to discuss the matter with McCarthy, but McCarthy was adamant in his stand that this was censorship and he would not submit to it. . . . Senator Warren Magnuson [who had been scheduled to deliver a Democratic rebuttal to McCarthy's speech] . . . was greeted by McCarthy and McCarthy called on him to be a witness. . . . I got the impression that Magnuson wanted no part of it and he told McCarthy that he didn't know what was going on."

The station finally announced on the air that McCarthy had refused to go on, a statement "to which McCarthy took rather violent exception." A member of McCarthy's entourage called the *Post-Intelligencer*, and soon McCarthy was on one phone giving his version of the incident to the press while Otto Brandt was on another phone, giving the King Broadcasting Company's version.

The station had faced down the witch-hunting senator from Wisconsin. The station hadn't picked the fight; it had simply followed the same cautious legal procedures with McCarthy that it would have followed with anyone else. But the incident reflected the character King Broadcasting had already displayed. That same year, KING had produced a show on integration and "we got a lot of calls from people who were furious," Elizabeth Wright Evans recalled fifteen years later. "I stood there crying, and along came Dorothy Bullitt. . . . People were violent. How dare I show Negroes and whites in these situations? Mrs. Bullitt said, 'Never you mind; if you did what you thought was right, this station will back you up the full way. Don't you worry about it.'" The McCarthy episode may have shown less devotion to principle, but it took some fortitude. At that point in American history, a lot of people would have gone out of their way to avoid getting on McCarthy's bad side. Before the senator left the studio, he threatened to have the FCC revoke KING-TV's license. He actually tried to do it, though he didn't get anywhere.

Cain subsequently lost the election to Henry Jackson, who would remain in the Senate until his death thirty-one years later. But Eisenhower led a great Republican sweep, and other Democratic candidates didn't fare as well. Mitchell lost the gubernatorial race to Langlie, leaving Mitchell's assistant, Ancil Payne, out of professional politics. And Stimson Bullitt lost his race for Congress to Tom Pelly, short-circuiting Bullitt's own professional political career. Bullitt ran again in 1954, and then gave up on electoral politics.

―――――

King Broadcasting Company was particularly eager to stay on the FCC's good side. In the summer of 1952, the agency ended the freeze on new stations, and the inevitable scramble for channels started. The end of the freeze meant that KING-TV would finally face competition in Seattle. But it would also create opportunities in other cities, which would be allowed to have television stations for the first time. The FCC's list of candidate cities for new television channels included Portland, Oregon, and Spokane, Washington. Andrew Haley suggested to Dorothy Bullitt that King try for a station in Portland; there was a lot to gain, he figured, and very little to lose. She decided to take his advice.

There would obviously be competition for the Portland channel, and the FCC would have to choose the applicant that would, in its opinion, do the best job. Eventually, four different companies, including huge, diversified Westinghouse Electric, applied for permission to broadcast over Portland's Channel 8. The FCC would make its decision after a formal hearing in Washington, D.C. King Broadcasting would have to start laying a foundation for its application and hearing testimony right away. The first step, Haley pointed out, would be lining up some Portland investors; the FCC would look for local involvement, and Seattle wouldn't be local enough.

A couple of Portland businessmen had already been talking about television. One of them, W. Calder McCall, president of the McCall Oil Company, said in 1953 that his interest "developed the first time I ever saw television. [Paul L. Murphy, president of Gas Heat, Inc. and Oregon Iron and Steel] and I were in New York at the time when the Kefauver [hearings] were on. We were staying in a hotel where they had television sets . . . there were days when I never left my room, they were so fascinating. . . .

"At a party at my home one night . . . Mr. Murphy and Henry Kuckenberg [president of the Kuckenberg Construction Company] were there and I mentioned to Mr. Kuckenberg that I thought this was going to be a tremendous business, and I thought we ought to see if we could get into it."

In 1952 McCall, who had just returned from a trip to New York and Washington, D.C., was playing golf with Murphy, when "Mr. Murphy said to me . . . 'I know a way that we might be able to get into this television business. . . . While you were gone . . . Henry [Kuckenberg] and I had a visit from Mrs. Bullitt.'"

The three men flew to Seattle on July 12, 1952, and met all morning with Dorothy Bullitt. Around one o'clock, they took a long lunch and talked until it was time for Henry Owen to drive them to the airport. Back in Portland, the three businessmen kept discussing the idea of starting a television station, and on July 16, they met with Dorothy Bullitt at the University Club. The Portland men argued that if they formed a new company to pursue a television license, it should be split fifty-fifty between King Broadcasting and themselves. Dorothy Bullitt wasn't about to give them half. Her company would supply the expertise, she said, and she expected control. She didn't care what the exact numbers were, but King Broadcasting was going to have more than 50 percent. She won. King Broadcasting and a group of Portland investors—McCall, Murphy, Kuckenberg, Gordon D. Orput (the Oregon general agent for the New England Mutual Life Insurance Company), and Prescott W. Cookingham (a partner in a Portland law firm)—would form a new company, North Pacific Television. It would acquire a radio station and apply for a television license. The Portland group would own 40 percent of the company and control the radio operation. King Broadcasting would own 60 percent and control the television operation. And the tail would not be able to wag the dog: if Dorothy Bullitt ever decided to sell King's 60 percent, the Portland people would have to sell their 40 percent at the same price.

The next year King and the Portland investors acquired Pioneer Broadcasting, which operated Portland's oldest radio station, KGW. The station had gone on the air in 1922, had made its network debut in 1927 by broadcasting a speech of President Calvin Coolidge, and had produced what were arguably the nation's first audience-participation show, first quiz show, and first singing commercials.

As the FCC hearing approached in early 1953, North Pacific Television was busy finding out what Oregon wanted its first television station to be. To satisfy the FCC, broadcasters were forever surveying their communities' alleged programming preferences. These surveys ignored what people really wanted to watch (viewers were not asked if they'd prefer more sex and violence) and did not affect the *quality* of news or cultural programming. The company hired a friend of Gloria Chandler's named Helen Platt, who had written scripts for Chandler's "Books Bring Adventure," to find out what was important to Oregonians outside Portland. Platt, with whom Dorothy Bullitt subsequently stayed when she visited Portland, was a great-granddaughter of Henry Clark, a missionary who had arrived in Oregon on horseback in 1840. Chandler assured Dorothy Bullitt that

Platt knew all there was to know about Oregon. She was certainly at least willing to find out; Platt borrowed a car and drove to every county in the state talking to politicians and academics. She "would go to a little town and stop at the drugstore or the court-house or some place and say, 'Who's the mayor and where is he,'" Bullitt recalled. "Someone would reply, 'Well, his last name is Jones, and he's got an orchard over there. I think you'll probably find

Dorothy Bullitt's success in broadcasting would not have been possible without the knowledge and skill of Andrew Haley, her adviser and friend.

him out in the orchard picking apples.' So she would plow through rough ground until she found the mayor. Or maybe he was in the pool hall so she'd go to the pool hall and interview the mayor." Dorothy Bullitt and Gloria Chandler pumped people for information, too. In Portland, "Gloria and I went to the three top religious leaders of the city. And we followed the rabbi. . . . He wouldn't answer the telephone and we couldn't find him at home and we finally caught him coming down the steps of the synagogue and we jumped out of the car and cornered him on the steps."

The big showdown with Westinghouse and the two lesser competitors started in February 1953. Andrew Haley orchestrated North Pacific's performance before the FCC from start to finish. Gloria Chandler left for Washington, D.C., at the beginning of February to help him prepare. She, Dorothy Bullitt, and Jim Middlebrooks were holed up in the Mayflower Hotel when the hearings began. Middlebrooks shuttled between Washington, D.C., and Seattle; at one point, he flew east with 350 pounds of exhibits.

On February 8, 1953, Dorothy Bullitt was "up early and worked all day searching through renewal applications of all Westinghouse radio and TV stations for 1948 and 1949, comparing and analyzing program schedules . . . personnel, staffing, etc." On February 9, she spent "all day digging through Westinghouse exhibits." Haley had her make up a list of questions he should ask her, then make up a list of answers. Routinely, she "worked until 11:30 each night." Some nights she had a real dinner and went back to work. Other nights, she just went out for a cheap hamburger at the nearby White Tower.

Westinghouse was represented by the blue-chip New York law firm now known as Cravath, Swaine and Moore. North Pacific was represented by Haley's firm, Haley and Doty. "The Westinghouse group came in their wedge formation . . . in their swallowtail coats," Ancil Payne remembered Dorothy Bullitt's description years later. "They just looked like they were going to be ambassadors to the world or something."

Payne talked years later at a cocktail party with a Portland executive who had been part of another group competing for the television license. The man remembered, "This big guy named Haley was roaring along at the head of the team. Behind him came two women. One looked like she should be president of the Junior League and the other one looked like she should be president of the American Garden Club. I said, 'If we can't defeat those two old women, we should take the night train out of here.' And before they finished they had run our heads through a pencil sharpener. We did leave in the middle of the night. I never took such a beating in my life."

I said, 'If we can't defeat those two old women, we should take the night train out of here.' And before they finished they had run our heads through a pencil sharpener. We did leave in the middle of the night. I never took such a beating in my life.

Otto Brandt flew to Washington to appear before the hearing examiner. He stressed KING-TV's history of corporate virtue. King Broadcasting was a charter subscriber to the National Association of Radio and Television Broadcasters code of conduct, which established voluntary standards of taste and decorum for television programs and ads. (Dorothy Bullitt was the only woman on the five-person board that established the first code, and she served as a member of the Code Board for eight years.) Even before the code existed, Brandt said, "We operated with a code of our own. . . . For example, we would not permit beer advertising earlier than seven o'clock. We would not allow crime programs to be broadcast prior to nine o'clock."

Nevertheless, Brandt recalled, "While we were here in Washington for the hearing . . . the University of Washington was having a conference of various experts, teachers and others, interested in drama, and . . . we put on . . . a dramatic skit which had been written by Glenn Hughes, who is the head of the University of Washington drama department, and . . . some language that people might object to was telecast by KING-TV. My face was . . . very red and I . . . [had] the producer-director who worked that show suspended for a week."

Haley knew what the FCC examiner wanted. Gloria Chandler testified at length about children's programming. Well-drilled by Haley, Dorothy Bullitt made it clear that she could remember company finances down to the last dollar.

The Westinghouse lawyers tried to create the impression that she was a lot sharper and better versed in North Pacific's corporate subtleties than the Portland investors were. Paul Murphy was asked if he realized that he was "putting in the hands of a Seattle group the right to decide at any future date that Portland people's participation in your station could be wiped out?"

"I think we were aware of that," Murphy replied.

The Westinghouse lawyers pursued the same point with another Portland investor, Prescott Cookingham. "If Mrs. Bullitt herself were to be the purchaser of the stock in North Pacific held by King," Cookingham was asked, "she, in effect, could force the Portland stockholders to sell out to her, is that not true?"

Cookingham said he thought that "the question of good faith might be involved. . . . If, for instance, she should decide to buy the King stock at $35 a share instead of $100 and force us to sell our stock at that, I do not believe that would be enforceable."

Dorothy Bullitt and King Broadcasting met the corporate giant Westinghouse in a battle for a television license—and won. KGW became Portland's first television station.

The Westinghouse lawyer kept at it. "But you would not apply that [reasoning] to the purchase of King stock by a member of the [Bullitt] family, would you?" he asked.

"No," Cookingham conceded. "I think she is entitled to transfer her King stock to her own family [and] they could elect to demand the sale of our King stock."

This exchange had no noticeable effect on the FCC, but it embarassed the Portland investors. "The Westinghouse lawyer humiliated them," said Dorothy Bullitt. "They threatened to go home that night, and Andy had to hold them together and walk them up and down the hall until they agreed to finish out the [hearing]."

After the incident, relations between Dorothy Bullitt and most of the Portland group were permanently strained.

For now, she and the Portland investors needed each other, at least until the FCC made its decision. Her alliance with Hearst, on the other hand, had outlived its usefulness. In March, the North Pacific people noticed that Westinghouse's lawyers had amassed stacks of documents about the King Broadcasting Company's relationship with Hearst. Politically right-wing and historically associated with sensational yellow journalism, the Hearst organization was controversial and certainly no more homegrown than Westinghouse; King's Hearst connection could conceivably be used against North Pacific. A nasty fight in a public hearing might not be good for Hearst, either. There was an easy way around the problem. Dorothy Bullitt and Henry Owen went to New York and talked with Hearst's president. She named a price. He said it was fair. On Friday, March 13, Dorothy Bullitt bought back Hearst's 25 percent of the King Broadcasting Company. On April 1, when she began her testimony before the FCC, Haley asked her if there were any changes in her biography. "Yes," she replied. "On page two, at the top of the page, my stock in King Broadcasting Company is listed as 64.45 percent and it is now 85.93." The Westinghouse lawyers objected vehemently, but there was nothing illegal about the transaction, and the deed was done.

Ultimately, Westinghouse did a lot to cut its own throat. "Will you tell me why Westinghouse Electric and Westinghouse Radio Stations are interested in owning and operating radio and television stations?" the company's own attorney asked its president, Gwilyn A. Price. "We have been in [the broadcasting business] because it has proven to be, on the whole, a profitable business," Price answered in the presence of an FCC commissioner who wanted to hear about public service. In addition, Price said, "We feel that . . . if we operate our stations in the public interest as they should be operated then they reflect credit on the company and they directly serve to keep our name before the public and they indirectly result in building up an acceptance for our industrial products . . . and our consumer products." In other words, as Dorothy Bullitt summed it up later, "broadcasting helped Westinghouse advertise its refrigerators and toasters."

Price talked at some length about the Westinghouse-owned broadcasting stations. Asked if he could recite the frequency, power, and operating hours of those stations, he answered, "No sir." Asked where Westinghouse's Portland station was located, he replied, "I am not familiar enough with the city of Portland to be able to tell you exact locations." So much for the issue of local control.

When the hearings finally ended in July, Dorothy Bullitt and her colleagues had to go home and wait for the FCC to make up its mind. They waited nearly a year. Finally, in June 1954 the hearing examiner recommended awarding the license to North Pacific. The King group's significant local ownership and King Broadcasting's record of children's programming tipped the scales. The hearing examiner's "decision comes as a surprise," reported *Variety*, the entertainment industry journal, on June 30, "and a blow to the Westinghouse interests, which had spent considerable funds in pushing for the grant. In fact Westinghouse some time back had even made overtures to CBS for [a network] affiliation, so confident was it of winning the coveted channel."

The decision was a personal triumph for Dorothy Bullitt. "If the examiner's recommendation is made final," *Variety* observed, she "will become the leading woman in the broadcasting industry."

Haley was quick to warn her that the apparent victory could still be snatched away—the FCC didn't have to accept the examiner's recommendation—and that Westinghouse would do its best to snatch it. "Now that the flush of our initial victory has cleared away," he wrote to her on July 6, "we must take a very sober and hard look at what we face to achieve the final victory.

"[One of the attorneys who represented Westinghouse at the hearing] reported to me that [a Westinghouse attorney] stated that he is determined to go all the way to achieve the final victory. We may expect him to redouble his confidential agents and spies in an effort to obtain some positive proof that we are not in a position to perform as we testified in the hearings. . . .

"Westinghouse has been wining and dining the commissioners at an accelerated pace for the past year, and you may rest assured that its influential men are in and out of the White House and other centers of information in Washington and elsewhere. . . . Westinghouse will leave no stone unturned in an effort to reverse the examiner."

Caution may have been in order, but that didn't lessen the sense of triumph. A couple of weeks earlier, when word of the hearing examiner's recommendation reached Seattle, Schulman wrote to Dorothy Bullitt, "When the news hit here I could feel Jim [Middlebrooks] smile all the way through the walls. I don't think I've ever heard Otto sound quite the same as when we broke the news to him on the phone in Portland. Henry came back last night looking like the cat who had swallowed the canary. . . .

"It's the greatest thrill I've ever known. . . .

"It's a long, long way from an August day in 1949, isn't it?"

It certainly was. King Broadcasting could play in the big leagues now. For the rest of Dorothy Bullitt's long life, beating Westinghouse in the contest for Portland was one of the things she remembered with the greatest satisfaction.

CHAPTER FOUR

A REGION PLUGS IN
1953–1961

ESTINGHOUSE'S POST-HEARING WINING and dining of FCC commissioners—if it really took place—was a waste of money. In June 1955, the FCC announced that it would award a license to North Pacific Television. At the beginning of the year, Andrew Haley told Dorothy Bullitt that he was afraid they had lost. In March, though, Warren Magnuson called Dorothy Bullitt and Henry Owen to let them know that the FCC commissioners had taken a confidential vote, and North Pacific had won, five to two. Haley called right afterward and warned them to keep the news to themselves. A representative of another group competing for the license offered King $50,000 to drop out; Dorothy Bullitt and Owen didn't consider the offer worth discussing. A few days later, Owen arrived at her house late at night with an insider who told her that the FCC meeting had been deadlocked, but that the only female commissioner, Freida Hennock, had persuaded a couple of her colleagues to switch to North Pacific.

Hennock's support for North Pacific can't have surprised anyone. There weren't many women in broadcasting beyond the level of secretaries, and if that didn't give Hennock and Bullitt enough in common, they had also been allies in fighting to have the FCC set aside a vacant channel in each city for educational television. "As a female FCC commissioner in the late 1940s and early 1950s, Freida Hennock was a conspicuous enough Washington anomaly," wrote Mary Ann Watson in *The Expanding Vista: American Television in the Kennedy Years.* "But the politically ambitious Truman appointee also had brassy manners and a proclivity for publicity. Although these qualities irritated her male colleagues, Hennock put them to use for a good cause." Irritating or not, she won her battle for educational television: thanks largely to Hennock, when the freeze ended, channels were set aside in twenty-five cities that had educational institutions which might be able to run nonprofit stations. "If it had not been for Freida Hennock, there might have been no educational channels," Dorothy Bullitt said. "She fought for it hard, and she held to it like a puppy to a bone."

"Blessings on Freida!" Dorothy Bullitt wrote when news of the FCC's confidential vote reached her in 1955. Having friends in high places didn't hurt. But she was aware that some of her friends might be a little overzealous. Around the same time, she wrote, "All our friends are pulling for us, but it could so easily be overdone and do more harm than good." King and its allies didn't make any crucial mistakes; at last, the FCC awarded Portland's Channel 8 to North Pacific Television.

By the time the FCC made its announcement, the Portland investors' tense relationship with Dorothy Bullitt had passed the point of no return. The Portland men may have brought the situation upon themselves, or Dorothy Bullitt may have planned from the start to get rid of them as soon as she got the license—or both. A group of successful businessmen in the early 1950s may have resented being led by a woman. Men used to running their own companies may have wanted to run this one. But the relationship may have been doomed whatever the Portland investors did. Dorothy Bullitt probably never envisioned having less than full control of the Portland station.

The only member of the Portland group whom Dorothy Bullitt considered a friend was W. Calder McCall, who quit after arguing with Paul Murphy at a board meeting. "They got mad at each other and one called the other a liar," Bullitt recalled. McCall "got up and walked out of the room, slammed the door, and never came to another meeting. He said, 'I don't have to! I don't have to put up with that!' So he was out." McCall left the board and unloaded his stock.

At the end of 1955, after some nasty negotiations (during which Bullitt thought that Andrew Haley and Henry Kuckenberg might actually come to blows) King Broadcasting bought an extra 20 percent of Pioneer Broadcasting, thereby gaining control of the radio operation. In January 1956, Pioneer merged with North Pacific Television. In April, the name of the entire company was changed to Pioneer.

By that time, Dorothy Bullitt was prepared to dump the Portland investors once and for all. It wasn't hard. RCA had submitted a bid to build the new Portland television station. The contract with RCA was all ready to sign. In June, Dorothy Bullitt went to a Portland lawyer and had him draw up two resolutions, which she took to a Pioneer board meeting. The board members reviewed the RCA engineering contract, and she gave Gordon Orput, the Pioneer president, a resolution that called for accepting the contract. The board voted for it without much ado. "Then I slid the other [resolution] over and his face blanched." The second resolution called for all the stockholders to actually pay the money they had pledged for their shares. The money was needed to pay for RCA's equipment and services under the contract that they had just signed. But the Portland men had never planned to risk much capital in broadcasting. "In a few minutes [Orput] said, 'Come out in the hall,' and he said, 'I can't put that up.' And I said, 'You have to.' He said, 'The roof's going to come off. I can't do it.' And I said, 'I'm not going home without it.'" The Portland men would have to put up or shut up. Orput suggested putting off the decision until the next morning at nine. Before nine, Orput called Dorothy Bullitt at Helen Platt's house, where she was staying, and told her not to come back yet. She, James Middlebrooks, and Platt "sat there playing gin rummy waiting for the telephone and the telephone rang again. And he said, 'We're making some progress, but still don't come down.' About dinner they said, 'We've got a deal. Will you meet us in the lawyer's office this evening?'" They called and put off the evening meeting, too, but eventually Dorothy Bullitt and Middlebrooks met the Portland men, who offered a one-page agreement. The Portland investors would simply give up their television stock. King Broadcasting would buy out their radio stock. King would own everything. The Portland operation would all be hers. (She acquired their stock in June 1957 and merged Pioneer Broadcasting into King that December.)

———

Long before King Broadcasting forced out the Portland investors, KING-TV lost its monopoly position in Seattle. It could no longer pick and choose among all four networks' programs. After the FCC freeze ended, all the networks except ABC switched to other stations. Tacoma's KTNT-TV started broadcasting CBS and Dumont network programs in March 1953 (Dumont folded soon afterward, and KTNT-TV quickly lost its CBS affiliation to KIRO-TV), and Seattle's KOMO-TV went on the air with NBC programs in December.

The end of the FCC freeze was less traumatic than Dorothy Bullitt had feared in the spring of 1951, when she was negotiating with Hearst and thought it might end any day. At that time, she went to a King board meeting "full of jitters" and offered to buy everyone else's shares of the company. The other board members were willing to stick it out, and she was "quite touched."

Now, in 1953, there was no talk of buying out the other board members. Even after being abandoned by CBS and NBC, KING-TV was still way ahead of the pack.

While the new stations were definitely competitors, in a sense they were clones of KING-TV. Lee Schulman, the only person in Seattle with television production experience, had taught everyone at KING-TV how to do things, and as opportunities expanded, his pupils moved out from KING to staff the other stations. Early television in the Seattle area was produced largely by people who had learned their trade from Lee Schulman.

New pupils kept arriving at KING. Kit Spier directed plays at the Tacoma Little Theater. His wife, who was doing a KING-TV show once a week for the *Post-Intelligencer*, encouraged him to try directing television. At the beginning of 1953, he went to see Schulman. Schulman took him down to the Smith Tower, where the executives still had their offices, to meet Otto Brandt. "Otto," he said, "I'd like you to meet our new director." Spier stayed at King for years; he played a key role in translating Schulman's visions into reality.

Although KING-TV still had most of the local expertise and the lion's share of the local audience, the end of the freeze left it with the weakest major network and, for the first time, the station had to work to hang on to its viewers.

Jack Fearey had been working for a Bellingham radio station in the early 1950s. His wife and the wife of KING-TV sports announcer Bill O'Mara had been sorority sisters, and at the end of 1953 O'Mara arranged an interview with Lee Schulman. Fearey drove down to Seattle to talk with Schulman. "What makes you think you can do this job?" Schulman asked. "What made you think you could do this job when you came out from New York?" Fearey answered. Schulman told him, "I want you to come and join the family." He did.

Fearey soon discovered the lengths to which Schulman expected his "family" to go for a story. The next year, Fearey was sent with cameraman Ted Simpson to cover an attempt by Florence Chadwick, who had swum the English Channel—a big media event in those days—to swim across the Strait of Juan de Fuca. Feary and Simpson accompanied Chadwick in a rowboat, with a seasick Fearey at the oars. They delivered their film to a barge, from which a helicopter took it to a developing lab set up in Port Angeles, from which it was taken to Seattle. Chadwick didn't make it, but KING's audience got to watch her try.

Although KING-TV still had most of the local expertise and the lion's share of the local audience, the end of the freeze left it with the weakest major network. For the first time, the station had to work to hang on to its viewers. In 1955, when ABC was angry at KING-TV for not running more network programs, Otto Brandt wrote to network president Robert Kintner, "The first five years of KING-TV's operation were accomplished during the period when ABC was not a real program source. At the time we became an 'exclusive' ABC affiliate, the network still was not ready to provide ample programming. This situation, together with our determination to stay in the number-one spot in this market, meant that we had to operate virtually as independent."

Brandt described KING-TV's early post-freeze experience in a letter he sent to the owner of a Tulsa television station that was about to face competition for the first time. "The most important fact of television life that we have learned as a result of competition is that we were wrong in our belief that a good local live personality or program built up over the years would be a match for almost anything new competition could throw against it," Brandt wrote. "The audience is a great deal more fickle than that and so an old-time local favorite is going to have to be a better program than the film shown against it. The audience is not going to watch . . . for old times' sake."

Dorothy Bullitt didn't like being stuck with ABC after the freeze. She didn't like ABC's image. The network made itself competitive with NBC and CBS during the mid–1950s, but only, in her opinion, by emphasizing trashy entertainment. "It was really a Hollywood sort of network, show biz," she remembered later. The people who represented ABC in Seattle struck her as Hollywood, too. Her attitude toward them was colored, evidently, by the fact that they were Jewish. Dorothy Bullitt hired Jews, she worked with Jews, but she referred to her ally, Freida Hennock, as a "Jewess," and clearly, she felt that Jews were different. "The owner was a type that I didn't like very well," she said later about ABC. He was "the wrong kind. Some of them I like very much. Some of them I can't stand. They lied and pushed and did whatever for an extra dollar. That wasn't the way we were trying to build a station."

Lest this be considered an expression of simple anti-Semitism, one should realize that she coveted an affiliation with NBC, which was also run by a Jew; in fact, the particular Jew who ran it, David Sarnoff, the chairman of RCA, was one of NBC's great attractions for her.

Sarnoff had emigrated from czarist Russia to New York as a boy, had grown rich as the chairman of RCA, and had been the great promoter of television before World War II. He was autocratic, self-important—but, in many ways, a man after her own heart. In 1937, Sarnoff hired the great Italian conductor Arturo Toscanini to conduct the NBC Symphony Orchestra, luring Toscanini to New York not only with money but also with the promise that he could handpick an entire orchestra to play under him. Years later, watching television in his London hotel room, Sarnoff remarked that the state-run BBC was closer to his original vision of the medium than American commercial programming.

Dorothy Bullitt tried, well before the freeze ended, to persuade NBC to choose KING-TV over the television station KOMO would form. She got Hearst's vice president for radio and television, Don Provost, to talk with NBC. She talked with NBC herself. She kept getting turned down. In April 1952, she made a kind of breakthrough when NBC asked her to send information about KING-TV to its headquarters in New York. But Provost wrote her on April 14, 1952, "After a talk last week with several people at NBC, I can only report that their reaction is negative. . . . The way it looks now I think action would come only on an order from General Sarnoff."

She repeatedly visited NBC's vice president in charge of affiliates, "a great big fat funny man" named Harry Bannister who "told the truth, which was a rarity in the network business." She pestered Bannister so often that he later toasted her as "the woman I have said 'no' to more than any other." According to her notes of the mid-1950s, Bannister "hates the country, fresh air, etc. Loves N.Y., smoke-filled rooms, etc. Drinks, smokes, wears a baseball cap at his desk to keep air conditioner off his bald head. Usually does not leave his office during day." She remembered that "at one appointment, the World Series was on and he never took his eyes off the screen, and I sat there watching the World Series and our time ran out. There was all sorts of funny treatment. But he was honest with me. He said, 'Listen, I'm going to tell you the truth. I think you're all right. In Seattle we are affiliated with the Fishers [who owned KOMO], who are running a sloppy operation. We know it's sloppy, but Mr. Fisher is a friend of the general's and they play cards together. Whenever Mr. Fisher is East they go out to long lunches. And we can't make a move without the general. Now, if he should say "make a change," I would, but he is not about to. So there's your problem.'"

In November 1953, a chance to take the first step toward winning over David Sarnoff fell into her lap. The Navy had built the world's most powerful radio station in the Cascade Mountains near Arlington, Washington, north of Seattle. With twelve big steel towers and thirty miles of antenna wire, the 1.2-million-watt station could send low-frequency signals to Navy submarines under the polar ice cap and to other vessels literally all over the world. The equipment had been built by RCA in Camden, New Jersey, and hauled across the country to Washington on twenty-seven freight cars. Naval officers, politicians, and local business leaders were invited to the dedication ceremony. Sarnoff flew in by private plane. Dorothy Bullitt arranged to get her name on the guest list. She also discovered that the Fishers had made no plans to have dinner with Sarnoff, so she invited him to dinner at her house on Capitol Hill. Her daughter, Patsy, and her son, Stimson, and their spouses were invited, too. At dinner, she asked Sarnoff to tell the story of how, as a young telegraph operator in the Marconi wireless station at Wanamaker's store in lower Manhattan, he received the first news of the *Titanic*'s sinking and stayed at his post for three days and nights—America's only link with the disaster in the north Atlantic. The general was happy to oblige. The dramatic story formed part of the Sarnoff legend, although, according to Sarnoff's biographer, Kenneth Bilby, it probably wasn't entirely true. Everyone at least pretended to listen raptly and Sarnoff, who wound up in the pantry mixing his own martini, had a fine time.

Dorothy Bullitt was determined to ingratiate herself with Sarnoff, and was willing to do whatever it took. She made notes on the personal characteristics and preferences of Sarnoff, his wife, and other key people. She found out that the general's wife was head of volunteer services at the New York Infirmary for Women, and spent Mondays, Wednesdays, and Thursdays in the hospital gift shop—so Dorothy Bullitt waylaid her in the gift shop. The general's wife had a "very limited social life" because "her husband's friends are principally business associates," so Dorothy Bullitt invited her to lunch. The general's wife "doesn't like to fly," so when Dorothy Bullitt and the Sarnoffs attended a dinner in Washington, D.C., she assumed they would return to New York by train. She caught the eleven o'clock train herself and sat outside their stateroom until Sarnoff came out, saw her, and invited her to sit with them the rest of the way to New York. She made no secret of her desire to hook up with NBC, and before they left the train, Sarnoff's son, Bob, said, "You have nothing to worry about but your patience." One way or another, she kept turning up in Sarnoff's life.

And she kept turning up in NBC executives' offices. According to her notes, Bob Sarnoff told her, "It is [NBC's] unanimous wish to affiliate with us [in Portland] but not now. Hopes we can wait." CBS too "would like to affiliate with us, but not just now—can we wait a little while? Sounds like a record. Same answer as NBC." In March 1958, she holed up in a New York hotel room, laying siege to the network. Haley "says we must stay and live close to NBC here in N.Y.. . . . Stayed in all eve in hotel—Otto going home this eve. Wish desperately I could go too." In April, she had lunch with Mrs. Sarnoff, Gloria Chandler, and two doctors from Mrs. Sarnoff's favorite hospital, giving little key-chain music boxes to her guests.

Her persistence finally paid off. General Sarnoff's son phoned her in Seattle and told her to come to New York. She had Haley join her there. (There was a lot of intrigue going on. CBS was interested in affiliating with KING, too—like NBC, it probably welcomed the prospect of getting stations in both Portland and Seattle—but it didn't want anyone to know it was interested. Consequently, CBS executives wanted Dorothy Bullitt to stay away from their offices; they talked with her in the doorway of Saks Fifth Avenue and other public spots.) Dorothy Bullitt and Haley met with NBC's president and chief counsel to talk about switching KING-TV and KGW-TV to NBC. After a while, the president told his secretary to bring champagne. That was when Harry Bannister, who had been invited to the office, proposed his toast to Dorothy Bullitt. They all drank champagne, then Bannister took her out to dinner.

Bannister and Brandt announced NBC's new affiliation with KING-TV in New York on October 15, 1958. KOMO complained that "NBC's announcement . . . came as a complete surprise to us. . . . We do not know what political, economic, or ulterior forces were brought to bear on NBC to destroy thirty-two years of successful partnership. . . . We are amazed that NBC would have the audacity to make a 'package' deal, involving Portland and Seattle, which sells one of its oldest friends and staunchest supporters down the river." KOMO filed an anti-trust suit, but settled out of court for $130,000, of which NBC paid two-thirds. *Seattle Times* television columnist C. J. Skreen wrote, "For a network suddenly to drop a station with KOMO's longstanding prestige, position, and years of affiliation is virtually unprecedented." It was the first time a network had ever voluntarily switched stations. The change took place on June 14, 1959.

————

Long before Dorothy Bullitt drank champagne at NBC headquarters, even before she invited General Sarnoff to dinner, she had started looking for grander television studio space. Late in 1951, when she noticed a lack of pedestrian traffic past the display windows of the big Baron's furniture store on Highway 99 (Aurora Avenue North)—then part of the main north–south highway between California and Canada—she was pretty sure the store would be willing to part with at least half of the building. The Stimson Realty Company acquired part of the property at the end of 1951 and in February 1952 leased it to King Broadcasting for five years. (Later that year, Dorothy Bullitt changed the Stimson Realty Company's name to the Bullitt Company.) The

*It didn't take long for King Broad-
casting to outgrow its Queen Anne
studio space. The new King headquarters (shown here), a former
furniture store, would serve as corporate headquarters for the next
three decades.*

station started remodeling the space that it would occupy—although
it would subsequently expand—for the next four decades.

In the basement, right in the middle of the studio space, a huge
column supported the structure above. The column could have been
moved and the building supported in another way, but the operation would have been expensive, and Dorothy Bullitt didn't want to
spend the money. "The building is progressing nicely," she wrote at
the end of 1952. "There is not an unnecessary or fancy feature in
it. It will be a factory, but I think an attractive one." Cameramen
and engineers simply had to work around the column—for the next
thirty years.

Although King was growing, acquiring new studio space and
maneuvering to get a channel in Portland, the company retained its
small-town, family-business atmosphere. By mid-1954, King
Broadcasting had lent money to more than a dozen employees,
including Fred Stimson, who borrowed a small sum in the fall of
1953, and a cameraman who borrowed a much larger sum in 1952
after his wife had a heart attack. For years, Dorothy Bullitt and
Henry Owen would meet at the station on Saturday mornings, go
into the coffee shop, raid the refrigerator—which she always called
the ice box—and talk.

At times, the family atmosphere led to almost familial resentments and jealousies. Dorothy Bullitt's journals report a conflict between Lee Schulman and Jim Middlebrooks: "Apparently I am the unconscious cause of some of it as each seems to resent seeing the other coming out of my office. Will have to take every precaution not to aggravate this."

Most people who worked at the station in those years remember having fun. Commercials were still shot live. Newscaster Chuck Herring would drop an Alka Seltzer into a glass of water and say you could hear it fizz because off camera, someone else dropped a whole bottle of Alka Seltzer into a glass of warm water to make a fizzing noise loud enough for the microphones to pick up. The fizzing was recorded and used later for the sound of bacon frying.

The station went to more elaborate lengths to televise the hydroplane races each year. The early hand-held cameras were not easy to use, especially in the summer sun. They were heavy. They were battery-operated, so the person carrying one had to sit down in the van and change the batteries every half hour. And they didn't work well in the heat, so the operator had to carry an ice pack around with the camera.

The telephoto lenses that KING rented to cover the hydroplane races left something to be desired, too. A commercial telephoto lens was mounted on the front of a camera so that no other lens could be used at the same time—wide-angle and long-range shots would require separate cameras—and the telephoto lens projected a full 40 inches beyond the camera. This was clumsy, and the lens tended to be unstable: a strong wind made it impossible to get a sharp picture. Al Smith, by then a cameraman, and a KING-TV engineer named Earl Thoms, who had built telescopes, decided to make a better long-range lens that could be mounted on the side of the camera. Grinding their own mirrors, they first developed a 40-inch lens to use at the hydro races, then built a 60-inch lens and a 100-inch lens. The KING-TV lenses worked better than the ones that were commercially available at the time, and they allowed other lenses to be used on the same cameras. Soon the networks were borrowing

In 1951, KING-TV engineers Earl Thoms (in foreground) and Al Smith (in back) developed and produced the nation's first 100-inch camera lens, designed to capture close-ups of the hydroplane races. The lens was loaned to the networks when similar shots were called for.

KING-TV's long-range lenses to cover the Rose Bowl and other football games. KING-TV used them until zoom lenses reached the market in the 1960s.

———

Gloria Chandler joined King Broadcasting as a regular employee in 1952, and soon made children's programming a KING-TV trademark. It started with "Televenture Tales," a television version of Chandler's radio show, "Books Bring Adventure." In November 1953, KING launched a show for very young children called "Wunda Wunda" that attracted older kids and their parents, too. Ruth Prins, who had read aloud on "Televenture Tales," now dressed in a pointed hat and tights and became the Story Lady in "Wunda Wunda." Elliott Fisher Brown composed original music for the show and played it on an organ. Gloria Chandler was the first producer. "Wunda Wunda" aired at noon, when kids were home for lunch, and the show quickly grabbed two-thirds of the audience in that time slot. Prins invited her young viewers to write in. What name did the kids suggest for the poor little no-name dog? What did they think the Music Man looked like? The letters poured in: by the middle of January 1954 the show had

Wunda Wunda (Ruth Prins) was a familiar figure to children who grew up in Seattle in the 1950s. "Wunda Wunda" won a Peabody Award for children's programming.

received more than 2,000 of them. When a camera was moving in for a shot of a miniature set on "Wunda Wunda," the lens knocked over some of the buildings. Cameraman Al Houston reached in to set them back up. The camera caught a close-up of his freckled arm. Ruth Prins ad libbed something about "the great speckled snake," and the snake became a regular character on her show. In 1957, "Wunda Wunda" became the first television show produced by a local station to win a prestigious Peabody Award.

"Wunda Wunda" wasn't the only kids' show on KING. By 1955, Stan Boreson and Art Barduhn decided that their show had reached the end of the line. Barduhn took his trio and went off to play in Las Vegas. At Lee Schulman's suggestion, Boreson developed a program for kids, which he based on a clubhouse motif. At the start of every show, a camera dollied up to a knothole, then the picture would switch to a second camera, creating the illusion that the viewer had entered the clubhouse through the knothole. Boreson and his colleagues decided that the show needed a mascot. First, they held a contest for kids to decide what kind of animal the mascot should be. The kids chose a dog. Then, they held another contest in which the kids chose the breed, a bassett hound. Finally, they had a contest to name the bassett hound. At the time the Slo Mo Shun boats dominated Seattle's hydro races, and a little girl suggested naming Boreson's torpid dog "No Mo Shun." The station gave her a bicycle. She was one of six children and her family hadn't been able to afford a bicycle. Boreson was delighted.

Boreson kept the dog at his house. After about six weeks, No Mo Shun ran out into the street and was hit by a car. The dog needed surgery. Boreson's son had been operated on by a heart surgeon, so Boreson called the surgeon and asked if he could recommend a vet to operate on No Mo Shun. The doctor himself arrived by ambulance at a vet's office in Lake City, accompanied by a nurse and an anaesthesiologist, and operated on No Mo Shun. He couldn't save her. But he never billed Boreson for his services. "People have forgotten what a neighbor is for," he said.

Boreson didn't want to tell his viewers what had happened to No Mo Shun. He needed a new bassett hound that he could pass off as the old one. He found a dog that looked almost right, but she was younger and thinner than the original No Mo Shun. He trained her to sleep in No Mo Shun's basket and just let her nap during the show, "because if she stood up, everyone would know it was the wrong dog."

Dorothy Bullitt hadn't forgotten about educational TV. The FCC had reserved Channel 9 for a Seattle educational station, and a group of people was trying to start an educational station at the University of Washington. But the university, whose teachers and administrators looked down on TV, wasn't especially interested. Dorothy Bullitt feared that if the university didn't make a move, the opportunity would simply disappear.

KING-TV had a used but serviceable transmitter and cameras that Dorothy Bullitt wanted to give the university for the new educational station. The university didn't want the transmitter. The

"Zero dachus, Mucho Crackus, Hallaballooza Bub. . . ." For eighteen years, Stan Boreson (right), "Hey You" the clown (left), and canine pal "No Mo" entertained children in "KING's Klubhouse."

school's acting president said, as Dorothy Bullitt recalled, "'It's obsolete, it's old, it's worn out, they are throwing it out. Why do we have to be the victim and take it on? We don't think we will accept this.'"

The university eventually changed its mind. KING's used equipment, valued at $182,000, was the largest single donation Channel 9 received before it went on the air at the beginning of 1955.

———

Commercial television had its educational moments, too. In 1954, KING provided same-day coverage of the hearings that marked Senator McCarthy's downfall. One of McCarthy's aides, G. David

Schine, had been drafted and stationed at Fort Dix, New Jersey. The Army said that McCarthy and members of his committee had used "improper" methods to get preferential treatment for Schine. McCarthy claimed that the Army had been holding Schine as a "hostage" in order to force the senator to abandon his investigations. The hearings essentially focused on who was lying. They lasted thirty-five days and were watched, at one point or another, by an estimated twenty million people, an unprecedented audience for the time. "The great audience was far more interested in the players and their relationship one to another than in the larger conflict of ideas and institutions," wrote Richard H. Rovere in *Senator Joe McCarthy*. "Every

In 1954, when KING-TV asked viewers to write letters about how television affected their lives, the station found that for many women, "television alleviates the loneliness of hours formerly spent caring for small children or filled with the activity of younger years."

face was a study, every voice a revelation of the man from whom it came. On camera, McCarthy was not the genial assassin who might be encountered in the [Senate] corridors. He snarled, and he roared." King was able to broadcast the McCarthy hearings the same way the station had provided same-day coverage of the World Series before coaxial cable reached the Northwest: each day KING had hearings kinescoped in Chicago, then immediately flown to Seattle so that they could be aired that night.

As the huge audience for the McCarthy hearings indicated, television had gained a significant place in American culture. In 1954, when KING-TV asked viewers to write letters about how television affected their lives, the station found that for many women, "television alleviates the loneliness of hours formerly spent caring for small children or filled with the activity of younger years." The letters revealed as much about the situations of women in the early 1950s and the character of the Seattle area as they did about television. "Actually, more loneliness was expressed by those [women who were] married or living with families than by those who mentioned living alone." The station reported that "companionship . . . was stressed particularly by newcomers to Seattle or to the state. They implied considerable native unfriendliness. . . . Servicemen's families particularly felt unwelcome."

The letters also suggest that television provided an antidote to the stress of living in the early 1950s. "Many . . . cited the high pressures under which we live today and said that these would be unbearable if they could not 'escape' via the television. Women mostly cited television as a cure or relief from loneliness, frustration, or boredom. Men stressed relaxation and the fact that television eases tension and worry [created] by the pressure of their jobs and/or debts."

Viewers described a disintegration of family life in the early 1950s, and praised television as a force that could hold families together. Since buying a television set, one viewer wrote, "Our family is together more often. Our children are kept off the streets." Another wrote that television had created or restored "closely knit family ties. My daughter is not at the neighbor's. My husband is not in a tavern." A third viewer noted, "My little boy has learned to talk better. My husband stays at home much more. And my oldest son does not want to run the streets at night."

Despite these positive sentiments, some people were worried about television's negative effects on children. The tube wasn't just making children more sedentary—although the KING viewers' survey offered some evidence of that: "Even the teenagers find life a little too much for themselves," the station found. "At least forty-two wrote that they find TV 'relaxing' . . . they like television because they don't have to 'move'—they can just 'sit.'"

"Television broadcasters insist they are educating your youngster, not driving him away from his books," the Associated Press reported in late 1953.

Already there were questions about the effects of televised violence. "In 1954—the same year the frozen TV dinner first appeared in American supermarkets . . ." writes Mary Ann Watson, "Senator Estes Kefauver . . . led a Senate inquiry into juvenile delinquency. Television violence was a prime suspect."

The television images that gained such a hold over the country were primarily black and white. On May 18, 1954, KING-TV broadcast a test pattern of vertical colored stripes for ninety-five minutes, giving the estimated thirty-five people in the Seattle area who had invested in color sets their first opportunity to see color on the small screen. (People who owned black-and-white sets could see the stripes in various shades of gray.) On July 1, KING-TV became the first station west of the Rockies to broadcast a program in color. In August, KOMO-TV became the first station in the Northwest to broadcast a network program live in color—although

KING helicopters took off from the station's roof and could deliver cameras to breaking local news faster than anything on the ground.

the program it ran, an Army Signal Corps demonstration of the use of television in warfare, may not have been a big improvement on KING's colored test pattern. In August, KING-TV telecast a network color production of "Alice in Wonderland."

As things developed, KING-TV was actually slow to convert its operation entirely to color. Portland's KGW-TV, which started out with state-of-the-art equipment, was all color when it went on the air ten days before Christmas 1956. KING-TV, in contrast, ran network shows in color but didn't produce live color programs until the Seattle World's Fair in 1962; its local news didn't go all color until 1967.

If the company took its time switching to color, it was quick to acquire other new tools and gimmicks of the trade. In 1954, King Broadcasting Company opened the Northwest's first private heliport on the station roof, so that helicopters could take KING-TV cameras to fires, car crashes, and other news events. Three years later, it snapped up the first videotape machine ever sold to anyone but the networks themselves. At the National Association of Broadcasters convention in 1956, Jim Middlebrooks got a sneak preview of the Ampex Corporation's display, which included the first videotape recording machines. Middlebrooks immediately ordered one for KING-TV. Dorothy Bullitt approved. The prototype models went to the networks. In November 1957, the first production model out of the factory went to KING-TV.

The new machine revolutionized television production. It also marked the end of old-time live television. People could try shooting a studio scene more than once; if somebody made a mistake, they no longer had to keep going. KING-TV didn't shoot everything on videotape until the 1970s, but during the 1958 Gold Cup hydro races, when the *Miss Thriftway* hit a Coast Guard picket boat at 160 miles per hour, driving its prow into the larger boat's side and sinking it, the audience got to see the collision twice. KING-TV's videotaped images of a Coast Guard crewman climbing out through a hole in his sinking vessel's hull and crawling along the hull toward safety ran as still photos in the next day's *Seattle Post-Intelligencer*.

———

By that time, Dorothy Bullitt was rather confidently building an empire. In 1955, Ray Hamilton, the Chicago media broker who had been at her house when she bought her first television station, wrote to tell her that KREM-TV in Spokane might be for sale. The station was owned by Lou Wasmer, who had owned radio stations since before World War II and had sold a couple of them for what at the time were very large sums. Wasmer had figured he could run a television station as he had run his radio holdings—without investing much time. "He thought this could be handled on a more or less remote control basis," Hamilton explained. He discovered that it couldn't. "It now develops that he is spending too much time at the office," Hamilton explained. "He and Mrs. Wasmer want to be able to travel. . . . The last time I was in Spokane, Mr. Wasmer told me that he was sixty-five and doesn't want to keep on 'hitting the ball' as

KING was an innovator in the industry. A later version of the original Ampex [videotape recording] machine is shown here. In 1956, KING-TV was the first independent television station to own a videotape machine (shown here).

he has during the past many years." In other words, he was ready to sell the television station, along with KREM-AM and FM. King Broadcasting was ready to buy. In the summer of 1957, King and Wasmer reached an agreement. King Broadcasting formed a new subsidiary to run KREM and acquired majority ownership, but kept Wasmer as president. In early 1958, KREM began broadcasting in Spokane. Wasmer hadn't wasted much money on equipment. Ken Hermanson later described KREM as a "technical disaster." The television station had management problems, too. King started trying to shape it up—without wasting too much money of its own.

KREM itself may have been rather threadbare, but Dorothy Bullitt was glad to have it. When the sale went through, she wrote King Broadcasting employees, "We now have KREM . . . (as of three o'clock this afternoon) to complete the triangle. We should really be able to do a job in this good old Northwest." The memo began with a jubilant "Whee!"

KGW-TV wasn't operating in the black yet—it lost nearly $343,000 in 1957—but it would turn the corner in 1958. Even before it got out of the red, KGW-TV was such an obviously valuable property that people wanted to buy it. In October 1957, when the station was losing money and the King Broadcasting officers' policy committee was talking about "business alternatives available in the event these losses continue," the company had already turned down a $4 million offer for the station. A letter asking Dorothy Bullitt "if someone from our office can call and discuss the possibility of a sale at a high price" had led nowhere. Dorothy Bullitt wasn't interested in selling KGW-TV. Before the station went on the air, she talked with her son about selling Portland but "he has talked with both girls and they all agree we should not sell it but build up." That was evidently what she wanted to hear; there is no indication that she seriously considered any of the offers.

King continued to branch out. In 1959, King Broadcasting acquired Musiking, the company that held the Seattle franchise for Muzak, which provided background music in elevators, offices, and other spaces full of captive listeners. In November 1961, the company was merged into King, but a few months later, it was sold.

While King Broadcasting was still working to acquire KREM and make KGW-TV profitable, KING-TV took its cameras into new locations. Starting in 1957, for a weekly series called "Success Story" that was sponsored and produced by Richfield Oil, KING-TV crews carried cameras and ran cable through factories and offices to create live portraits of local businesses. The people who worked for those businesses were not used to being on television. Even when the KING crews tried to rehearse them, there were surprises. Once, the day crew at a plywood plant rehearsed, but the shift changed before the show started, so KING wound up shooting the unrehearsed night workers. On the night shift at the Mission macaroni plant, all the workers seemed to speak only Italian. A member of the KING crew spoke Italian, too, so the television people communicated with the workers entirely in that language. One of the workers seemed quite confused; he just didn't seem to follow what was going on. Finally he asked, "Why is he speaking Italian? My name is Peterson, and I don't understand a thing."

The company also started sending cameras to major regional events. In the spring of 1957, the U.S. Army Corps of Engineers completed The Dalles Dam across the Columbia River at the upstream end of the Columbia Gorge. The new dam wasn't the first federal dam across the river or the largest, but it was a major regional project, and the water backed up behind it would flood the ancient Indian fishing site at Celilo Falls, where fishermen with long-handled dipnets stood on platforms above the rapids. Archaeological evidence indicated that the site had been used for perhaps 8,000 years.

Lee Schulman decided that completion of the dam was a historic event, and that KING-TV should cover it. The station had the telephone company install microwave relays along the Columbia Gorge from The Dalles to Portland and then north to Seattle. To catch the closing of the floodgates and the filling of the reservoir, the station sent eight cameras and a crew of twenty-five. One camera was positioned on top of the dam, another at the base of the spillway; a third camera on a platform was lowered by crane into the space behind the dam, along with news editor Charles Herring. KING-TV cameras caught the first thin stream of water flowing over the crest of the spillway. The timing—the cameras were ready exactly when the water reached the top of the spillway—added to the Schulman legend.

Historic events did not dull the station's appetite for hydroplane racing. In 1957, King Broadcasting Company sued successfully in Chelan County Superior Court for access to the Apple Cup race on Lake Chelan, where the race organizing committee had given exclusive rights to KOMO-TV. The Apple Cup was the first of nine hydro events KING-TV covered that year. For a race on Lake Coeur d'Alene in 1959, KING cameramen loaded the remote truck onto a barge, hauled the truck to a point that was not accessible by road, and drove it off the barge onto the sand and rocks of the lakeshore in order to get the shot they wanted. Hydro racing had become so much a part of the station's identity that when Stan Boreson was on vacation, the dominant hydro driver of the time, Bill Muncey, filled in for him.

Each year, KING-TV brought the excitement of hydro racing live to the small screen.

At the beginning of 1959, KING-TV broadcast the first live coverage of the state legislature. Some Democratic senators objected that their colleagues might vote differently—especially on revenue and appropriations bills—if they knew the cameras were covering them live. In the House of Representatives, Speaker John O'Brien didn't mind live coverage, but he said, "It has tended to make ham actors out of legislators."

The camera tended to make ham actors out of many people. Early one evening in February 1958, a woman called news director Ted Bryant and asked where an "escapee could turn himself in." A twenty-five-year-old man who had been diagnosed as paranoid schizophrenic and held under maximum security had escaped two weeks earlier from Northern State Hospital. Now, he wanted to surrender—and he wanted a TV reporter to go with him.

The next afternoon, Bryant showed up on a street corner in downtown Lynnwood, and the man's mother took the reporter to a private home west of town. The escaped mental patient walked out of the woods. Bryant and his cameraman filmed an interview, then drove with mother and son to the Snohomish County Sheriff.

An hour and a half later, the interview ran on KING-TV's "Early Edition" news.

———

By the late 1950s, KING was ready to produce special programs more often. In 1959 the station hired Bob Schulman (no relation to Lee Schulman), who had been Northwest bureau chief for Time-Life magazines, as director of special features. Bob Schulman's first project was a documentary about the Port of Seattle entitled "Lost Cargo." The ninety-minute film, which appeared on the evening of June 25, was not only KING-TV's first documentary, it may have been the first locally produced television documentary made anywhere.

The Port of Seattle had fallen on hard times. It relied on the piers and warehouses it had used at the end of World War I. It had a reputation for high costs, frequent work stoppages, and poor service. The Seattle Port Commission was unwieldy, and some port officials skirted the far edge of ethical behavior. The lion's share of the Northwest's cargo passed through the Port of Portland.

Bob Schulman's documentary pointed out the port's inability to attract high-value packaged cargo, its loss of passenger business, its crumbling piers, the low productivity of its longshore workers, and its lack of cranes that could handle heavy cargo. The National Bank of Commerce (which later became Rainier Bank) agreed to sponsor the program. On the night KING-TV aired "Lost Cargo," the company invited executives from the bank and its advertising agency to the Camlin Hotel for cocktails and dinner, after which everyone watched the documentary. Bank officials were delighted. The day after "Lost Cargo" appeared, a KING-TV secretary reported that the bank's advertising manager "called to say the bank was getting a very strong favorable reaction on 'Lost Cargo.' He seems real pleased and said the various officers were continuing to get calls congratulating them for 'their program.'"

A month later, KING flew a moderator out from New York, rented the Moore Theater, and held a "Town Hall Meeting" at which a port commissioner, a longshore union leader, a shipper, and a Seattle businessman answered audience questions about the port.

The documentary didn't create the only pressure for reform. The Seattle Municipal League convinced the port to hire a consultant, and televised hearings on port management were held. All these things had an effect. Before long, Seattle voters passed a $20 million bond issue to improve the port, and they replaced the three paid port commissioners with five unpaid ones. In the 1960s, the port's leaders gambled early and successfully on the shift to containerization of ocean cargo, and over the next couple of decades, Seattle developed into one of the nation's leading container ports. In the 1980s, the Port of Tacoma came to rival Seattle as a container port, but it couldn't have attracted container cargos if the ships hadn't already been coming into Puget Sound—and they might never have done so if "Lost Cargo" hadn't helped focus public attention on the Port of Seattle.

It's usually hard to figure out whether a television show has affected public opinion, much less what its effect has been; but no one doubted that the showing of "Lost Cargo" helped inspire a drastic alteration of Seattle's port.

"Lost Cargo" may have been the most influential documentary the King Broadcasting Company ever made. It's usually hard to figure out whether a television show has affected public opinion, much less what its effect has been; but no one doubted that the showing of "Lost Cargo" helped inspire a drastic alteration of Seattle's port.

———

Small-screen images, in color or black and white, had started shaping political decisions all over the country. On a national level, television had arguably become the most politically influential mass medium. It had a visceral effect that nonvisual media couldn't match. Television's impact on national politics became clear during the presidential election of 1960, when the televised debates between the photogenic John F. Kennedy and the jowly, perspiring, unshaven-looking

Richard M. Nixon were generally given credit for Kennedy's narrow margin of victory.

Television's political potential was recognized at least as early as the nominating conventions. At the time of the 1960 Democratic convention, Mary Ann Watson observed, "Print journalists sensed that television was making inroads into their sphere of influence. They were distressed . . . to find that broadcasters were given preferential treatment by the Democratic National Committee in the allotment of premium working space at the convention hall. Most newspaper reporters actually found themselves and their typewriters housed in a tent outside the Los Angeles Sports Arena. . . . Newspaper reporters realized they needed to monitor the television networks to keep abreast of the news."

Print journalists also soon realized that they had to keep their eyes on the screen to know who was winning. Russell Baker tried covering the first Kennedy–Nixon debate for the *New York Times* without watching the screen. He later realized that he had made a big mistake: "I thought Nixon had a slight edge in what little argument there had been," Baker wrote. "But as I talked to more and more people it was clear they thought Kennedy had indeed won a great victory. . . . I missed it completely because I had been too busy taking notes and writing to get more than fleeting glimpses of what the country was seeing on the screen. . . . That night television replaced newspapers as the most important communications medium in American politics."

Around the same time, King Broadcasting deliberately set out to influence electoral politics in the Northwest. During the 1960 political campaigns, Bob Schulman noted in a memo to Dorothy Bullitt, Otto Brandt, and Henry Owen that "hate literature of the most scurrilous type is being circulated widely throughout Oregon. . . . Accusing . . . Oregon Democrats at the Congressional level of opposing actions 'which no one but a traitor would oppose' and of sponsoring 'terrible Red bills' . . . is the least of the defamations." Portland's daily newspapers had ignored the hate literature, Schulman said, and he believed that "here is the occasion when KGW should make its dip into editorializing."

No King station had ever broadcast an editorial, but Dorothy Bullitt liked the idea. She discussed the situation with Ancil Payne, whom Henry Owen had hired the year before as his assistant. After Payne's old boss, Congressman Hugh Mitchell, lost his race for the governorship of Washington in 1952, Payne had gone to Alaska, where he had been president of a trucking company and was active in the campaign for statehood. He had then moved to Portland, where he had run a brokerage firm. Payne had grown up in Oregon and he knew Oregon politics. Dorothy Bullitt asked him if he thought an editorial would be a good idea, and when he said yes, she asked him how soon he could leave for Portland. The two of them hurried south and met with KGW-TV program manager Tom Dargan, along with Maureen Neuberger, who was campaigning for the U.S. Senate (she won), and Tom McCall, a KGW-TV news announcer who would eventually become governor of Oregon. After hours of conversation, Payne drafted an editorial. McCall wasn't enthusiastic about reading it on the air—he had political aspirations and he evidently feared that the editorial would alienate potential voters. Dorothy Bullitt insisted; she wanted the editorial read, and she wanted it read often.

It was. On November 4, McCall told Portland viewers that "the material in these documents is loathsome and evil, . . . the same brand of hateful innuendo and appeal to prejudice that has marred politics [this year] at the national level. . . . It is not enough for party leaders to clear their skirts of the authorship or circulation of such smears," McCall said. "We ask them to rise up against these dangerous tracts with unequivocal denunciation." The editorial ran for four days.

———

By 1960, King Broadcasting had outgrown its space on Aurora Avenue. Fortuitously, the furniture store that owned and occupied the north end of King's headquarters building was going bankrupt. The Bullitt Company acquired the rest of the structure at the end of 1959—after agreeing to keep quiet about the purchase until the new year, so that the news wouldn't cut into the furniture company's Christmas sales. King spread out into the other half of the building in 1960.

Before that, the two halves of the structure were separated by solid walls, and one could walk from one to the other only by going through a door in the basement. One night in 1960, a burglar was seen crawling through a window into the furniture store. Police came to investigate. The only way they could get into the locked store without breaking glass was by going through KING-TV's basement studios and opening the connecting door. They arrived as Ruth Prins, director Al Smith, and a crew were shooting an episode of "Wunda Wunda." The police walked through the set, past a mock stone wall and a painted pastoral backdrop, and disappeared through the door. Smith put "Wunda Wunda" on hold and trained the lights and camera on the door. The police soon emerged leading a forty-six-year-old man with his hands cuffed behind him. KING-TV showed the arrest on its next news broadcast.

As the company grew at the end of the decade, it hired people who would play key roles years later. One was Ancil Payne, who would manage the Portland operation and then serve as the company's president for sixteen years. Eric Bremner, a University of Washington communications graduate who had worked for United Press International in Olympia, was also hired that year. Bremner, who would manage KING-TV, become vice president in charge of broadcasting, and serve as co-president after Payne retired, was hired as an assistant to promotion director Mel Anderson. His first job was mailing out lengths of tarred hemp rope with "Lost Cargo" shipping labels attached to promote the station's groundbreaking documentary.

In the spring of 1961, Dorothy Bullitt hired a new vice president for engineering, Jay Wright. Wright had been chief radio engineer at CBS and then president of a broadcasting company in Salt Lake City. Andrew Haley recommended Wright to Dorothy Bullitt. She phoned Wright out of the blue and offered him a job. Wright needed time to think about it. His first move was to call Jim Middlebrooks, who by then was working in California. Wright had known Middlebrooks through the network and had run into him at conventions over the years. Middlebrooks had good things to say about King Broadcasting Company, so Wright flew out to Seattle to look for himself. It was obvious, he later recalled, that "this was a different kind of company." He stayed at King until he retired twenty years later. Engineer Ken Hermanson was quickly impressed by Wright's grasp of the broadcasting business, as well as the technicalities of transmitting signals, and by his ability to pore over sheets of statistics until they suggested new things to do. Wright helped Hermanson develop "a sense of professionalism."

———

Although the 1950s were, in some respects, a simpler and happier time than the decade that followed, they were neither as simple nor as happy as some people's memories later made them seem. At the end of the 1950s, the whole broadcasting industry came under attack. In 1956 and early 1957, a young Columbia University English instructor named Charles Van Doren had won money week after week on the quiz show "Twenty One," dazzling viewers with his knowledge and becoming a kind of pop-culture celebrity. When Van Doren left the quiz show, he signed a television contract of his own to appear on the morning "Today Show." In 1958, though, rumors circulated that Van Doren had been given answers to the questions in advance. In the fall of 1959, Van Doren admitted this was true. The quiz show had been rigged. Right after Van Doren came clean, the Payola scandal broke: disc jockeys had been taking money from record companies to play their records on the air. "American Bandstand" host Dick Clark was called before a Congressional investigating committee and a New York radio disc jockey went to jail. In the spring of 1960, a letter from Dorothy Bullitt to King stockholders noted that "[t]he year 1959 brought about the most violent and active attacks on the broadcasting industry of any year in its history. . . . The quiz scandals will be remembered far longer than some of the many fine things [the industry] has done. . . . It will take a long time . . . to rebuild the reputation for integrity. . . . The hue and cry of Payola followed closely on the heels of the quiz investigation."

Closer to home there was no scandal, but there was certainly no lack of personnel problems. In 1961, Otto Brandt told chief television engineer Bob Ferguson that Ferguson seemed unhappy, that something seemed to be bothering him. Ferguson replied, Brandt reported, that "at times he does become quite unhappy and that a certain amount of this unhappiness stems from the problem of getting along with Lee Schulman. Fergie added that for many years he has been one of Schulman's supporters and defenders, but that he is tiring of this role and admittedly is losing patience."

So many employees drank heavily that alcohol wasn't generally considered a problem, but sometimes an employee's drinking was impossible to ignore. One night, Brandt was working late in his office when he turned on KING radio. The announcer's "production was sloppy and his speech was slurred. . . . I went up to radio and as soon as I walked into the control room, [the announcer] remarked, 'I'm drunk and you'd better take me off the air.'" Brandt got someone from the newsroom to take the microphone, then he and the announcer went into the record library to talk. The announcer said he was an alcoholic who belonged to Alcoholics Anonymous and hadn't had a drink in five or six months, but that night he had gone to the cocktail lounge of the Benjamin Franklin Hotel with another King Broadcasting employee, also an alcoholic, and had gotten drunk. The other man was so drunk that the announcer had had to carry him out of the hotel. The announcer had then driven to the station and gone on the air. After telling the whole story, the announcer "launched into a highly emotional attack on KING. . . . He had been promised a raise that had never materialized. . . . KING is a penny-pinching operation. . . . Morale . . . is at an all-time low." Brandt let him go on for half an hour. When he showed signs of sobering up and said that a friend was driving over to get him, Brandt walked him out of the station, told him not to drive, and left him standing in the parking lot. The next morning, the announcer came in and apologized.

The company was still paternalistic—Dorothy Bullitt doled out bonuses as she saw fit—and it was resolutely indifferent to modern recordkeeping. One executive would stuff all unpaid bills—those addressed to his department and those addressed to him personally—under the blotter on his desk.

This was a broadcasting company that operated television and radio stations in three cities. It generated tremendous stacks of paper. Each day, the station compiled a ten-page log and distributed six to eight copies. Dorothy Bullitt saved everything. Periodically she would tell accountant Frank Yanagimachi something like, "Let's look at 1948," and they would be able to dig out the complete financial records. But she could have stored them as well in her basement or attic. Nothing was automated. Yanagimachi had to fight for money to microfilm the records. The company's voluminous papers were piled in a big safe. Anyone who wanted to consult them had to haul a stepladder into the safe to reach the top piles.

Dorothy Bullitt had realized for some time that the company could be organized more efficiently. She wasn't—and knew she wasn't—the person to shape King into a modern corporation. She was committed to a family business dynasty, though. A few years later, to defuse persistent rumors that one or all of the stations were for sale, she wrote to employees that "as principal shareholder, I assure you this is the farthest [thing] from my intentions. The permanence and continuity of the company has been carefully provided for. The *New York Times* has not built its standing in one generation." It was clear that when she stepped down, she would hand over control of the company to one of her children. Some employees hoped she would choose her daughter Harriet. That was never likely. Although Dorothy Bullitt had succeeded as a woman in what was still overwhelmingly a man's world, she wasn't about to turn the company over to one of her daughters. Her son, Stimson, by then a forty-two-year-old Seattle lawyer, had been running the real estate company since 1954 and had been consulted on broadcasting decisions for years. On November 1, 1961—reluctantly, from a sense of family obligation, with misgivings about leaving the practice of law and a fear that Dorothy Bullitt would find ways to maneuver around him and keep control—Stimson Bullitt became president of King Broadcasting Company.

Dorothy Bullitt continued as chairman of the board and majority stockholder. It was effectively her company. She probably assumed that her son would keep her people and take her advice. He didn't.

A lot of people—including Stimson Bullitt himself—later believed that he was clearly the wrong person for the job. He had never wanted it. He didn't like day-to-day administration. He didn't like the broadcasting salesmen who brought in the advertising dollars or the Hollywood types who produced programs. And he didn't like broadcasting.

CHAPTER FIVE

AGAINST THE GRAIN
1961–1971

STIMSON BULLITT BECAME PRESIDENT of King Broadcasting Company in the brief, heady period during which John F. Kennedy was president of the United States. Bullitt's background was, in many respects, Kennedyesque: both men had gone to Ivy League schools, Kennedy to Harvard and Bullitt to Yale. Both had won medals as naval officers in World War II. Both had published estimable books. (Bullitt had actually written his, *To Be a Politician,* which was reviewed respectfully by the *New York Times* and the *New Yorker* after it was published in 1959.) Both had run for public office. Both valued physical accomplishment (Bullitt had boxed at Yale and later took up mountain climbing).

Bullitt was not unusual in his disdain for television. Virtually no one of any intellectual pretension had much use for the medium. (The University of Washington professors who scorned television in the 1950s were typical.) Kennedy appointed as chairman of the FCC an Indiana lawyer named Newton Minow, who quickly antagonized the industry when—in a 1961 speech to the National

Association of Broadcasters—he characterized commercial television programming as "a vast wasteland." In case the broadcasters wondered what he meant, he gave them a list: "[a] procession of game shows, violence, audience participation shows, formula comedies about totally unbelievable families, blood and thunder, mayhem, violence, sadism, murder, western bad men, western good men, private eyes, gangsters, more violence, and cartoons. And, endlessly, commercials—many screaming, cajoling, and offending." Minow suggested that things had better change. "I want to say to you now," he told the broadcasters, "renewal [of your broadcasting licenses] will not be pro forma in the future. There is nothing permanent or sacred about a broadcast license."

Stimson Bullitt's impatience with commercial TV and his lack of respect for the industry paralleled the statements of the new FCC chairman. There was some reason to think that the industry might actually change (though Bullitt himself wasn't very optimistic on that score). Minow was not the only person pressing commercial broadcasters to reform. People hadn't forgotten the Payola and quiz show scandals, and critics still thought that there might be some link between television violence and juvenile crime. In 1961, Senator Thomas Dodd of Connecticut started three years of hearings on juvenile delinquency, focusing heavily on television's role.

"At the same time the Dodd hearings were going on . . . the FCC was . . . engaged in a formal inquiry into TV practices," writes Mary Ann Watson in *The Expanding Vista*. "And, again, the networks were portrayed as the bad guys—as the ones allowing ratings and advertisers to debase popular entertainment."

The networks responded to the criticism, eager to clean up their images (albeit not to change their programming in any fundamental way). Watson writes, "The quiz show and Payola scandals that rocked the broadcast industry . . . led to more public service programming by the networks in an attempt to mollify the civic, religious, and educational constituencies offended by the fraud. . . . After the Vast Wasteland speech, the amount of documentary programming that erupted on American television was phenomenal."

Not much really changed at King Broadcasting during Stimson Bullitt's first year. He realized that it would not be easy for a quiet man whose mother had founded and run the company to establish himself as a leader in his own right. But the organization could run itself while he learned the ropes, a task he didn't find especially satisfying or even interesting.

King was not a typical commercial broadcasting company even before Stimson Bullitt started to reshape it. Its stations ran a lot of mindless network entertainment, but at the start of 1962, KING-TV taped four debates between "the Father of the H-bomb," Edward Teller, who argued that dropping the bomb should not be unthinkable, and Gilbert Seldes, a journalist and educator, who thought it should. In April *Newsweek* suggested that "'forthright' is if anything too mild a word" for the "highly articulate, totally uninhibited verbal brawls on the subject of disarmament, the H-bomb, and human survival" between Teller and Seldes. "Dispensing with TV's usual amenities—moderators, panels, rigid time limits, and commercial interruptions—Teller and Seldes wage as sharply defined a debate between the use-it-if-necessary view and the it-must-never-be-used view as has ever been recorded in this country."

Later in the year, KGW-TV ran a documentary entitled "Pollution in Paradise," which focused attention on Oregon's water and air pollution problems. "Population and industrial expansion . . . have turn[ed] the Willamette [River], in particular, into a giant test tube," commentator Tom McCall told the television audience. "Health experts say water that is safe for waterskiing and swimming cannot have more than 240 units of disease-bearing bacteria in samples taken for checking. But the average number of such bacteria discovered in the Willamette, from Salem downstream to the mouth, was . . . 43 *hundred* [units]. . . . In and near Portland, the count was up to 70 *thousand*."

On November 20, 1962, the day before the documentary was shown, the *Oregonian*'s television columnist wrote that "[b]rownish purple sludge flowing into the sparkling blue waters of the Willamette looks particularly untasty in color, but Tom Dargan,

KGW-TV program manager . . . assures us that it will appear equally unpalatable in black and white. Certainly the shots of smog-bound Portland or trash fish fighting over sewage will pack a wallop no matter how you watch it."

KGW-TV showed the documentary again in January 1963, just in time for the opening of the state legislature. Bombarded by letters and calls, the legislature passed a law that for the first time permitted the state to shut down a polluting factory. The commotion gave McCall so much notoriety that he went public with his desire to be governor. In 1965, he became secretary of state, and the next year, he was elected governor. McCall served eight years, during which Oregon became known as the most environmentally conscious state in the union. One of his regime's clear triumphs was cleaning up the Willamette River.

While KGW-TV was developing "Pollution in Paradise," KING-TV backed the first of what would be several mass transit proposals put before Seattle voters. Actually, Eric Bremner, who started writing the transit piece, did his research and concluded that for Seattle at that time, a heavy-rail transit system made little sense. Bob Schulman and Dick Riddell, who were strong transit backers, took him to lunch and tried to persuade him to change his mind. Bremner wasn't told to change anything, and he didn't alter his script. But before he finished the job, he seized an opportunity to work as Otto Brandt's assistant and dropped the project. Schulman rewrote it into a pro-transit piece. Voters turned the proposal down anyway.

Although Seattle wasn't ready for rail transit, the city was eager to step into the national spotlight. The year 1962 was the year of Century 21, the Seattle World's Fair, which for much of the post-war United States put the city on the map. Before the fair opened, Lee Schulman decided to scout the fairgrounds for camera locations. The top of the 605-foot Space Needle seemed a logical place to put a camera that could scan the whole fair. Although the structure was still under construction, Schulman put on a hard hat and took the elevator to the restaurant level for a look. The restaurant site, 500 feet above ground, was just an open slab of concrete, and Schulman later recalled "getting out of the elevator and crawling on hands and knees, because we were frightened beyond comprehension, to the edge."

KING-TV covered the World's Fair opening, live, in color, for NBC. The station had amassed barely enough equipment to broadcast the event entirely in color. Fair coverage was supposed to run live in New York on the "Today" show at 7 A.M., so for a week, KING-TV camera crews were out shooting at 4 A.M. KING-TV put a remote truck on the Alaskan Way viaduct to provide shots of the city, and other cameras on golf carts rolled throughout the fairgrounds. The Goodyear blimp was in town for the fair opening, and Schulman wanted it in a shot of the Space Needle. The camera panned up the Needle, Schulman said, "Cue the blimp," and, sure enough, the blimp drifted into the shot.

Stimson Bullitt did not object to covering the fair but, in general, he was not out to give the public what it wanted. "If audience feedback governs a station's operations, the public's whim is its command," he wrote in 1963. "This . . . permits a station to delegate some of its chief decisions to rating services and other measuring devices." The rating services would determine broadcasters' choices more and more over the coming years. Bullitt did not want them to dictate King's.

There was no obvious reason to move the broadcasting operation in radically new directions. In 1962, KING-TV received national attention when it won a DuPont Award. *Newsweek* said that most TV stations didn't bother producing their own documentaries or children's programs if the networks offered anything in the same area, but "exceptions do exist . . . and in the state of Washington last week one of the most outstanding of them won a long-overdue Alfred I. DuPont Award for 'a consistent policy of responsibility toward community needs and interests.'" *Newsweek* reported that the awards committee "took special note of KING's initiative in supplementing network programming with 'programs for children and a series of forthright documentaries on controversial public issues.'"

And, just as Dorothy Bullitt had always wanted, the company was doing well by doing good. In October 1962, Stimson Bullitt told the board that King Broadcasting Company's combined net income from broadcasting in Seattle, Portland, and Spokane for the first three quarters of the year was double the net for 1961.

Dorothy Bullitt was still very much around, although she did not try to run the company herself. "Once, when an executive wondered aloud where Stimson Bullitt was taking the station," Emmett Watson recalled years later in the *Seattle Times*, "Mrs. Bullitt replied in low, measured tones: 'I don't care if he runs the company broke, he's got the authority.'" As she became more of a legend, she became more a figure from a different era. An *Oregonian* reporter suggested that "[s]he dresses and talks like the headmistress at an expensive boarding school." In the early 1960s, she still drove to work in a 1954 Ford. Many people at the company thought she should buy something classier, but she saw no need. She also saw no need to have her own reserved parking space. Parking was always tight in the King lot, and sometimes when there was a show with a live studio audience there would be no free spaces. When that happened, Dorothy Bullitt didn't mind parking on the street and walking. Some King executives wished she wouldn't; they couldn't very well get their own reserved parking spots if Dorothy Bullitt didn't have one.

Stimson Bullitt, so different in style from his mother, seemed to share her dynastic sense of the business. In the spring of 1963, he denied persistent industry rumors that one or all of the television stations were for sale, announcing that "[f]or the foreseeable future . . . the company is to be kept by the clan which holds the controlling interest . . . as both a permanent investment for profit and an institution for the pursuit of ideals and the fulfillment of responsibilities. . . . It is not to be treated as just another asset to be turned into cash if a high enough offer comes along."

But a commitment to family ownership did not mean a commitment to the managers who had guided the company through its first fifteen years. In 1963, Bullitt had the board of directors create a new position, vice president for business, which would oversee everything except broadcasting and engineering. Ancil Payne was temporarily appointed to the new job. Henry Owen kept the title of executive vice president, but from then on, Owen would be responsible only for personnel. The old order had started to change.

King employees would probably have resented any significant changes in the company, no matter who had made them. As it happened, many employees came to resent Stimson Bullitt personally. Some sensed a new corporate coldness. Dorothy Bullitt manipulated people shamelessly, but they didn't mind. With her Victorian good manners, she made everyone feel they were liked, that she cared about what they were saying, and agreed with their ideas. People believed they were her personal favorites when in fact she made it clear in private that she didn't much care for them. She treated King employees with a certain deference: when she wanted something done, she'd always add "if you have time" or "if it wouldn't be too much trouble."

Stimson Bullitt did not have those particular gifts. He didn't manipulate people, but he often

Stimson Bullitt didn't manipulate people, but he often left them feeling ill-treated or ignored. Shy and intellectual, he seemed more unapproachable than he actually was.

left them feeling ill-treated or ignored. Shy and intellectual, he seemed more unapproachable than he actually was. And some people who did speak with Bullitt found that he maintained a certain distance. One young writer, talking with him in the coffee shop, addressed him as "Stim." The company president informed the writer that their relationship had not progressed that far; the name was "Mr. Bullitt." Stories proliferated. Bullitt would walk out of a meeting and people would assume he had gone to the men's room, but he wouldn't return. Once a group of men from King's national advertising representative flew out from New York to make a presentation. Bullitt came into the meeting with a black briefcase, opened it, and read through its contents, never looking up while the New Yorkers performed for his benefit with flip charts and graphs. After about fifteen minutes, Bullitt closed his briefcase, stood up,

Philosophical by nature, Stimson Bullitt was not a businessman content with profit alone. He set out to modernize the company and to diversify King's holdings into other creative media. Not all ventures were successful, but many of his innovations were credited for King's later success.

excused himself, and walked out, leaving the stunned New Yorkers standing with their flip charts.

The main sore spot, though, was not his manner but his hiring policy and what it seemed to say about his regard for broadcasting and for local talent. Bullitt hired people who were culturally different from those who had built the company and who continued to build most of its profit. Some veteran King employees had a sense that Bullitt himself was on a different wavelength. When he came out with a new comprehensive company policy manual, recalled Al Smith, "Most of us looked at that and thought, 'What the hell is he talking about?'"

In 1963 Bullitt laid out a new company hiring policy. It was all very logical: people were the heart of the company. Therefore, the company should go out and hire the best people it could find. King Broadcasting was in no position to out-bid larger organizations for established talent. Therefore, to have any chance of attracting the best people, King would have to hire them young, as raw talent, before they had a chance to establish themselves. "'Rather than buying expensive, big-league stars, we're getting younger sandlot players and betting on their potential,'" Bullitt told Shelby Scates of the *Post-Intelligencer* in 1966. (Scates felt that the "sports simile . . . seemed slightly curious coming from him.") With limited resources, the company couldn't afford to look everywhere for new talent. Instead, it would have to search in a relatively few places. The places with the deepest pools of young talent were the elite colleges and universities. Therefore, King would recruit at those schools. Talent was more important than training and King's own training was better than anything offered at communications schools, so the company wouldn't go after people with communications degrees. In filling entry-level jobs, King would look for pure potential.

> *Talent was more important than training and King's own training was better than anything offered at communications schools, so the company wouldn't go after people with communications degrees. In filling entry-level jobs, King would look for pure potential. This policy went very much against the Seattle grain.*

This policy went very much against the Seattle grain, which at the time was provincial in the extreme. By the mid-1960s, many national-level news organizations—the *New York Times,* the *Washington Post,* the *Wall Street Journal*—hired promising people directly out of prestigious colleges. In Seattle, the attitude tended to be "spend five years paying your dues in Omak, then come talk to us." Bullitt was making King Broadcasting more like the kinds of national elite organizations to which Dorothy Bullitt hoped it would be compared—but less like Seattle. Bullitt was breaking out of the inbred Seattle broadcasting community in which virtually everyone had learned television from Lee Schulman.

In 1962, Bullitt hired a print journalist named Herb Altschul, who had been Associated Press bureau chief in Bonn and worked for the Sunday *New York Times* but had no broadcast experience, to deliver regular television commentaries. Altschul wasn't the only unusual hiring. Bullitt soon concluded that a Seattle lawyer named Irving Clark, who could stand up at a party and talk coherently on any topic under the sun, was more literate and better versed in current affairs than any radio talk personality in Seattle. So in 1964 he hired Clark to do a regular radio program.

These and other hirings minimized the importance of technical expertise. "I am looking for people who have something to communicate," Bullitt told Scates. "Mass communications is too important to leave to technicians, just as war is too important to leave to generals."

Bullitt realized that this approach contained pitfalls: the new recruits might be seen and resented as a favored elite, and their presence might cause dissension in the company. He wanted to avoid that. He couldn't.

King never gave itself over entirely to amateurism. It never stopped hiring experienced people for engineering or managerial positions. And it never insisted that everyone have a fancy education; one Bullitt manager was a high school dropout with a conviction for armed robbery.

Nevertheless, the Ivy League graduates who arrived from points east knowing nothing about television became symbols of the new regime. Dorothy Bullitt considered them East Coast snobs and never liked the idea of hiring them. Graduates of local communications schools felt slighted. Local people with practical experience felt that they had become second-class citizens. They had spent years learning their trades, and now management assumed that any bright kid with a good general education could come in and quickly learn to do the same things.

Not only did Bullitt hire newcomers with Ivy League degrees for entry-level jobs; he also started non-broadcasting subsidiaries and brought in outsiders to staff and run them. The first was *Seattle* magazine.

Bullitt had been thinking seriously about starting a magazine since the late 1950s. Peter Bunzel, an associate editor of *Life* who was hired to start and edit *Seattle*, wrote in 1970 that he and Bullitt had first discussed launching a publication over lunch at the Rainier Club in downtown Seattle when Bunzel visited the city during the summer of 1957. Bullitt talked to him about starting a publication for the people who listened to FM radio—at that time a very small, highbrow audience. "Mr. Bullitt and I corresponded periodically over the next several years," Bunzel wrote, "and every once in a while he would corporealize . . . in my *Life* office, always commenting on the splendid view of downtown Manhattan from my thirthieth-floor office." In the spring of 1963, Bullitt got the King Broadcasting board to approve his proposal for starting a magazine and he hired Bunzel to edit it. Bullitt had envisioned a rather drab but serious journal with a focus on public affairs. He did not envision color photographs on slick paper. Bunzel, who had just been working at the biggest, slickest magazine in the country, argued successfully for higher production values. In April 1964, the magazine published its first issue—on slick paper in color—depicting a silhouette of a man holding an umbrella on a rainy Seattle day.

For a man who had Bullitt's fondness for the printed word, a magazine made personal sense. In addition, city magazines seemed to be an idea whose time had come; although other broadcasting companies weren't rushing out to start publications, city magazines were springing up in many places. King wasn't straying from the communications business, just branching out into a different part of it. (And Stimson Bullitt wasn't straying as far as people assumed from his mother's own precedents. The people who considered Bullitt's venture into print publishing one of his flakier ideas probably never realized that in 1951, during the brief partnership with Hearst, his mother had tried to get a right of first refusal to buy the

Seattle Post-Intelligencer.) Besides, the 1960s were a time during which branching out was encouraged; the smart guys in business schools were advising corporations to diversify. Starting a magazine was a step toward diversifying King.

It was also a step toward diversifying the print media in Seattle. At that time, Seattle newspapers were politically conservative, stylistically stodgy, and reluctant to criticize local leaders or institutions. Stories about Boeing, the area's dominant employer, read like corporate press releases—which in many cases they probably were. The magazine would give the city a new voice.

But it was never a realistic business proposition. It never even made the most of an inherently hopeless situation. The business side of the operation always got short shrift. Bunzel himself had no experience with the business side of magazine publishing—he had worked for magazines that discouraged contact between the advertising and editorial staffs—and knew very little about it. The publication lost money from beginning to end.

Seattle also inspired bad feelings within the company because its editor, Bunzel, was exactly the sort of Ivy League carpetbagger whom many employees resented and because Bullitt so clearly cared more about the magazine than he did about broadcasting (Bullitt actually went over the grammar in longer articles, and made sure that they were ideologically satisfactory, stepping in to decide, for example, that a profile of Senator Henry Jackson should be more critical).

The tone of the magazine contributed to the sense that the people who produced it thought they were better than the locals. Explicitly or implicitly, Seattle was always being compared to the East Coast. Ancil Payne suggested that the magazine always had a kind of expatriate quality. The city of Seattle's prevailing tone was as subdued as the region's gray winter skies, but the magazine was unabashedly smart-assed. Its style, so unlike Stimson Bullitt's, seemed of a piece with Bullitt's hiring policy and the East Coast intellectual elitism with which he was associated. The publication was therefore viewed as another reflection of the company's president—although it never provided the intellectual analysis of public affairs that Stimson Bullitt had envisioned, and its editorial brashness made him uncomfortable.

Dorothy Bullitt never liked the magazine. Neither, unfortunately, did a number of Seattle's largest retail advertisers. At least during the publication's first couple of years, advertisers avoided it largely because it couldn't deliver many readers for the money. Roger Hagan, who served as *Seattle*'s business manager from mid-1964 to mid-1966, knew that many potential advertisers complained about the magazine's editorial policies, "but I never had the impression that they would have advertised anyway." The politically conservative managers of downtown department stores were clearly hostile for ideological reasons, but other retailers, whatever their politics, looked beyond the magazine's attractive demographics to its low readership numbers. Regular advertisers tended to be people who wanted to see the magazine succeed, rather than those who figured that advertising in it was a sound business proposition. *Seattle*'s circulation grew, but the magazine depended on advertising revenue, and when the community's major advertisers turned away, it had no chance of breaking even.

The broadcasting divisions were making enough money to cover the magazine's losses comfortably, but the drain on broadcasting revenues became another source of resentment within the company. The employees in broadcasting not only felt neglected, they felt it was unfair that the revenue they generated was being siphoned off to support one of Stimson Bullitt's pet projects.

———

For the American broadcasting industry, 1963 marked the end of all that disturbing talk about reform. Newton Minow left the FCC, John F. Kennedy was assassinated, and the country soon had other things on its mind.

After Kennedy was shot, people kept their sets on to get news of the assassination. In the process, millions saw the president's alleged assassin, Lee Harvey Oswald, gunned down in front of a live NBC camera: Oswald, flanked by detectives, walked from an elevator. Dallas nightclub owner Jack Ruby rushed toward him. Oswald doubled over and fell as Ruby's bullet struck him in the stomach. An NBC correspondent shouted, "He's been shot! He's been shot! Lee Oswald has been shot! There is absolute panic. Pandemonium has broken out." The scene was replayed again and again all over the nation. Kennedy's funeral was subsequently watched by more people than any previous event in television history—and, therefore, than any previous event in the history of the world.

No one criticized the way television covered the Kennedy assassination and its aftermath. Mary Ann Watson writes in *The Expanding Vista: American Television in the Kennedy Years*, "Television critics in every city wrote in superlatives about how the medium heroically rose to the tragic occasion. . . . The message from the halls of Congress was that TV bashing was no longer a fashionable activity." Television coverage of Kennedy's assassination and funeral made it clear that the screen, not the printed page, was now the nation's main news medium. A Roper poll taken in November 1963 indicated that television had supplanted newspapers as the main news source for the largest number of Americans. Two years earlier a Roper poll had found that TV was already more trusted than newspapers. Reform was dead.

KING-TV, KGW-TV, and KREM-TV carried network footage of the assassination and funeral. But when a catastrophic earthquake struck Alaska in 1964, the nation's first network pictures of the event came from KING-TV. As the early news from Alaska came in, everyone at the station knew it was an event that had to be covered somehow, but people just milled around not knowing what to do until Lee Schulman arrived. Eric Bremner remembered that Schulman walked in, stood on a landing above the newsroom, and announced, "I'm here." People stopped milling and got organized. Before long, cameraman Phil Sturholm and reporter Al Wallace were on a plane to Anchorage. As the plane flew over the ruined city, passengers started to weep. When Sturholm and Wallace reached the airport, they found no taxis or rental cars, so they hitched a ride with a Dutch flight crew from KLM to the heart of downtown Anchorage. Sturholm shot eleven minutes of film, and they drove back to the airport. The plane that had arrived after theirs was returning to Seattle in a couple of hours, and they asked a stewardess to take the film to Seattle. It was impossible to make a phone call from Anchorage; they couldn't tell Schulman or anyone else at KING-TV that the film was on its way. They didn't have to. When the plane from Anchorage arrived at SeaTac airport, Schulman had a helicopter waiting. The film was flown directly from the airport to the processing laboratory. It was the first film of the earthquake to arrive. Other stations sent film of the quake damage to Seattle, too, but KING-TV had the lab tied up. The other stations had to wait in line. As the first footage of the Alaska quake ran in Seattle, KING-TV newscaster Ted Bryant ad-libbed a commentary, and it all went out over the network.

The next year, the station chalked up another first. Telstar, the first satellite that relayed television broadcasts across the Atlantic, had been launched in July 1962 and operated experimentally until early 1963. Now, in April 1965, a commercial broadcasting satellite called Early Bird was launched. It was experimental, too, and television networks could use it for free. Nearly everyone assumed that the satellite was open only to network broadcasts. But Schulman had the chutzpah to ask if King Broadcasting could use the satellite, and the company reserved Early Bird's last free-time slot. King had twenty minutes during which its news people would talk and conduct interviews simultaneously from London, Paris, Washington, D.C., and Seattle. First it had to get its correspondents into place. Phil Sturholm and Herb Altschul were already overseas reporting on European politics and social conditions. The two men had been to the U.S.S.R., Hungary, Czechoslovakia, East Germany (where they had been thrown out for filming too close to the Berlin Wall), and much of western Europe, and were sitting in a cafe in a small West German town when a waiter told them they had a phone call. They were surprised that anyone knew where they were. Altschul took the call. It was Schulman, who seemed pleased to have tracked them down. He wanted Altschul in London as soon as possible for the satellite broadcast. Altschul and the other KING correspondents got into position, the station's engineers locked onto Early Bird, and KING-TV, KGW-TV, and KREM-TV became the first local stations to bounce signals off a satellite, the first local stations to broadcast live from Europe.

Although it was now technically feasible to send signals directly from London to Seattle, it still wasn't possible to get decent television reception in a neighborhood surrounded by hills, which distorted broadcast signals. However, a cable system could deliver a clear signal in any terrain. King's vice-president for engineering, Jay Wright, figured that the company could make money by delivering a better signal to viewers in hilly areas and he urged Stimson Bullitt to get the company involved in cable TV. Cable systems had existed since the early days of commercial television, but at that point, there was no indication that cable would become a rival to broadcast TV. (Wright did figure that once a cable system was plugged into people's homes, it would be able to run movies and other programs that could draw viewers away from regular broadcasts.) Bullitt asked Andrew Haley if any cable systems were for sale. Haley said yes, a system in Tujunga, California, was available, and Wright flew down to check it out. King bought its first cable system in 1965. A separate division, King Videocable, was formed that September.

The systems that King started buying tended to be mom-and-pop operations. A local television distributor might start a cable system and run it out of his home. After a while the recordkeeping would get too complicated to handle, and he would be eager to sell. Once Stimson Bullitt ventured into the cable market, people started coming in and offering to sell their small cable systems to King. The company was always ready to buy. A cable system required a sizable investment up front and took years to pay off, but it was a straightforward business proposition: just hook up the customers, maintain the system, and send out the bills. The opportunity was so attractive that the price didn't seem terribly important. By late April 1966, King had picked up the Tujunga system in California and small Washington systems in Montesano, Elma, and Ocean Shores, plus a half-interest in the Cowlitz system. To keep buying, Bullitt told the board it would have to raise the corporate borrowing limit of half a million dollars that it had imposed just the previous December. By the end of the year, the company had picked up the Sun Valley cable system in California, and was negotiating with the Prudential Insurance Company for a loan that could finance more cable, plus color equipment for KING-TV, studios for KREM-TV, and film production, and provide enough cash to pay off short-term loans. At the end of 1966, the company also joined with its competitors, KOMO and KIRO, to acquire and run most of the cable systems in Seattle. King would accelerate its purchasing of cable systems in later years, but the groundwork for its cable holdings was laid in the 1960s.

Cable was a meat-and-potatoes investment that did not capture Bullitt's imagination. He was more interested in the magazine and in two other ventures he launched during 1966: documentary filmmaking and feature films. Their attractions were easy to grasp—not only was Bullitt reluctant to leave all the company's eggs in one basket; he found a number of other fields more appealing than television. Besides, one assumes he liked the idea of succeeding in realms that his mother hadn't already conquered. Making King Broadcasting *his* company rather than Dorothy Bullitt's was a natural enough impulse. But the company couldn't really be separated from Dorothy Bullitt's personality or legend. Nor could Stimson Bullitt educate the community as he had hoped. Even in the 1960s, serious programs about serious issues had trouble competing in the circus atmosphere of commercial television.

Producing documentary films was not, of course, totally unprecedented for King Broadcasting. The company's stations in Seattle and Portland had produced them for years. Until 1965, KING-TV and KGW-TV documentaries had been made by people in the stations'

Cable was a meat-and-potatoes investment that did not capture Bullitt's imagination. He was more interested in the magazine and in two other ventures he launched during 1966: documentary filmmaking and feature films.

news and other departments. Then Stimson Bullitt decided to decentralize the management of the broadcasting empire. He sent Ancil Payne, at the time vice president for business, south to be vice president in charge of King's Portland operations. There Payne was able to create his own largely independent fiefdom, insulated from the policies and politics that were creating so much turmoil in Seattle. He soon pulled together a group of unusually talented people whose main mission would be to produce documentaries. One of the group's first efforts explored race relations in Portland, pointing out that there were no blacks employed as retail clerks, waiters, gas station attendants, or cabdrivers in the whole city.

Some of the people Payne had making documentaries in Portland were the kind of young, inexperienced Ivy Leaguers who were stimulating such resentment in Seattle. Payne also recruited talent at Ivy League colleges, but he was never identified, as Bullitt was, with the Ivy Leaguers.

A couple of the filmmakers came from Harvard. (One, Charles Horman, was later murdered in Chile during the U.S.-backed coup against Chile's elected president, Salvador Allende. His disappearance became the subject of the film *Missing*.) Jim Compton, who would become a KING-TV commentator and an NBC network correspondent, came from Reed College in Portland. Compton had just graduated and was working as a janitor at the college while he waited for a ship in the merchant marine. He was mopping a floor when the dean walked up and asked if he'd be interested in interviewing for a job with a local radio station. Compton had never given radio much thought, but a free lunch was part of the interview, so he gave it a try. He found himself doing radio news for KGW. Compton was interested in TV, so when the documentary unit had a job available, he snapped it up.

Bullitt liked the documentary-makers, and in 1966—over Payne's objection—he moved the whole unit to Seattle as the nucleus of a new filmmaking division, King Screen Productions. Roger Hagan, *Seattle* magazine's business manager, was made general manager. Hagan hadn't even known that Bullitt was contemplating a screen division, much less that he himself would wind up running it. In April, when the board voted to establish King Screen, it also agreed to bankroll two feature films by an independent filmmaker named Michael Roemer. Bullitt had been impressed by Roemer's 1964 film *Nothing But a Man*, and had phoned him out of the blue to talk. (The filmmaker had assumed Bullitt was looking for a job.) He liked Roemer, who became a personal friend. But Roemer had never made a commercially successful film. Backing his next feature, *The Plot Against Harry*, led to a financial abyss.

Although *Harry* was produced in New York with no King employees, King Screen Productions soon rivaled *Seattle* magazine as an object of resentment and a symbol of the new order. Like the magazine, it employed Easterners with elite educations, lost piles of money, and seemed to interest Bullitt more than the bread-and-butter broadcasting division did. Payne has suggested that broadcasting people reacted to King Screen as older siblings react to a new baby in the family.

The magazine, two years old at the time King Screen started, was arguably hitting its editorial stride. Cover stories explored the controversy over the then new birth control pill, the problems of local anti-poverty programs, the "fish-ins" for Indian fishing rights. Future novelist Tom Robbins wrote about the mystical paintings of Morris Graves, the epic films of Akira Kurosawa, and "The Anatomy of a Go-Go Dancer." But the magazine's provocative approach to the region continued to antagonize the conservative local business establishment. The headline of one cover story asked, "Why Would Anyone Want to Live in Tacoma?"

Despite King Broadcasting's reputation for hiring Ivy League graduates, some local boys still applied for jobs. In early 1966, a Washington State University graduate named Mike James, who was working part-time for three different radio stations, went to King's offices on Aurora Avenue and filled out an application. The woman who took it told him that the company wasn't exactly looking for WSU graduates, but she was one herself, so she'd get him interviews with King executives that same day. The news director asked him about Vietnam and what he knew about the background of the war.

Stimson Bullitt asked him about books he had read lately and books that had mattered to him in college. Nobody, except Personnel director Eric Bremner, asked him about his experience. James was hired.

Another local boy, Don LaCombe, took a part-time job on the telephone switchboard while he was still a student in the communications school at the University of Washington. A strike in 1967 gave him an opportunity to fill in as a reporter. That, in turn, gave him enough visibility within the company so that he was hired to fill a temporary vacancy for a floor director, the standard starting job in television. After that, whenever a temporary job as a floor director came up, LaCombe had the experience to fill it. Soon he had so much experience that he was asked to train new people who arrived to take permanent floor directors' jobs. But he wasn't hired for one of those permanent jobs himself. In the atmosphere of the time, he assumed the company didn't hire him because he didn't have an Ivy League degree. In retrospect, he figured maybe the company wouldn't hire him because he hadn't yet graduated from college. LaCombe finally graduated and got a floor director's job at KING, subsequently becoming a director, a producer, and KING-TV production manager. (King's local hiring didn't make a dent in Stimson Bullitt's reputation for bringing in outsiders. When Emory Bundy, a college professor with no broadcasting background, was hired in 1969 as KING-TV's director of public affairs, he found that he was resented as one of "Stimmy's boys." But Bundy hadn't been hired by Bullitt. And he wasn't an East Coast carpetbagger: he had grown up in Seattle and gone to the University of Washington. His background was so different from the company stereotype that a KING-TV promotion director took him around Seattle and introduced him to people as evidence that KING really did hire local talent.)

The hiring process could be a little strange. Bob Faw, who had no previous television experience, became a KING-TV reporter in 1967. During Faw's employment interview in Stimson Bullitt's dimly lighted office, Bullitt asked him about the writing of Columbia University sociologist C. Wright Mills. As part of Faw's visit to KING, he had dinner with commentator Herb Altschul. Altschul said

Faw really shouldn't go into television at all. It's a cesspool, he told the younger man—but if you want to get involved with it, KING is a good place to start.

Faw, who went on to a network career, found that the job at KING was "a golden opportunity." On one hand, he felt some resentment from long-term employees, because "you were looked upon as one of Stim's guys." On the other, "you'd go from Stim and talk to Dorothy and there was this *legendary* figure." More than that, the station gave him a tremendous amount of freedom.

LaCombe found a lot of freedom, too. He wanted to learn how to shoot film, so he was invited to collect the unused ends of film rolls, splice them together, borrow a KING camera, and experiment. In 1970, when the Beatles broke up, although LaCombe was just a floor director, he was allowed to make a half-hour special about the Beatles.

Mike James started out doing radio news, coming in at four in the morning and telephoning the police and fire departments to find out what had happened overnight. The local crimes and fires and the "rip and read" wire-service news might not have added up to much satisfaction for a guy who was reading a lot about Vietnam and interested in policy issues, but he got to write scripts for Ted Bryant, the TV news anchor who came in to read the radio news twice a day. The disc jockeys who ran the morning music shows would walk into the studio to talk with him on the air about Vietnam and other issues. James felt he got a chance to *use* everything he learned.

When James moved from radio to television news in 1968, he found he had enough time to cover a beat the way a print reporter could. James saw television crews from other stations come into city hall, spend fifteen minutes at a meeting, and leave. He was free to hang out there, spend all day at a hearing, and then, when the story had finally developed, call in a camera at 2 A.M. He wasn't sure that viewers cared about or even recognized the difference (and in the late 1960s, KING's news ratings went downhill), but he found the experience satisfying.

Reporters and writers weren't the only people who got all the freedom they could reasonably want. In 1966, Eric Bremner was sent to Spokane to manage financially troubled KREM. Bremner was thirty years old and had never run a television station before. But no one looked over his shoulder. No one talked to him. He was in Spokane for a month, and no one from corporate headquarters even called. Finally, Bremner called Seattle to get in touch.

The whole broadcasting industry was becoming bigger, slicker, more routinized. The live variety-show programs that KING had run for twenty years had become anachronisms.

Young employees might relish their freedom, but not everyone was having fun. King Broadcasting wasn't a little family business, and it could no longer be managed like one. Between 1958 and 1966, the number of employees rose 41 percent; Seattle employment, including King Screen, rose 57 percent. Inevitably, the company acquired new layers of management and a more rigid corporate structure. Shortly after taking over in 1961, Stimson Bullitt had his managers start going through a formal budget process every year. In 1967, it switched from machine accounting to computers.

The whole broadcasting industry was becoming bigger, slicker, more routinized. The live variety-show programs that KING had run for twenty years had become anachronisms. Stan Boreson did his last show in 1967. (On his last day at KING-TV, Dorothy Bullitt appeared in his office and said she'd be his date for the day's two retirement parties. She accompanied him to both parties, then invited him to her house, where they had coffee into which, much to Boreson's surprise—it was only 10 A.M.—her maid poured shots of brandy.) Bea Donovan's cooking show went off the air in 1968. Charles Herring, who had been *the* news commentator in Seattle during the 1950s and early 1960s, left in 1967. Elizabeth Wright Evans, who had made public service programs since 1953, left in 1968.

In 1968, a KING manager who had spent years with the company (and had turned down a job at 50 percent more pay with a different broadcasting company only two years before) resigned. In a letter to Dorothy Bullitt he wrote, "As we take the Stan Boresons off the air, move the Wundas to weekends, do remotes only when sold . . . we remove the last . . . creative element from the program department." Actually, he didn't think all the creativity had left the company; it had just gone to parts of the company he didn't much like: "A logical outlet [for the letter-writer] would have been King's Screen for some creative energy, but I am not in sympathy with the hippie element down there."

The process of bureaucratization left other casualties. KING-TV was going to hire its first general manager in 1965. Lee Schulman wanted the job. Though he had been acknowledged as a great program director, he was not considered good at managing people. The board doubted he was the right person for the position—when the subject was discussed, Henry Owen said he gave Schulman no better than fifty-fifty odds of success—but he clearly deserved a chance. Schulman got the job, but he didn't keep it for long. He left KING in May 1966. Bob Schulman had already moved on. At least seven other people left around the same time. The company for which Lee Schulman became a general manager was not the same company for which he had worked since 1948. "The torment, the frustrations, the anxieties—the flailing at windmills; all of it has been heartbreaking," Schulman wrote Dorothy Bullitt in spring 1966. "I'm sorry," he told her, "that all of the unsaid hopes we have shared really never materialized."

The year before, in the same management shuffle that had sent Payne to Portland, Henry Owen had become vice-chairman of the board and had lost all operational responsibility. At the beginning of 1968, Otto Brandt was forced out. Brandt had evidently assumed he would be able to run the company with a free hand after Dorothy Bullitt stepped down. He became extremely frustrated with the way Stimson Bullitt ran King. An assistant once found him sitting at his desk red-faced with anger. "When he came, I thought he was a genius," Brandt said. "He isn't." Bullitt, for his part, resented the way Brandt patronized him, asking his advice about simple-minded business problems, taking phone calls while Bullitt waited to talk with him. Bullitt consequently belittled Brandt at meetings, showing little respect for the man who had once been ABC's boy wonder vice president. With Brandt gone, more responsibility for actually running the company fell on Bullitt's shoulders.

Andrew Haley was gone, too. He died in September 1966. Stimson Bullitt had never gotten along especially well with the flamboyant Washington lawyer—hardly surprising given the difference in their personalities and Haley's tendency to patronize the younger man. Bullitt never relied on Haley as his mother had.

Dorothy Bullitt was still around every day, walking the halls and hanging out in the coffee shop. She was still chairman of the board, but she had, in effect, been exiled to the old brick apartment building behind the station, to which Henry Owen and Gloria Chandler also moved. Her big desk and her oriental carpets now filled a ground-floor room in "the brick house." Her old friends—Henry Owen, her cousin Fred Stimson, Gloria Chandler, and John Leffler, Dean of St. Mark's Episcopal Cathedral—were still together, and would sometimes go out to the horse races at Longacres, but they were no longer at the center of things, and Dorothy Bullitt, for one, clearly missed it. In 1967, she and Owen officially retired as chairman and vice-chairman of the board. That same year, when Owen—the man who had run the company for her—spoke to employees of *Seattle* magazine, they didn't know who he was.

And King wasn't Dorothy Bullitt's company anymore. For the first several years of Stimson Bullitt's reign, she had stayed out of the way, had let him make his own changes and his own mistakes, but

Dorothy Bullitt was still around every day, walking the halls and hanging out in the coffee shop. She was still chairman of the board, but she had, in effect, been exiled to the old brick apartment building behind the station. King wasn't Dorothy Bullitt's company anymore.

King Broadcasting had still been hers—she personally owned roughly 85 percent of the stock. In 1965, looking ahead to her death and trying to save the family inheritance taxes, she distributed much of her stock to her three children. She remained the largest of the four major shareholders, and her family still owned almost all of the company, but she no longer held a controlling share.

The year before, the first strike in the company's history (the same strike that gave LaCombe his chance to work someplace beyond the switchboard) reflected the divisions that had developed within what had once been a close-knit corporation. King Broadcasting had always had good relations with its unions. Henry Owen and Dorothy Bullitt had kept the peace, even when other broadcasting companies were having problems. This time, the engineers at the AM and FM stations and KING-TV demanded more money than management wanted to give them. But the real issue at KING-TV wasn't money, it was the resentment that had built up among much of the broadcasting staff. The resentment wasn't directed toward Dorothy Bullitt. People felt that she hadn't changed. But they did resent the new order; they felt that the company's current management was trying to force the old guard out.

> *The divisions within the corporation mirrored the generational and cultural splits that were developing in American society.*

Managers, sometimes working twelve to eighteen hours a day, kept the station on the air. When the strike ended two months later, the engineers got only seven cents per hour more than the company had originally offered, $4.57 an hour instead of $4.50. Settlement of the strike didn't resolve the underlying conflicts. King Broadcasting was no longer one big happy family.

The divisions within the corporation mirrored the generational and cultural splits that were developing in American society. Age per se was becoming a sign of differing attitudes, and there were significant age gaps at King. In 1966, the average age of all KING-AM, -FM and -TV employees was 38.4 years. The average age of magazine employees was 29.3. Anyone looking for a source of cultural conflict between the magazine and the rest of King could start right there.

At King as in the rest of American society, young people were more likely to have long hair (although in the mid-60s, the magazine staff was a pretty short-haired, buttoned-down group); more likely to smoke pot (although virtually everyone in the company drank, some to frequent excess); and more likely to oppose the Vietnam War.

In 1966, despite all the complaints made later by frustrated soldiers and bureaucrats about the mainstream press turning the American people against the war, the press supported the war effort. Reporters for the *New York Times* and other publications had made it clear that the war was not going as advertised, but their editorial boards hadn't caught on. In the broadcast industry, regulated by the FCC and always looking over its shoulder at regulators and advertisers, there was no hint of dissent.

Stimson Bullitt made some large waves, therefore, on December 23, 1966, when he read the nation's first television editorial against the Vietnam War. Characteristically, Bullitt had thought the issue through, reached his conclusions, and saw no reason not to state them. Would advertisers flee KING? There would be more advertisers to take their places. Television was making money hand over fist. Bullitt didn't worry about losing a few ads.

"War always poses the question whether the purpose justifies the whole cost," Bullitt said. "In World War II, it did. In this war, I submit that it does not." Bullitt followed his own editorial with a series of guest commentaries. At the end of December, Senator George McGovern of South Dakota told KING viewers that "it was a mistake . . . to have bombed North Vietnam at all." In January 1967, John W. Lewis, an associate professor of government and Asian studies at Cornell, explained that "the United States has been misled by its confusion of the spread of Communism with the expansion of China." Later in January, *Washington Post* columnist

Joseph Kraft said that there could not be peace until "the pattern of American escalation [is] broken."

Reaction to King's anti-war editorials was mixed. According to Jack Fearey, who had succeeded Lee Schulman as KING-TV's program director, "People said, 'My God, they'll take our license away.'" Dorothy Bullitt was nervous. Some local advertisers did flee. But the sky didn't fall. Profits declined in 1967, but the company still netted some $700,000. The *New York Times*' television critic, Jack Gould, wrote on January 22 that "[i]n some respects, the most intriguing broadcaster of the current season is Stimson Bullitt. He is the first video station owner to go on the air with an editorial challenging President Johnson's conduct of the Vietnamese war and urging a cessation of the bombing of North Vietnam."

Within the company, the editorial deepened the existing generational and cultural divisions. Some younger employees, feeling management was on their side, slapped anti-war stickers on company cars. Veteran broadcasting people, who already felt beleaguered, now felt that the tide had clearly turned against them. Dorothy Bullitt didn't like the editorial either. She didn't disagree with the ideas, but she didn't want the company to antagonize people.

In the context of the time, King's editorial position did not simply reflect Bullitt's individual views. It staked out one end of a political/cultural continuum. In some people's minds, the editorial linked the broadcasting company to the beards-and-sandals protesters or at least linked it more closely to the Ivy League elite, a major source of early anti-war sentiment. By committing the station to an anti-war position—however principled and, in retrospect, however sound that position may have been—Stimson Bullitt was making a kind of cultural statement.

With hindsight, taking a position against the Vietnam War does not seem like such a radical act. A little more than a year after Bullitt's anti-war editorial, the nation's best-known and most avuncular television commentator, Walter Cronkite, returned from a tour of Vietnam and concluded that the United States couldn't possibly succeed in winning the war. By the end of the year, President Lyndon

Johnson, succumbing to popular discontent, had stopped bombing North Vietnam, and had decided not to run for another term. Richard Nixon was elected president in 1968 at least partly on the strength of his secret plan to stop the war (although he didn't actually pull out the last U.S. troops until 1973).

But in 1966, opposing the war took courage, or at least an absence of the fear—of regulators, of advertisers, of offending people—that shadowed most of the broadcasting industry. King's reputation in the Northwest as a crusading liberal company stems in large part from that era, and the Vietnam editorial had a lot to do with creating it.

Even before Stimson Bullitt delivered his anti-war editorial, King Screen made a film about the people who worked in a napalm factory in Redwood City, California, and their attitudes toward their product and the war. The film won a grand prize at the 1967 Cracow film festival—less of an honor than met the eye, perhaps, given that the film was implicitly critical of the American war effort and Cracow was located in then-Communist Poland. Still, it was an international award. KING-TV never aired the film.

King Screen's biggest prizewinner was a 1967 film written by Mark Harris and sponsored by the Sierra Club about threats to the California redwoods, which were being logged at an alarming rate. The film won a 1968 Oscar for best short documentary.

Critically and aesthetically, King Screen was a success. Financially, it was a disaster. And no wonder. It had not been conceived of or managed by experienced film people. There simply wasn't a market for much of what it did. From the isolated vantage point of Seattle, there had seemed to be no reason why King Screen couldn't make documentaries on subjects of national significance and sell them to the networks. But the networks didn't want documentaries. Bullitt and Roger Hagan, novices in the business, hadn't realized that, and no one had told them. Even Otto Brandt, who may not have known the film business but certainly knew the networks, encouraged the venture and actually set up a meeting with people at NBC. For Hagan, the meeting provided "a dose of reality." The only films King Screen had to show the network executives were documentaries such as *Huelga!*—a sympathetic picture of the Delano, California, grape pickers' strike that won a half dozen awards but reflected the unashamed left-of-center political bias of the company's young filmmakers. The network didn't want anything to do with them. Actually, the network didn't want anything to do with any hard-news documentaries from independent sources. The only documentaries that might possibly have interested NBC were "soft" features that it could turn into entertainment. The example the network people gave was Sophia Loren in Rome.

Bullitt might have been satisfied to just make documentaries, even if they didn't turn a profit. Hagan, however, felt some obligation to try to earn his keep, so he pushed ahead with commercials and industrial films. But the people who made documentaries had no experience making commercials or industrial films, and weren't interested in making them anyway. So Hagan hired extra staff. "The thing grew faster than it should have," Hagan realized in retrospect. "We had too big a group right from the start." Most production companies hired people for specific projects and laid them off when the projects were completed; King Screen paid the salaries of a permanent staff all year around. Costs were clearly too high. But no one even knew how much things *should* cost.

King Broadcasting Company watched its film division's budgets closely, but no one did anything to stop the losses. After Payson Hall, a former publishing executive, became the company's vice president for finance and planning in 1968, he summoned Hagan to his house once a week for tutorials in business and economics, but that was about all. Whenever King Screen showed a profit for the month, people congratulated Hagan, but he knew that any month in the black was simply an artifact of the screen division's billing cycle; it was never the start of a more profitable trend. As King Screen continued to lose money, it continued to stir resentments within the company. The news and program departments were always more commercial and more conservative than the new ventures. Most King Screen productions were never shown on KING-TV. There was

SEATTLE

THE PACIFIC NORTHWEST MAGAZINE   60 CENTS · OCTOBER 1968

'Hey Chief, I hear you're
looking for black policemen'

Black Panther Captain
Aaron Dixon

SEATTLE

From racism and homosexuality to living in Tacoma, no subject was too controversial for Seattle *magazine. The magazine's writers were young, brash, and intent on giving the city a new voice.*

still a perception of favoritism: Bullitt cared more about the screen division than he cared about television. This was true. But it was also ironic, since some screen division people came to feel that Bullitt had lost interest in them. He might not even attend the screening of a new film, or he might go and then walk out without saying anything. The documentary makers didn't know what he was thinking. They "got the impression he did not approve of what they were doing," Hagan said. "They got the impression he was a disapproving parent." The rest of the company wasn't aware of these feelings.

If the management of King Broadcasting was naive about documentaries, it was totally ignorant about features. Hagan went to Hollywood and talked with Warner Brothers about *The Plot Against Harry*. A Warner Brothers executive, who had just been yelled at by Warren Beatty about the studio's handling of *Bonnie and Clyde*, proceeded to yell at Hagan. How could King Broadcasting possibly have let Roemer's feature get this far along without nailing down a distribution deal and getting the distributor to invest money in the film? It was absurd. "He was very rude and very loud," Hagan discovered, "but he was right." Hagan went back to Seattle and told Bullitt about the conversation. Bullitt didn't think a distributor was needed at that point. Roemer kept working on the film.

———

In a somewhat desperate attempt to be noticed, *Seattle* magazine started running covers that caught people's attention but seemed to epitomize the magazine's too-hip-for-this-city attitude. Perhaps the best of them showed Seattle Black Panther leader Aaron Dixon behind the wheel of a city police car saying, "Hey Chief, I hear you're looking for black policemen." Another cover featured a local homosexual businessman, which was startling for a time at which most homosexuals stayed deep in the closet. Some newsstands refused to sell these issues at all. "In short order," Bunzel wrote, "we lost a variety of prime [advertising] accounts. These included . . . the Seattle First National Bank, whose representative told our advertising manager that the appearance of their ad on the inside back cover of the Panther issue doomed any chance of retaining them; major corporate depositors had complained in the most forceful terms. Thus, the very reasons for our high newsstand sales ended up decreasing our ad revenues."

The new ventures weren't the only parts of the company that were having trouble. KREM-TV, which had been merged into the King Broadcasting Company in 1965, continued to struggle financially.

Although the station erected a new tower and saw its ratings and earnings rise around the time of the merger, in 1968 the King board was seriously contemplating selling KREM if things didn't get better.

King radio had been losing money for years. It was in a very competitive business, and King Broadcasting's management didn't give it enough time or attention to have much chance of success. But radio never stirred up internal resentments. People evidently assumed that King should be involved in radio. They did not assume that it should be involved in magazine publishing or documentary films.

Some television people resented the magazine and screen divisions partly because they thought that the money spent on documentaries and print journalism should be spent on new broadcasting equipment; they worried that the company was falling behind technologically.

Some television people resented the magazine and screen divisions partly because they thought that the money spent on documentaries and print journalism should be spent on new broadcasting equipment; they worried that the company was falling behind technologically. "We needed equipment," Al Smith recalled. "We were patching stuff up." Certainly, King Broadcasting was no longer being run by someone who had Dorothy Bullitt's desire to be the first on her block with the latest gadget. But really, her desire for innovation had had pretty tight limits; she wasn't about to throw large sums of money after expensive toys. She bought the first production model videotape machine in the country. She equipped the new station in Portland with the latest color cameras. But she didn't rush to update the threadbare hardware in Spokane, where capital investment would pay off slowly at best. And she never did junk all the existing hardware and switch Seattle to color; all the flagship station's local programming was still black and white when she turned the company over to Stimson Bullitt. More than five years later, in early January

1967, the local news went color; by the end of the month, KING-TV had finally abandoned black and white.

The company may have been slow to embrace color, but it was significantly ahead of its time in hiring minorities and women. The commitment to hire people other than white males for responsible positions stemmed from Stimson Bullitt's own personal conviction. Arguably, Bullitt was the only high-level executive who was committed to hiring women and minorities. Like KING-TV's opposition to the Vietnam War, this is a policy that with hindsight doesn't seem so remarkable; within a few years, more companies were hiring women and minorities. But in the mid-1960s, virtually no one was hiring them—and King Broadcasting Company wouldn't have hired them, either, if Stimson Bullitt hadn't insisted.

Dorothy Bullitt didn't go out of her way to give other women a chance. She gave her friend Gloria Chandler and other women prominent roles in traditionally women's areas—children's programming, public affairs—but that was about all. She generally expected women to work as secretaries. She was quick to overlook male associates' behavior that in later years would be condemned as sexual harassment, if not prosecuted as sexual assault. She did not hire women as camera operators or reporters. She never put her own daughters onto the board of directors. Not that her attitudes about hiring women and minorities were in any way behind the times; they just weren't noticeably ahead.

Stimson Bullitt, on the other hand, not only put his sisters on the board of directors—Patsy joined the board in 1961, Harriet in 1965—in 1968, he personally recruited the company's first black cameraman, and he recruited other minority workers. After a while, Bullitt simply insisted that his managers hire women and minorities. Managers had to keep track of the ethnic backgrounds of the people in their departments and specifically justify not hiring minorities. (In the mid-1960s, Al Hunter, managing KREM in Spokane, called Eric Bremner, then serving as the company's first personnel director, in frustration; he needed people but Bullitt wouldn't approve his hirings.) The minority hirings did not always work out well. Some people who weren't especially competent got hired. Others who were competent came in groups after less than a year on the job to ask why they hadn't been promoted. Managers were afraid that they were being asked to hire the unqualified, and they resented Bullitt usurping their right to hire and fire the people working under them. Eventually, executives revolted. King had serious problems and they needed competent people. If Bullitt was going to tell them whom they could hire, they would quit.

Many of the people who joined King Broadcasting in the later 1960s were considered representatives of the so-called "counterculture." The cultural division within the company became obvious at the annual Christmas parties. In the late 1960s, the party would be channeled into two separate rooms. In one room, a traditional "combo" played pre-rock dance music. In the other, a well-amplified band played rock. The station's sports editor, Rod Belcher, always sang a couple of numbers with the traditional group. One year, the rock band in the other room was so loud that no one could even hear the more traditional group. Frustrated, Belcher walked next door and pulled all the wires out of the rock band's amplifiers. The Christmas party was obviously reaching the end of its useful life. At the very last one, someone spiked the cookies and a magazine editor threw up on the table in front of the always-decorous Dorothy Bullitt.

In addition to the war and the rise of the counterculture, the late 1960s saw the spread of racial tension and urban violence. The Watts riot of 1964 had been a relatively isolated event. The unprecedented urban riots of 1967 struck a number of cities and even some suburban communities. Then, in the spring of 1968, Martin Luther King, Jr. was shot, Robert Kennedy was shot, and there were bigger riots than there had been the year before. In Seattle's Central Area in 1968, racial tensions ran high, and edgy cops kept a close watch on the streets.

That year, Sturholm and Altschul dropped their annual trip abroad. The station's management figured that so much was happening in the United States that the two should explore political and social conditions closer to home. Instead of filming the Berlin Wall, they made a ninety-minute special on Seattle's own Central Area.

With racial tension high in the Central Area, KING-TV's African-American cameraman could cover stories that white KING-TV employees couldn't. But other King people covered the racial tension, too. News anchor Ted Bryant managed to spend time with members of the radical Black Panthers, which evidently convinced some Seattle cops that KING was on the other side. (African-American news people covering the ghetto could become a stereotype, too: when Bill Baker was television assignment editor, a black reporter complained to Baker that he was tired of covering the Central Area; he wanted to cover city hall.) In the spring of 1969, news director Bob Hoyt complained that KING's news staff wasn't staying close enough to the story, that people were needlessly avoiding the tension and demonstrations. One night, to prove his point, he and a KING secretary drove into the Central Area. Around 9:30 P.M., at the intersection of 23rd and Jefferson, their car got wedged between two others. Hoyt was dragged out and beaten. The secretary had her purse snatched. There were no more complaints from Hoyt to the news staff.

Simmons switched on the television in his Seattle hotel room and, as he later recalled, saw announcers unlike any he had ever seen on TV news—there was reporter Mike James with hair down to his shoulders—and whenever KING's call letters appeared on the screen, they were accompanied by the flashing message "Stop the war."

There was a thin and sometimes indiscernible line between covering the turmoil of the time and being part of it. Capable as the KING-TV people were, they did not seem to be—and in some cases did not want to be—objective reporters. The station did not project an image of objectivity. A California television newsman named Bob Simmons, who wound up as a KING commentator, saw KING for the first time in the spring of 1968, when he was covering Robert

Kennedy's presidential campaign. Simmons switched on the television in his Seattle hotel room and, as he later recalled, saw announcers unlike any he had ever seen on TV news—there was reporter Mike James with hair down to his shoulders—and whenever KING's call letters appeared on the screen, they were accompanied by the flashing message "Stop the war."

Some people felt that KING's news biases went well beyond the realm of hairstyles and editorial policy. When John Komen, former news director at KOMO and a New York–based network correspondent for ABC, returned to Seattle in 1969 and started reporting for KING-TV, he found that a number of people considered themselves part of "the movement," working for political and social change. This was, after all, a time at which otherwise rational people talked seriously about revolution and those who didn't want history to leave them behind liked to think of themselves as radical. Actually, Komen thought the same attitude was permeating television news all over. "Television news, largely in the past five years, has almost destroyed its credibility," he said in a speech quoted in the *Seattle Times* television column. "It has done that by a snobbish, intolerant, arrogant blurring of the dividing line between news and opinion." Komen inevitably rubbed some of his colleagues at KING-TV the wrong way.

Komen was politically more conservative than most of his colleagues at the station, but he wasn't the only observer who felt that KING-TV's news coverage lacked objectivity. Ancil Payne, very much an insider—and the man who would soon be running the company—felt the same way.

———

King Broadcasting kept investing in mundane businesses with the sole idea of making money. The company acquired more small cable systems. It also launched a mobile production unit. KING engineers had put together a remote production unit by cramming equipment into an old diesel truck that the post office had once used for sorting mail on the fly along Oregon highways. The company sometimes rented the truck out to NBC and to other stations. Jay Wright, vice president of engineering, figured the company could make more money with the mobile unit if it bought better equipment and rented the truck out more. To be sure of turning a profit, King would have to get all three of its own television stations to rent the truck. Wright talked to the managers of all three stations, but none would commit to renting it. Bullitt told Wright to go ahead and buy equipment anyway. In December 1968, the board voted to establish Northwest Mobile Television as a new profit center. The mobile unit quickly became a success. Before long, it was covering the space program, as well as sports, and by the time the company was sold, it was the largest mobile production unit in the world.

During the summer of 1968—considering not only another source of capital but also the attractions of a tie-in with movie theaters and the advantages of being part of a larger organization—the board talked repeatedly about merging with the Walter Reade theater chain, which operated seventy theaters across the country and also produced and distributed films. In July, the King board decided to offer Walter Reade a proposal to merge by exchanging stock. The executive committee dropped the negotiations, but the merger idea didn't go away, and King Broadcasting soon brought Walter Reade, Jr., who owned the theater chain, onto its board. (The theaters were managed from New Jersey, but Reade himself—the son of the theater chain's founder—was a kind of Hollywood figure who wore flowers in his lapels and diamond rings and brought a show business manner to the board meetings. In 1973, he was killed while skiing in the Swiss Alps.) The company was also contemplating a public stock offering.

While King Broadcasting branched out into cable systems and mobile production, into magazines and filmmaking, it remained totally separate from the Bullitt Company's real estate holdings. On one hand, the separation made sense because broadcasting and real estate were distinct businesses with nothing in common. On the other hand, the companies shared ownership and management, and over the years the real estate company had lent money and leased property to the broadcasting company. At least as early as 1951, the outside accounting firm of Haskins & Sells had suggested the advantages of merging the two companies. Running the two companies together would enable the real estate operation to use King's data processing and accounting systems and would produce some economies. It would also erase the broadcasting company's debt to the real estate company, boosting King's stock value. Dorothy Bullitt may have considered a merger, but she had never acted. Now, Stimson Bullitt decided to go ahead. On September 18, 1968, the King board voted to merge with the Bullitt Company. In October, the shareholders approved. Dorothy Bullitt didn't like the idea of a merger—she felt quite hurt by it—but her son was running the companies, so when the papers were put in front of her, she signed. On February 28, 1969, the two companies were formally merged.

The merger broadened King Broadcasting's holdings from the unusual to the bizarre. Some King employees believed that the company had deliberately made strange investments in the late 1960s, compounding the sins, real or imagined, of the magazine and screen divisions. Actually, the truly strange acquisitions were baggage that came along with the Bullitt Company.

They had been odd enough ventures for the Bullitt Company alone. In the early 1960s, Dick Riddell, King's attorney and Stimson Bullitt's law partner, had invested in a plywood mill on Okinawa, a Japanese possession that was still occupied and governed by the United States. Riddell persuaded Bullitt to invest. Without really planning to, Bullitt and Riddell became embroiled in a struggle with another investor for control of the company. They won. Bullitt soon wished they hadn't.

Once the Bullitt Company had the plywood mill on Okinawa, it acquired timber concessions in the Philippines and a log trading company headquartered in Hong Kong. When the plywood mill needed money, the Bullitt Company provided loans, so Bullitt and his colleagues had to take an active part in the plywood company's affairs.

Okinawa Plywood started out badly, and with hindsight Bullitt and Riddell probably should have recognized the omens. In 1962, the company's resident manager wrote from Naha that "[a]bsenteeism has been a real problem of late. . . . This morning we are unable to run the core lathe because of a lack of people. Yesterday and last night was some sort of lunar holiday. Getting this last shipment out was a real struggle. Tom and I took our shirts off and pitched in with the rest of them for about four days."

But the Seattle investors persevered. When America poured troops into Vietnam after the Gulf of Tonkin incident in 1964, the plywood mill had a virtually unlimited market selling building materials to the Army and Marines. There was certainly some irony in that: on one hand, Stimson Bullitt's broadcasting company was running unprecedented and courageous editorials against the war. At the same time, his real estate company's subsidiary was making money from the war.

The ethical conflict, if there was one, didn't last long. When the United States started withdrawing troops from Vietnam, the market dried up, and the plywood company—facing competition from Korean mills subsidized by American foreign aid—began a complicated slide toward oblivion.

The mill had caused its share of trouble and embarrassment even before the market went bad. In 1964, its Okinawan workers went out on strike. The mill's 131-foot smokestack was a landmark visible from all over the city of Naha. Four striking workers climbed the stack with a sheet of plywood, erected a platform on top, and camped out there. The plant shut down. The strike had distinct political overtones. The plant employed Okinawan workers with Japanese managers—just the way the Japanese had run things before the war— and the Okinawans resented it. The strike was finally settled. The mill would, in effect, become more Okinawan: it would hire Okinawan managers, set up a company commissary that sold cheap rice, even establish a company baseball team.

Now this distant, troublesome plywood mill was part of King Broadcasting Company. In June 1969, the board talked about selling it. In fact Bullitt wanted to sell, but Riddell and King's corporate secretary, Jonathan Whetzel, didn't. At that stage, King's newly acquired Far Eastern operations were profitable.

At home, the screen division was still losing money. It had managed to sell some commercials and industrial films, but advertisers would have only small projects done in Seattle; for major West Coast commercials they looked to Los Angeles. In 1969, Hagan proposed moving the commercial-making venture to San Francisco, where it might be able to corral a portion of the advertising business from the Bay Area north, but the proposal fell on deaf ears. King's executive committee discussed King Screen's problems repeatedly without reaching any decision. At the end of 1969, Bullitt reported to the board that King Screen had changed its management and its focus. The division's original general manager, Roger Hagan, had been replaced by Bernard Roederer, who had been the company's director of research. Staff had been cut, ambitions had been scaled back, and the division was now concentrating on educational films. But King Screen still couldn't find markets. As a result, its still relatively large staff of bright young men was chronically underemployed. On Fridays, some would check movies out of the public library and spend the day watching them, drinking beer and smoking marijuana on the job.

Television remained the goose that laid King Broadcasting's golden eggs, but it was perhaps laying fewer of them than it should have been; the company's net profit and its shareholders' return on investment had started to drop. Some people blamed Stimson Bullitt for squandering the lead that the FCC freeze of the late 1940s and early 1950s had given Dorothy Bullitt over her competitors. That was unrealistic. By 1970, the freeze had been over for almost twenty years, and sooner or later the competition was going to catch up.

Nevertheless, the company's flagship Seattle television station would have made more money if Bullitt had been more interested in profit and less interested in principle. Some advertisers had been driven away by the company's position on Vietnam. Others left after the station presented evidence that the University of Washington football coach was a racist—Bullitt got phone calls from community leaders angry over that one, but he didn't back down. Nor did he follow the other local media and downtown business interests in backing the city of Seattle's redevelopment plans for the Pike Place Market.

Bullitt's problems with the local business community were compounded by his distaste for business socializing. He did not go to

Rotary meetings. He did not go out of his way to explain King's editorial policies to business leaders who disagreed with them. He did not pretend to like or even remember people who didn't interest him.

Local news, originally a kind of public service that wasn't expected to make money, was becoming a major source of profit for television stations all over the country. During most of the 1960s, KING-TV had the highest-rated local news shows in Seattle. But news ratings were—and are—tied closely to personalities, and the personalities change. KING's anchor, Ted Bryant, who had joined KING in 1956 and was the best-known news anchor in Seattle, didn't like working for news director Bob Hoyt. Hoyt, who had arrived in November 1968 with no previous experience in TV news, talked about San Francisco's public television station, KQED, as a model. At the beginning of 1969, Bryant had coffee with station manager Eric Bremner at a motel coffee shop near the station and presented a list of demands. If the demands had been met, he would have been in control of the news. Bremner said he couldn't do it. Bryant left KING-TV, and the station's news ratings sank.

In good times, people might have taken this more in stride. But the end of the decade was not a good time in Seattle. The mid- and late sixties had been boom years in Seattle largely because Boeing was doing so well. In 1967, the aircraft manufacturer employed more than 100,000 people in the Puget Sound area. But the aircraft industry has always been notoriously cyclical, and Boeing started reducing its work force. Before the end of 1971, it laid off nearly two-thirds of its Seattle-area employees. At the start of 1971, Washington State's unemployment rate hit 15 percent. This was not an ideal time for selling ads.

But Stimson Bullitt never worried much about the company's survival. There didn't seem much reason to. In 1968, exclusive of the real estate operations, King earned a net after-tax profit of just under a million dollars. When Bullitt told the board in early 1970 that broadcast revenues were suffering from the recession, he also told it that King had made more than a million dollars profit the year before. A network affiliation still all but guaranteed success. King might be making less money than it could, but he felt no compulsion to accumulate wealth.

Nevertheless, during the first four months of 1970 the broad-casting and cable operations earned only $163,000. Clearly, there were problems; Bullitt did not have many illusions about his ability to solve them singlehandedly, and he asked Payne to move back from Portland to Seattle. In June 1970, the board created the position of executive vice president—the company's chief administrative offi-cer—and elected Payne to the position. "Stim was getting frustrated," Payne recalled. "He came down and said, 'I want you to come back as executive vice president.'" Payne was reluctant to make the move. He was happy in Portland. Besides, he didn't like the prospect of sharing authority with Bullitt, and he figured that being executive vice president when the president's family owned the company sounded like a bad deal. But Bullitt told him that someone else would be hired as executive vice president if he refused, and Payne decided that for his own self-preservation he had better take the job.

The company's management had grown obsessed with the prob-lems of its non-broadcasting subsidiaries. When Bremner started managing the Seattle television station in 1968, he wanted advice about the business side of the operation, but King's financial people were so busy figuring out what to do about King Screen and the magazine that he literally couldn't get anyone to talk with him. He threatened to hire his own accountant before he finally got help.

By mid-1970, *Seattle's* condition had become terminal. Bunzel had proposed abandoning the color and slick paper to save on pro-duction costs. Bullitt rejected the idea. He considered it a retreat. On September 10, 1970, Peter Bunzel told the King executive board that *Seattle* would lose a projected $125,000 for the year and that getting the magazine into the black would require a 100-percent increase in advertising. Bunzel recommended pulling the plug. The next week, the board voted to fold *Seattle* by the end of 1970. Three days later, Bunzel told the magazine's staff. "The deathly silence which greeted my remarks made me feel desolate. Halfway through the meeting, I noticed Dorothy Bowen [who worked in the magazine's circulation department] fighting back tears, and this almost undid me."

Michael Roemer's film *The Plot Against Harry* was finally completed in 1970, four years after King decided to finance it. The idea had been to show the film in theaters, then later on TV. But the film was shot in black and white, and by that time, young people—even then the prime audience—expected color, so there was little interest among theater owners and essentially no interest from TV. In October 1970, Roederer reported that the film had been screened by Warner Brothers, Paramount, National General, Allied Artists, Universal, United Artists, Embassy Pictures, and Walter Reade. All "indicated that they had no interest in distributing the film—not even if we were to offer them a very advantageous contract." In other words, King couldn't give it away. Not only was the film black and white, it was perceived as too "ethnic" and not flashy enough. Some critics liked it, but the company had dropped $600,000 on the project, and *The Plot Against Harry* became another symbol of ways in which Stimson Bullitt had led King Broadcasting Company off the deep end.

Network television affiliations in three cities could still cover a multitude of financial sins, and while management was concentrating disproportionately on the company's troubled non-broadcasting divisions, the cable acquisitions continued. In 1968, the company bought cable systems in Portland, Oregon, and in Ellensburg, Washington, and in 1970, a system in Lodi, California. By 1971, on an investment of $4.2 million, the cable operations were bringing in $1.2 million a year in revenues and more than half a million dollars in profit.

Around that time Stimson Bullitt started buying property along First Avenue in Seattle, in the rundown area between the Pike Place Market and Pioneer Square. The property lay on the west side of First Avenue between Union and Madison Streets. In November 1970, he explained to the board that "the [geographical] relationship of the tract with the Central Business District and the financial district of Seattle, with two [proposed] urban renewal projects, and with the Seattle waterfront made the tract attractive at the appraised prices." The board voted to go ahead with the First Avenue purchases. The buildings belonged to a number of individual investors and if anyone discovered that King Broadcasting was trying to assemble a large, unified parcel, the price would have soared. Therefore, Bullitt "emphasized that . . . it was important that the project be kept confidential." At first, even most of the company's executives didn't know that their employer was assembling property on First Avenue.

Bullitt didn't simply want to develop real estate; he wanted to shape his community. In the late 1960s, he conceived "The Eighth Day," a series of programs about environmental issues in the Puget Sound area. Roger Hagan, by then working as an assistant to Bullitt, hired a local lawyer and environmentalist, Marvin Durning, to put the project together. When Emory Bundy arrived in 1969 to become KING's director of public affairs, he was also drawn into the project. Bundy found a grandiose concept budgeted at nearly $2 million on which no action had been taken. People involved in the project got the impression that Bullitt had lost interest; he had envisioned a series about city planning, and when the focus turned to the natural environment—not surprising in a year that began with the Santa Barbara oil spill and ended with Congressional passage of the National Environmental Policy Act—he withdrew. "Suddenly," Hagan said, "we found ourselves without him." Durning left. Hagan left. The project became Bundy's. He went around and assured people that King would do the series as planned. Then one day, station manager Eric Bremner called Bundy in and told him the project was dead. After he'd assured everyone that it wasn't, Bundy figured that he had better resign. He told Bremner he quit. King's management reconsidered. "The Eighth Day" would be made.

Early in 1970, "The Eighth Day" finally ran in eight half-hour installments over eight consecutive weeks. Each segment began with fifteen minutes of film, followed by a studio discussion in which experts argued from different points of view. The series explained that if development in the Puget Sound area continued in a straight line, this is what the region would look like by the year 2000, these would be the problems, these are some of the things that could be done to avoid them. People were encouraged to watch and talk about each installment in groups of neighbors or friends. Perhaps 5,000 did. Each installment ran once on KING-TV, then four times later the same week on public television, so groups could find convenient times to watch. Writing several years later in the *Seattle Argus*, David Brewster described "The Eighth Day" as the last in Bullitt's chain of high-minded failures. "It was startling in its visionary sweep, pitiful in its execution," Brewster wrote. That may be too harsh, or at least less than the whole story. One group of neighbors who gathered to watch the shows on Northeast 93rd Street started the citizens' movement that led to creation of the Burke-Gilman Trail, now regarded as one of the country's most remarkable urban foot and bicycle pathways. The series received the national Sigma Delta Chi award for that year. In 1971, KING-TV became one of fifteen stations—and one of only two commercial stations—to win a national *Saturday Review* award for its presentation of "The Eighth Day."

But the station could not continue producing such ambitious projects. On August 11, 1970, Frank Chesley reported in the *Seattle Post-Intelligencer* that "KING-TV . . . has for the past couple of months been going through some major changes in an attempt to overcome a few years of downward drift. Time and the changing competitive situation have eroded its once-unchallenged position of preeminence."

Ancil Payne brought Forest Amsden from Portland to Seattle as temporary news director. (The station had been running through news directors so fast that the turnover had become a kind of standing joke. The news director occupied an office with a window that looked out into the newsroom. Amsden's predecessor, Bob Hoyt, had hung curtains over the windows, so no one could see in or out. Within the curtained office, he kept the lighting very dim. Entering Hoyt's office, Mike James recalled, "was like going into a seance." After Hoyt left, the curtains came down.) Some people figured Amsden had been brought in specifically to get rid of commentator Herb Altschul. Altschul had built a wall along one side of the newsroom so that he and the people who reported for him had their own little fiefdom. Altschul came in one day to find that the wall separating him and his reporters from the rest of the newsroom was gone. He looked shocked. Soon Altschul himself was gone, to a teaching position at the University of Indiana.

The news department toned down its opinionated coverage a bit. "KING has a reputation as a liberal station with a strong sense of community service and no fear of controversy," Chesley reported in the *Post-Intelligencer*. "That reputation, well-deserved in the past, has suffered of late. As one critic said, 'When it comes to liberalism vs. the pocketbook, the pocketbook wins.'"

Some critics within the newsroom felt that Amsden tried to influence coverage of the debate over where to build a domed stadium for professional sports. He also tried to influence Bob Faw's analysis of another transit bond issue vote in 1971. Faw felt that the daily papers' coverage of the transit issue had been shamelessly slanted in favor of the transit vote.

> *The atmosphere in KING-TV's newsroom reflected a wider sense of corporate chaos. Some of the people who had resented Bullitt's hiring of young, inexperienced talent were still resentful. One actually yelled at news director Norm Heffron, "Will any of the older people ever get to do any good stories?"*

When Faw started a series of five television commentaries on the issue, he interviewed thoughtful opponents and tried to present both sides. After Faw's first two pieces appeared, Amsden said he wanted to see the script for the third. After reading it, he told Faw to change his conclusion. Faw refused. Amsden told Faw he would be suspended with pay. Faw said he'd be forced to resign, then stormed out and kicked a wastebasket across the newsroom. The end of Faw's third piece was rewritten by a committee and the rest of the project was given to Al Wallace. At the end of his suspension, Faw really did quit.

The atmosphere in KING-TV's newsroom reflected a wider sense of corporate chaos. Some of the people who had resented Bullitt's hiring of young, inexperienced talent were still resentful. One actually yelled at news director Norm Heffron, "Will any of the older people ever get to do any good stories?" Heffron didn't reply.

After work, news people complained over beers at the Dart Inn tavern just up Dexter Avenue from the King parking lot.

The company was still attracting good people. In 1970, Bullitt told the board that the quality of people applying for jobs with the company was better than ever before. Two commentators who would, as much as anyone, symbolize KING-TV in the 1970s, Don McGaffin and Charles Royer, joined the company that year.

After *Seattle* magazine folded at the end of 1970, David Brewster, who had been one of its staff writers, was hired as television assignment editor. Some broadcasting veterans viewed this move skeptically; here was another Ivy Leaguer with no broadcasting experience, someone who represented the defunct but still-resented magazine. The veteran news people came to accept Brewster, but there remained a tension between his public affairs and "high culture" orientation and the more traditional ideas of commercial television. Brewster would create a list of the day's stories weighted heavily toward hard news, and the station's executive producer, Bob George, would invert it, putting Brewster's top priorities at the bottom of the list, in an effort to get more action.

The newsroom was not really under the news director's control. McGaffin, who had been hired with the odd but explicit understanding that no one would tell him what to do or edit his work, didn't take orders from the news director. Neither did Charles Royer, whom Payne had told, "I'm going to give you an order: disregard any other order I give you." Brewster, McGaffin, and the brothers Charles and Bob Royer largely ran the newsroom, with Phil Sturholm the other main influence on day-to-day news coverage. (Sturholm was respected as a great cameraman. He was also considered a fanatic about doing things right. Once, when he and McGaffin disagreed about film editing, Sturholm, a former football star, picked up McGaffin, a former Marine, and stuffed him head-first into a large wastebasket full of discarded film. McGaffin's own pugnaciousness became part of the newsroom legend. In 1986, for a profile on Mike James in the *Seattle Weekly*, McGaffin told writer Jim Halpin, "I was having a screaming argument with [KING-TV assignment editor] Bill

Baker about coverage of the presidential election. . . . It actually degenerated into a pushing match. Mike got between us. He started shouting at me and jabbing his finger at me. He wouldn't back down and neither would I. I made up my mind that if his finger touched my chest, I was going to flatten him. . . . He didn't, and we've been friends for twenty years."

By 1971, with Payne and Stimson Bullitt dividing authority, there was some haziness about who was actually calling the shots. Payne was largely running the company, and Bullitt obviously wasn't happy with the arrangement.

By 1971, with Payne and Stimson Bullitt dividing authority, there was some haziness about who was actually calling the shots. Payne was largely running the company, and although Bullitt asked him to do certain things, Payne pretty much did as he pleased. Bullitt obviously wasn't happy with the arrangement. Dorothy Bullitt, though visible, was clearly not in day-to-day control. Stimson Bullitt was rarely visible. Payne was very visible but he tended to "wrap himself in a fog of humor" so that people weren't sure exactly what he was up to. Accountants and other professionals were racing around trying to fix things. "It was obvious that the sharks were beginning to circle," Faw recalled. He got the sense that people near the top of the company sometimes figured, "'Oh Jesus! Stim wants to do *this*!'" For the first time, employees got a sense that management was concerned about money.

In 1970, King's broadcasting and cable operations had earned a net income of $547,000, less than half the previous year's figure, and when the Far Eastern losses were added in, the company's net for the year was $236,000—a return on assets of less than 1 percent. The following year quickly shaped up as King Broadcasting's worst year.

The immediate prospects for television profits looked grim, or at least less rosy than they had for decades. Network TV still had all the competitive advantages of an oligopoly and Americans weren't throwing out their televisions. But in the short term, television was about to lose its largest single source of advertising revenue. After years of industry dithering about the morality of running cigarette commercials on the air, Congress finally decided that as of 1971, American television would no longer carry cigarette ads. Tobacco companies had bought more commercial time than anyone else. The broadcasting industry would clearly be able to attract other advertisers to fill the same time slots, but it would take time.

King's own broadcasting and cable revenues dropped while expenses rose. In the first four months of 1971, the broadcasting and cable operations lost $70,000. The company's downtown buildings lost tenants to the brand-new SeaFirst Building, Seattle's first modern skyscraper, which had became the most prestigious office address in the city.

The situation in the Far East had not improved. In June 1970, Whetzel told the board that the company could shut the plywood mill down at a complete loss or, theoretically, sell it—there were no potential buyers—or take the risk of expansion. The board voted to expand. But the mill didn't need more capacity. In March 1971, Bullitt told the board that "[t]he reduction of military effort in Vietnam together with some temporary oversupply problems in plywood has caused military purchases in Okinawa of plywood to be cut back substantially. In addition, a large cutback in civilian employees of the armed services in Okinawa announced just after [President Nixon and Japan's Prime Minister Sato announced that Okinawa would soon revert to Japan] has had a multiplying effect on the whole Ryukyu economy." In November, Whetzel reported that the Japanese market required higher quality plywood than the mill could produce. In June 1971, Bullitt told the company's annual meeting that the plant modernization was almost completed but "Okinawa Plywood is insolvent in the sense that it is unable to pay its debts as they come due."

The board authorized the company's officers to sell Okinawa Plywood and Hollymark Ltd. at any price they could negotiate.

In September 1971, Bullitt reported that Whetzel had negotiated a sale to the mill's manager, Harley Tawlks, for $250,000, of which only $25,000 was certain. In December, the board learned that the sale to Tawlks had fallen through, but that the company had finally sold Okinawa Plywood to an earlier manager—for $1,000. At the same meeting, the board heard that it had to increase Hollymark's line of credit by $150,000. If not, "Hollymark would be forced to close operations at a total loss." The board increased the line of credit.

King took more than a year to unload the rest of its Asian albatrosses. In September 1972, when the breakdown of the freighter *Chuyfung*, carrying Hollymark logs to Okinawa, put the Hong Kong company in a bind, the board extended Hollymark's line of credit further. In March 1973, it learned that Hollymark was finally gone— at a cash loss of $517,000 (albeit a book loss of only $80,000). King got rid of its Philippine timber concessions, too.

Even dumping the Far Eastern enterprises turned out to be complicated. The shells of Hollymark and King Timber Industry survived into 1976. When King lawyer George Willoughby went to Okinawa to wrap things up, the company's local representative suggested he take home some $30,000 in cash. Envisioning a U.S. customs agent opening his suitcase and finding it full of money, Willoughby refused. It took him a week to get the funds out legitimately.

After writing off losses for *Seattle* magazine and King Screen, the company actually lost money in 1971.

Even without cigarette ads, King Broadcasting was never in danger of going broke. Few people lost their jobs. Someone suggested that the company's executives take symbolic pay cuts, but they never did.

Although Stimson Bullitt wanted the company to earn a healthy profit, with his long view of history, his disdain for profit as a sole motivation, his ability to make money by practicing law, he simply wasn't very concerned about King's financial situation. But other people were growing anxious. Even people close to Bullitt felt that the company was in disarray.

Dorothy Bullitt had been feeling nervous for some time. Her office may have been in the brick building out back, but she was in the coffee shop every day, and she kept track of what was going on.

She would call accountant Frank Yanagimachi into her office to tell her how much people were being paid and how much things had cost. "I'm going to die in the poorhouse," she'd say.

She was upset to learn that the Los Angeles Times-Mirror Company had approached Stimson Bullit about a possible merger, and that he was at least willing to listen. His mother and sisters weren't. Dorothy Bullitt liked to say that anything was for sale if the price was right, but given King's financial problems, the price would clearly be rock-bottom. Above all, she and her daughters weren't prepared to give up the family business at any price. Harriet phoned her brother and told him to stop the merger talks.

Dorothy Bullitt tended not to say anything directly to her son. She was more inclined to call her daughter, Patsy, who lived in San Diego, and say, "Can't you do something about your brother?"

Her daughters were concerned, too—about their brother,

Although Stimson Bullitt wanted the company to earn a healthy profit, with his long view of history, his disdain for profit as a sole motivation, his ability to make money by practicing law, he simply wasn't very concerned about King's financial situation.

as well as the company. Stimson Bullitt had never enjoyed running the broadcasting company. And his experience was growing steadily worse. He hated going to work in the morning. He was obviously depressed.

Patsy Collins flew to Seattle and urged him to resign. His sister Harriet also urged him to go.

While the family started pressing Bullitt to step down, Payne was to some extent acting as if Bullitt had already done so. Payne had, in fact, been given administrative responsibility, and his personality tended to overshadow people even less reticent than Bullitt. Roger Hagan brought KING-TV managers together in Bullitt's office ("that hole of an office . . . airless, windowless," Hagan recalled) to coordinate their activities for the "Eighth Day" project. Managers seemed reluctant to cooperate, Bullitt was strangely silent, providing no sense of direction, while Payne seemed to deliberately embarrass him. Hagan recalled it as "the most shocking meeting I had ever seen."

Dorothy Bullitt and her daughters were upset to hear that Stimson Bullitt wasn't getting along with Payne, and that Payne was ready to quit. They felt that they needed Payne to lead the company out of its current predicament. They were afraid to lose him.

They also resented the fact that Stimson Bullitt's friend, Bagley Wright—a real estate developer whom Stimson Bullitt had brought onto the board in 1961—had been made chairman of the executive committee, in which capacity he seemed to be deciding how to spend their money without consulting them.

Patsy Collins and Harriet Bullitt went to see their brother in his office at King. They told him that they and their mother wanted to be on the executive committee, they wanted Wright off the executive committee, and they wanted Harriet Bullitt to become chairman in his place. Subsequently, Collins talked with Stimson Bullitt alone and asked him again to resign, leaving Payne to run the company.

Finally, Bullitt swallowed his considerable pride and went to Payne's office. Payne, technically the subordinate, acted very much in control. Bullitt had sent a memo that undermined his authority. Payne thought he was supposed to be running the company, but Bullitt was telling him to fire people. Bullitt had discussed a possible merger with the Times-Mirror without telling him. Payne had already typed out a letter of resignation.

Stimson Bullitt didn't want Payne to leave. He had no illusions about his ability to run the company alone. Payne had become essential. Bullitt knew that he himself was not essential. And he didn't like what he was doing, anyway.

He urged Payne to stay. He, Stimson Bullitt, would go. As Payne recalled the conversation, Bullitt said, "If I can't run the company with you, I can't run it without you, so I'll get out." At the board meeting on December 15, 1971, Bullitt officially resigned. Payne was appointed president in his place. Bullitt would continue as chairman of the board. Payne would have full responsibility for managing the company.

———

During the decade that began in 1961, King Broadcasting reflected several of the currents that characterized that remarkable—and quickly mythologized—period. With the Kennedy years, King Broadcasting shared some of the New Frontier glamour, the public display of intellectuality, the faith in a new era; also the hubris, the misplaced confidence that bright people without specific experience could solve intractable problems, the explosion of optimism followed by widespread disillusionment. With the early anti-war movement, King shared a sense of knowing better than the establishment smart guys, a willingness to challenge the established wisdom and antagonize the establishment itself. "It was a dizzy time [at King Broadcasting], rather like the 1960s in general," Brewster wrote soon afterward in *Argus*. "The personnel policy stiffened into a fondness for what Bullitt called 'superior novices' . . . some of them too ambitious to serve their visionary president well. The news grew irreverent and opinionated and suffered from a decline in production skills, reflecting the company's avoidance of trade school products. . . . [F]ew cared for television entertainment, so programming suffered. Ratings sank along with earnings."

Many of the ideas and attitudes that characterized King's leadership could be found widely at the nation's elite colleges and among the East Coast intelligentsia. But they were rare among people who ran broadcasting companies. As a result, King managed to be very much of its time—both for better and worse—and several steps ahead of its industry and its community.

The company was never oblivious to the bottom line. For all Dorothy Bullitt's alleged indifference to money, she was in fact passionately interested in her company's finances. Business was a game and profit was winning and she wanted to win. She wasn't obsessed with profit to the exclusion of everything else, but she certainly did not want to see her business in the red. Stimson Bullitt didn't, either. He didn't pursue wealth—in that respect, he was very much in tune with part of American culture in the 1960s—but he didn't start anything with the idea of *losing* money. He considered himself a businessman and viewed a purely aesthetic or critical success for one of his business ventures as a form of failure. "When you are employed to produce that for which others will pay and they do not," Bullitt wrote afterward, "a later discovery that you had been a patron of art does not make your experience any less a business failure." The magazine and the screen division were supposed to turn a profit. And they were supposed to be hedges against unexpected developments in the broadcasting industry—technological and economic changes that would make broadcast television less lucrative. In retrospect, some of his visions of the future seem to have been less wrongheaded than simply ahead of their time. While broadcast television hasn't disappeared, it has been left with a much smaller share of the market. Bullitt's vision of the competition that broadcast television would face was not that far off the mark. What worried him, Shelby Scates reported in the *Seattle Post-Intelligencer* the spring of 1966, was "the fear that local television stations could be short-circuited out of network TV programs. Two systems . . . could disrupt this method of distribution, just as television disrupted the neighborhood movie pattern in the late 1940s. One is a system of cables . . . the other is a system of space satellites. . . . 'I don't think this will happen for the next few years,' said Bullitt. 'It may not happen at all. . . . But we are certainly looking ahead for hedges, for alternatives.'"

This is not to say that the new ventures, conceived as hedges against technological and economic change, were *well* conceived. Bullitt himself came to believe that it was unrealistic to think a company could make money by producing documentaries, to enter a cutthroat enterprise without managers who knew the business, to enter a high-budget commercial venture without ever knowing what things should cost. He came to wonder whether *Seattle* magazine would have lasted longer without the slick paper and color photographs—or whether it would simply have made less of a splash and expired just as quickly. One is tempted to believe that if the magazine and screen division had been started and run with a keener eye for the bottom line, they might have succeeded. But the truth is that if anyone had shown a keener eye for the bottom line, these ventures would never have existed. And that would have been too bad. For all their excesses and eventual failures, both did some exceptionally good work, both provided launching pads for a number of careers, and both brought talented people to the Northwest.

Even the feature movie received a kind of vindication two decades after the fact. When *The Plot Against Harry* was shown at film festivals in 1989, critics praised it. *New York* magazine's film critic said it was "not a great film" but called it "consistently witty and enjoyable" and suggested that it was "one of the best and most comprehensive satires on Jewish American life ever put on film" (but noted that the movie still had no distributor).

Less than two years after Bullitt resigned as president, David Brewster wrote, "The KING of the 1960s probably was . . . the single most intriguing television station in the country."

CHAPTER SIX

DOING WELL BY DOING GOOD
1971–1987

THE KING BROADCASTING COMPANY would never again be managed by a Bullitt family member. Dorothy Bullitt remained a conspicuous—if chiefly symbolic—presence into the 1990s. Patsy Collins became chairman of the board in 1975 and held that post into the sale. Harriet Bullitt continued as chairman of the executive committee. They made decisions about hiring chief executives and buying or selling TV stations, cable systems, and other properties. By expressing personal interest in the content of broadcasting and not creating pressure for a quick return on investment, they helped set a tone, create an expectation that King wouldn't pursue the largest possible profit at the expense of quality. But they never managed the company's day-to-day operations. They never even saw King's operating budget. The family owned King without managing it from 1971 to 1992, almost half the time between the founding of Western Waves and the sale. Ancil Payne managed the company for sixteen years, longer than any family member had.

When Payne took over, Dorothy Bullitt was still very much around. She sat in the coffee shop, where she might bum unfiltered Camel cigarettes from a young public affairs cameraman or might try to plant an idea with a reporter, asking innocently, "Did you know . . . ?" She walked through the halls. She held court in the brick building out back.

Payne used her to legitimate his leadership. He would sometimes justify a decision by saying it was what Dorothy Bullitt wanted. And he cultivated a sense in the community that King was still her company. Even Seattle business leaders who had soured on King Broadcasting Company had nothing but good words to say about Dorothy Bullitt. As Payne explained later, she made such a wonderful corporate symbol that any businessman would have been a fool not to use her. A lot of people probably would have believed that she was still guiding King even if he hadn't. Dorothy Bullitt *was* King in the public's mind throughout the 1970s and even most of the 1980s.

The person really at the helm was, of course, Ancil Payne. He and Dorothy Bullitt agreed on that early in his presidency. The catalyst was a routine, if grisly, crime story. A child disappeared near Seattle Prep on Capitol Hill. Search parties combed the area. The child was found dead in a ravine. After a KING-TV camera crew spent time inside the parents' house, the mother complained that a newsman had read some letters that he had seen lying on a desk. Dorothy Bullitt was understandably angry and wanted the newsman fired. Payne told her the company couldn't fire him for something like that. She was adamant. Finally, Payne told her she'd have to decide who was running the company. She decided Payne was.

Payne gave the people under him a lot of autonomy—as did KING-TV general manager Eric Bremner—but no one ever doubted that he was in command. In fact, some people figured that Payne kept relatively weak managers in key positions so that he would have a lot of de facto control. Nevertheless, he backed up his managers. For years, news people had gone over the news director's head, complained to Stimson Bullitt, and seen the news director replaced. News directors came and went. When Ancil Payne took over, Bob

Hoyt was replaced by Forest Amsden, who was replaced by Norm Heffron, giving the station three news directors in one year. But that was the end of the revolving door. Soon after Heffron arrived from Portland, a group of news people went to Payne to complain about him. Payne told them to "talk to Norm." That was that. The news director was in charge—at least theoretically. With corporate officers just down the hall or in the lunchroom taking a personal interest in what KING-TV put on the air every night, people continued going over lower-level managers' heads. Some went around the news director to Payne and did largely as they pleased. Some tried to sell their ideas to Dorothy Bullitt, then told others that the great lady herself had approved.

Morale at the station soon improved. Here was a chief executive who actually walked around and talked to people. Employees may not have known what he was thinking, but they could all approach him. And here was an executive who would invest in traditional news-gathering rather than intellectualizing.

But that was all unofficial. Officially, Payne wouldn't undermine a manager's authority. People would have to follow the proper chain of command.

Morale at the station soon improved. Here was a chief executive who actually walked around and talked to people. Employees may not have known what he was thinking, but they could all approach him. And here was an executive who would invest in traditional news-gathering rather than intellectualizing.

Payne never shrank from expressing a point of view on the air. He himself would deliver liberal, good-government editorials for the next sixteen years, and he did not rein in the company's television commentators. Late in the decade, Bob Simmons delivered a series of commentaries about price-fixing by major oil companies. After each of the first three commentaries, Forest Amsden, who had taken over

Jean Enersen became Seattle's first television anchor woman, teamed here with news anchor Jim Harriott as they interview Dorothy Bullitt.

as KING-TV's station manager after Eric Bremner became corporate vice president for broadcasting in 1979, sent Simmons a memo defending the oil companies' point of view. Simmons began to feel a little nervous. Then Payne, who had read Amsden's memos, sent a note of his own, telling Simmons he was proud of what Simmons had been doing, urging him to keep pursuing the truth, and advising him not to listen to anyone else.

But that was commentary. Payne wanted the company's news reporting to be more objective—and he wanted more of it. Although money was tight—King Broadcasting Company was still operating at a loss in early 1972—he took Heffron's suggestion and doubled KING-TV's news budget. Money was tight for King Broadcasting's competitors, too—the recession and the loss of cigarette advertising had affected even companies that hadn't been making documentaries or running plywood mills on Okinawa—and Payne felt that the time was ripe to make a move. In 1973, KING-TV made Jim Harriott its late-news anchor, promoted Jean Enersen to an anchor spot with him—making her the first female news anchor in Seattle—and finally had the personalities the station needed to gain a larger audience for its newscasts. The company also spent money for new television equipment. Anti-war stickers came off company vehicles. Graduates of local universities once again had a chance. Employees who had felt disenfranchised under Stimson Bullitt now felt that the company had returned to the mainstream and that it was moving ahead.

By investing in news, King was going very much with the grain of American television. Stations all over the country beefed up their news budgets in the 1970s. But at KING-TV, where television people had felt neglected for a decade, the company's investment in news took on a symbolic value.

When Payne started, KING-TV was chasing KOMO-TV for the top news ratings. KING monitored the radio broadcasts from KOMO's traffic-spotting airplane, and KOMO knew it. So KOMO set KING up: the traffic plane sent a message about a big crash on the highway. KING-TV sent people out to cover it. When they arrived at the spot, they found absolutely nothing. KING's reporters were embarrassed. But by November 1973, KING's news ratings passed KOMO's, and people in the KING-TV newsroom broke out champagne.

By the end of the decade, KING-TV would be recognized for its programming and service, winning a Gabriel Award as television station of the year. It would channel more money into documentaries and public affairs than its peers. Its politics would remain staunchly liberal.

The urban Northwest was becoming less insular. And it was developing a new sensibility. Seattle citizens voted to preserve the Pike Place Market instead of destroying it with an urban renewal project and voted against building two planned freeways that would have sliced through urban neighborhoods. The old, stodgy Seattle city council was voted out. Seattle companies started to sell good coffee. Washington wine makers started to make good wine.

The company's editorial policies and hiring practices were no longer conspicuously out of step with their time and place. Of course, it was hard for a liberal company to be as conspicuously out of step in the 1970s as King Broadcasting had been in the mid- and late 1960s. Opposition to the war had gone mainstream. Opportunities for women and minorities expanded. At the end of 1971, Congress passed the Equal Opportunity Act and Washington State voters passed an equal rights amendment to the state constitution. Nevertheless, well into the decade KING-TV still provided more opportunities for women than other Seattle stations. In 1974 Linda Gatch, who was working at another Seattle TV station, heard that KING-TV was the only Seattle broadcaster to hire women for television production work. She had heard that KING-TV hired women for production jobs because King Broadcasting was owned by a woman. That was, of course, not true. King's hiring policies reflected the beliefs of Stimson Bullitt—and of Ancil Payne, who had been vice president in charge of Portland operations when KGW-TV hired the first female news anchor in the Northwest. Gatch wanted to get involved in TV production, so she applied to King Broadcasting, was hired for a job in radio, and the next year became a TV floor director.

Hydroplanes still roared across Lake Washington as part of the Seafair celebration every August, and KING-TV covered the hydro races, just as it had since 1951. But the city no longer needed an odd sporting event to put it on the map. The informed, educated public that Dorothy and Stimson Bullitt always had in mind had lost whatever fondness it may once have had for the hydro races. People who worked at KING-TV complained about having to cover the hydros.

Eric Bremner—who enjoyed a unique status at King Broadcasting headquarters as the only high-ranking executive who had worked his way up through the ranks—gave them no choice. He heard the grumbling. But he knew that covering the boat races was a great morale builder. It was the one project on which everyone at the station worked together, competing with other stations to get the earliest interviews, the best shots.

While Bremner built morale within King by covering the hydro races, Payne went outside to mend fences with the business community. Stimson Bullitt had staunchly avoided the traditional service clubs and meetings of the influential Downtown Seattle Association. The gregarious Payne joined the Chamber of Commerce. Bremner joined Rotary. And Payne twisted arms. Lamont Bean, who owned the Ernst hardware chain and had pulled his company's ads from King stations, was serving as president of Seafair, and he wanted KING-TV to run free public-service spots to sell fundraising pins for the festival. Payne told him he couldn't have free public service time if he refused to buy commercial time. Bean told his people to advertise on KING-TV again.

More than a decade had passed since KING-TV's first documentary, "Lost Cargo," called attention to the Port of Seattle's shortcomings. Since then, the Port of Seattle had grown: the nation's first major container line, SeaLand, had made Seattle its main site for shipping containers north to Alaska, and in 1970, six big Japanese shipping lines selected Seattle as their only Northwest destination for container ships. On the other hand, Seattle's port was locked in a costly competition for cargo with other Puget Sound ports. A second documentary on the port seemed to make sense. Payne figured that the documentary could make money and could help the company reestablish ties with the business community. The National Bank of Commerce, which had sponsored the earlier documentary, was enthusiastic about sponsoring a sequel to be christened "Seaport." In fact, the bank's advertising people came up with the idea.

The new documentary was made in 1972 by Bob Royer, who was twenty-seven years old and had been working as a news cameraman for all of six months. "Seaport" concluded that the competition among Puget Sound ports was wasteful, and wound up with anchorman Jim Harriott advocating a Puget Sound port authority that could coordinate the operations of all the ports. One of the people shown speaking in favor of a regional port was state Representative John L. O'Brien, a former four-term speaker of the house who had frequently been identified with the idea.

When higher-level executives from the National Bank of Commerce saw the documentary—before it went on the air— KING-TV's relationship with the bank quickly soured. The bank said it objected to the documentary siding with John O'Brien. It did not say that its president's brother-in-law, Frank Kitchell, was a Seattle port commissioner who opposed a regional port. The bank dropped its sponsorship. KING approached other banks, but apparently Kitchell had phoned their executives. No other local sponsor would step in to back "Seaport." Seattle Trust agreed to sponsor the documentary, but then backed out. With less than three weeks to go, KING was planning to run the documentary as an unsponsored special—that is, as a total financial loss. Finally, at the last minute, KING sold the time to General Mills, which was headquartered in Minneapolis and didn't have to worry about local pressures. The incident was sobering. Local advertisers still felt they should have some say in the content of shows they sponsored.

Although the company was making a concerted effort to ingratiate itself with potential advertisers, no one had even considered changing the documentary to please the original sponsor. Payne may have abandoned the aggressive anti-commercialism of the 1960s, but neither he nor the Bullitt family tried to impose a point of view on the company's reporters or commentators.

There were those who said Payne protested a bit too much about news coverage. He never set foot in the newsroom, but he caught news people in the lunchroom to give them his views on news reporting. Although he kept his hands off the news, he always knew what was going on. He never told people exactly what to say, but he would periodically announce that "we have to cover" something, and the Seattle station would.

He watched the news and cringed when reporters were ill-informed. As a former political pro and lifelong political junkie who often knew more than the reporters, he sometimes found the station's political coverage especially frustrating.

In the early 1970s, two adventurer-entrepreneurs named Ted Griffin and Don Goldsberry received permits to capture killer whales in Puget Sound for San Diego's huge Sea World aquarium. (During the mid-1960s, Griffin had displayed an orca named Namu—which had been caught accidentally in a British Columbia salmon fisherman's gill net—in a makeshift pen on Seattle's downtown waterfront. Before long, Sea World started displaying the first of a series of captive orcas named Shamu to much larger audiences.)

Ancil Payne (left) and NBC commentator John Chancellor (right) at the 1980 opening of King's corporate headquarters. Ancil Payne's personable managerial style restored employee morale after Stimson Bullitt's resignation. Payne managed the company for sixteen years—longer than any family member.

In August 1971, Don McGaffin was spending vacation time on Whidbey Island when he looked out over Penn Cove and saw a pod of orcas leaping in the water. He had never seen killer whales before, and he called KING to send up a cameraman. Cameraman Jeff Mart arrived the next day, and the two men hired a small boat to take them out to a U-shaped float with nets strung from the ends; within the nets, Ted Griffin and his partner, Don Goldsberry had penned thirty-three killer whales. A state fisheries agent was standing on the float along with Griffin, Goldsberry, and some men in wet suits. McGaffin talked to the fisheries agent, who explained he was there to keep an eye on things. The year before, the agent said, Griffin and Goldsberry had obtained a permit to capture killer whales. They had captured some whales but had then left abruptly. Later, killer whale carcasses, slit open and weighted with rocks, chunks of concrete, and old metal, had washed up on the island's beaches. Evidently, the captured whales had died and someone had tried to scuttle the evidence. The state legislature then passed a law requiring a fisheries inspector to be present whenever anyone captured killer whales. When McGaffin did a short stand-up commentary at the end of the film segment, he told viewers what the fisheries agent had told him.

The next day, McGaffin and cameraman Jeff Mart set out again with the boat owner and the boat owner's eight-year-old son. As they headed toward the float, the whale-catchers' boats formed a line across their path. One of the whale boats shot toward them at high speed. They swerved to avoid it, and a second boat bore down on them. The boats kept barely missing them, rocking them with bow waves, which threatened to dump all of them—McGaffin, the boat owner, the boy, and the cameraman strapped into his heavy metal "body pod"—into the water. They shot film of the attack and returned to shore, where they got the owner of the Captain Whidbey Inn to lock the film in his safe until an airplane arrived and flew it to Seattle. KING-TV ran news footage of the whale-catching boats' attack, and McGaffin subsequently won an award for a thirty-minute special on the whale captures. His film started the process of turning public opinion against orca captures in Puget Sound.

Three and a half years later, on a sunny Sunday morning, Goldsberry used a spotter plane and three power boats to corral a group of orcas in Budd Inlet—literally within sight of the Washington State Capitol and of many horrified people, including an aide to Governor Dan Evans. KING-TV filmed the whale capture, which was broadcast nationwide on NBC. Other local and national media ran coverage critical of the practice. Sea World received relentlessly bad publicity. Finally, as KING-TV's public affairs director Emory Bundy reported in a 1976 documentary, "Sea World agreed to give up the two whales [it still held] and never hunt whales again in Washington waters." Nevertheless, Bundy explained, "It has only been because of the capture and display of killer whales that the public has gained more understanding and sympathy for these remarkable creatures."

Other KING-TV film helped focus national attention on children's sleepwear. In the spring of 1972, Don McGaffin and Phil Sturholm produced a series of programs about the dangers of children's nightclothes catching fire. McGaffin read a tiny newspaper story about a girl being badly burned when her nightgown went up in flames and drove out to the then-new burn unit at Children's Orthopedic Hospital, arriving just as the girl—who had been burned from the neck down—was having her painful hourly bandage change. "Jesus!" he exclaimed years later. "I had never seen anything like that." He took Sturholm out to the hospital, arriving just in time for another bandage change; afterward, Sturholm went into a vacant room and wept. They subsequently defied the taboo against showing a naked human body on the television screen and let viewers watch the badly burned girl have her bandages changed. "The Burned Child" won a local Emmy and four national awards. In response to the KING-TV series, viewers bombarded the Commerce Department with thousands of letters. Senator Warren Magnuson had already been pushing the department to enforce the existing standards for children's sleepwear, as had Dr. Abe Bergman of Children's Hospital. But the *Washington Post* reported that "the criticisms hardest to bear were in many of the approximately 3,000 letters sent in response to a plea by Seattle's KING-TV at the end of a poignant documentary." After the Commerce Department decided to start enforcing the standards, Magnuson wrote to Ancil Payne, "I know that it was not until the Secretary of Commerce had viewed 'The Burned Child,' in the company of his top aides, that he made his decision to act in the manner he did."

The company not only continued to invest in TV documentary specials, it also kept acquiring California cable systems. Early in 1972, it decided to buy the systems that served Placerville, Sutter Creek, Jackson, and Angel's Camp. At the same time, King pruned away troublesome leftovers from the 1960s. King Screen's equipment and film library were sold in 1972, and by the middle of 1973, the last of the Far Eastern enterprises was gone. "We learned our lesson" from the bad investments of the 1960s, Patsy Collins recalled. "Don't try to do things you don't know how to do, especially in places you don't know."

King also unloaded its share of the Seattle cable system. The FCC ruled that after August 1973, television stations couldn't own cable systems in areas that they already reached with their broadcasts.

In early 1972—wanting to beat the 1973 deadline and eager to raise capital for its acquisition of other cable systems—King Broadcasting sold its 24 percent share to Viacom.

Finally, King split its broadcasting and real estate operations into separate companies, undoing the merger of 1969. The split made a lot of sense. King's board had gone along with the merger, but Stimson Bullitt had been the only person who really wanted to combine the two businesses. Now he was no longer running King. The First Avenue properties had made Dorothy Bullitt uncomfortable. First Avenue was lined with pawn shops, peep shows, and single-room-occupancy hotels, and King Broadcasting had acquired some pretty sleazy buildings. She could envision a prostitute killing a customer in one of King's crumbling brick apartments, scandalizing the FCC, or one of the buildings burning down, calling public attention to the fact that her high-minded broadcasting company was a major slumlord.

Dorothy Bullitt thought the company should pour its money and energy into broadcasting, not real estate. On a more personal level, she and her daughters had no desire to leave a large chunk of the family's capital tied up in property that would take at least a decade to pay off. (In March 1972, Jonathan Whetzel told the board that redevelopment of the area wouldn't be feasible for five to ten years. Actually, a decade turned out to be an optimistic guess. Financing proved hard to come by. Some of the old buildings were soon torn down, but some of their sites were still occupied by parking lots when King was sold twenty years later. A new building—flanked by a grand public stairway connecting First Avenue to the waterfront—finally opened on the First Avenue property in 1995.) Unlike Stimson Bullitt, who could earn money practicing law, the rest of the family depended on their income from King, so they were interested in much quicker payoffs. They also worried about the value of King stock, which would be depressed by the low revenues the company could expect to earn for years on its large real estate investments.

Finally and decisively, Stimson Bullitt wanted to leave King Broadcasting and, as he put it later, take his marbles with him. In 1972, the family found a way out of all these problems: Stimson Bullitt would take the company's real estate holdings into a new corporation and give up all his King Broadcasting stock. The basic idea appealed to everyone concerned, although plenty of details had to be resolved.

The family sat down several times for long, tense, strangely formal negotiations. Family members didn't negotiate directly with each other. Everyone was in the room together, but so were a lot of other people: Dick Riddell represented Stimson Bullitt's interests. Ancil Payne, along with King Broadcasting's chief financial officer, Payson Hall, and King's tax advisor represented the company's interests. Attorney Willard Wright represented the interests of Dorothy Bullitt, Harriet Bullitt, and Patsy Collins. And George Willoughby, who handled King legal affairs at Riddell's law firm, also took part. Inevitably, the process was emotionally difficult. There was a sense of sadness, of something coming to an end.

After two days, everyone agreed on the basics: Stimson Bullitt and his friend Bagley Wright, who was a minor King shareholder, would take the First Avenue properties, the 1411 Fourth Avenue and Logan Buildings, and the other real estate not associated with broadcasting studios, plus some of the company's stock holdings and a couple of the Washington cable systems—which the FCC had told King to get rid of, anyway—into a new corporation to be christened Harbor Properties. Bullitt and Wright would give up all their King Broadcasting stock.

On September 20, 1972, the board voted in favor of a split. Even then, the deal wasn't final. The Internal Revenue Service had to approve—neither Stimson Bullitt nor King wanted to wind up with a large taxable gain—and that didn't happen until March 30, 1973. The official exchange of property was dated March 31. At the end of April, the shareholders formally approved. Last but not least, Stimson Bullitt, the successful appellate lawyer, had to approve the fine print. On March 12, 1974, Payson Hall wrote to accountant Frank Yanagimachi, with copies to Payne, Willoughby, and others, that "we do have at long last an agreement . . . evidencing that all matters are closed between King and Harbor." He included "a particular nod of appreciation to George Willoughby, who achieved the miracle of the final negotiated and acceptable written document signed by Stimson Bullitt."

Stimson Bullitt resigned as chairman of the board. Patsy Collins replaced him. Against heavy odds, Dorothy Bullitt and her children had made the change without destroying either the family or the company.

————

In fact, King Broadcasting was prospering. The company's 1974 annual report told King stockholders that revenues were up 15 percent. Earnings, which had risen every year since 1971, had hit $1.2 million. King's management was no longer indifferent to the size of its audience. Most of management never had been, of course, but now its flagship KING-TV was a much more openly commercial station than it had been during most of the 1960s. In 1973, David Brewster wrote that part of Payne's strategy was to "[r]ecover a more youthful audience." To that end, "[i]nane game shows were installed in the slot between evening news and the prime-time shows—with a big jump in ratings." Viewers may not have objected to game shows, but some did object to certain commercials. Bremner reported viewer complaints to NBC in September 1972, explaining that a spot for Levi jeans "has an animated dancing doll with electric sockets on his feet. This supernatural hookup permits his [j]eans to reflect many psychedelic colors. It also, according to some callers, intrigues their youngsters into putting dolly's feet into the nearest light socket."

Bob Guy, who joined KING as program director—and whom Dorothy Bullitt referred to as "that awful man from Hollywood"— was largely responsible for bringing game shows to KING-TV and otherwise making the station more commercial. Guy was not the kind of employee most people associated with KING-TV. Enrique Cerna was working at KOMO radio when he heard that KING was about to fire one Hispanic and wanted to hire another one. Guy asked to talk with him and suggested meeting at the Dart Inn. Cerna got there and waited outside. A man who looked as if he might be homeless approached him. The man turned out to be Guy. The KING program director suggested they go someplace else in the neighborhood, and when they sat down, Guy ordered two drinks—VO and ginger ale with a twist of lemon—both for himself. Then he pulled out a pack of cigarettes and asked Cerna if he smoked. Cerna said no. Guy asked him, "Do you want to start?" Cerna didn't even know what the KING job was, but Guy assured him that if he wanted it, he could have it.

Some people who worked with Guy and heard his stories had trouble figuring out how much to believe. He told people that he had worked for military intelligence in the South Pacific during World War II. He said he had lived with the natives on the Japanese-occupied island of Ponape, east of Truk, and had later gotten information out to the American military. People assumed he was making this up. A young man who worked at KING joined the Peace Corps, which sent him to Truk for two years. When the young man returned, he stopped by to visit KING. Emory Bundy decided to play a trick on Guy. He asked the young man if people spoke the same language on Truk that they spoke on Ponape. The young man said yes, although the dialects were different. Bundy suggested that he say hello to Guy in that language. When Bundy ran into the young man again, he asked how the conversation had gone. The young man replied that Guy spoke the language like a native.

This complex and improbable man set out to boost KING-TV's audience ratings. At the beginning of 1973, he arranged to have the network game show "Truth or Consequences" move to Seattle and broadcast for several weeks in front of a live audience at the Seattle Center Arena. Years later it became common for network shows to broadcast from cities around the United States. Then, it was unheard of. But it worked. People lined up to be part of the audience, the station's ratings soared to number one in that time slot—and stayed there.

Not that Guy was interested only in producing popular schlock. He was fascinated with the historical figure of Galileo, and at a managers' meeting in 1977, he said it would be nice to have KING-TV produce something about the Renaissance astronomer. Bundy's secretary at the time, a poet named Art Wicks, read the meeting minutes, wrote a script for a show about Galileo, and got the script to Guy. Guy loved it, and the following year, on a very low budget, with people coming in on weekends to build sets and Guy's own office stuffed full of props, KING-TV produced an original half-hour dramatic program—with Guy himself starring as Galileo.

Guy was one of the many show-business people whose company Dorothy Bullitt seemed to enjoy. When she called him "that awful man from Hollywood," it was tongue-in-cheek. They would stand in the hallway together and smoke, and once a month they and Don LaCombe would drive to the Alaska Junction restaurant in West Seattle for drinks and lunch. They liked reminiscing about early run-ins with each other. One favorite story involved a plane trip Guy had taken when he was new at KING. Fresh from Hollywood, he had, of course, flown first class—and had been embarrassed to discover that Dorothy Bullitt was sitting back in coach.

LaCombe, by then a producer, joined the public affairs department. This wasn't considered a great career move—many TV people didn't take public affairs seriously. While Guy was making the station as a whole more commercial, LaCombe urged the public affairs staff to be more commercial as well. Too often, public affairs would create programs that were earnest and informative and would put them on the air whether anyone watched or not. LaCombe set about convincing Bundy and his colleagues that programs would be more effective if people actually watched them. He encouraged people to think of "Sammy Sixpack," and figure out "what will make him put his newspaper down." He persuaded the public affairs people to stop making what were in effect essays on film; instead, recalled Anne Stadler, who joined the station in 1973 and subsequently became public affairs director, "Don LaCombe taught us to tell stories."

Public affairs even tried a game show in which a pair of two-person teams competed to answer questions based on current affairs in front of a live studio audience. "The Great American Game Show" got unusually high ratings for a public affairs program. However, people tended to measure it against the networks' commercial game shows and to consider it a flop.

The news department was trying to educate people, too. Payne was disturbed by the pervasive voter apathy in the immediate post-

Watergate atmosphere of 1975. Bob and Charles Royer and Don McGaffin got his blessing to develop a series of programs called "A Political Chautauqua" designed to focus attention on issues in the 1975 elections. They first approached Heffron about the series, but he turned them down, so they went to Payne. The series used skits and cartoons as well as interviews, and explored not only state politics but also the way the Olympia press corps covered the legislature.

The series may have had Payne's backing, but that didn't mean that the whole company pitched in to make it work. KING-TV didn't promote "Chautauqua" at all. Frustrated, McGaffin and the Royers bought their own newspaper ad. After it appeared, Dorothy Bullitt called Bob Royer and asked who had done it. He told her the whole story. Within half an hour, a man from promotion was down in the newsroom finding out about the series.

KING-TV reporter Al Wallace was creating real educational programs, a series of shows entitled "How Come?" which explained to viewers in their early teens how all kinds of things worked. In 1974, with LaCombe directing and Bob George as executive producer, "How Come?" won a Peabody Award.

The company was still producing its share of high-minded and expensive programs, but it was making money again, and somehow, with the change in personalities and styles at the top, the production of ambitious money-losers no longer generated the same resentments. (After Collins and Willoughby got the company's profit- sharing plan changed to a pension plan, employees no longer saw money-losing ventures as taking cash out of their own pockets.) But some people still evidently thought the public affairs department siphoned money from the company's more productive enterprises. However, Emory Bundy found that the people who ran King Broadcasting didn't share those feelings. His job became somewhat easier after Payne wrote a memo saying that public affairs was just as important as anything else the company did. With Stimson Bullitt gone, top management's affection for things that didn't make money was no longer a big issue.

Although King no longer neglected local talent, it still hired Ivy Leaguers with no practical experience. One of them was Hal Calbom, who had grown up in Longview, Washington, but returned to the Northwest in 1976 after earning a masters' degree in English literature at Harvard and briefly playing professional basketball in Europe. Calbom approached an editor at the *Seattle Times* about a writing job. The *Times* wasn't interested in a twenty-four-year-old with no experience, and advised Calbom to try television. KING-TV had a reputation for hiring people like him, the *Times* editor said. Calbom applied at KING. Because he had never worked in broadcasting or journalism, his resume stressed his academic performance—all the way back to high school. He was hired. And his hiring wasn't an aberration. A few months later, news director Norm Heffron asked Calbom to evaluate another job applicant. The evaluation process consisted of reading a sixty-five-page Princeton undergraduate thesis. Sure, Calbom said, hire him. Heffron did. The new hire, Robin Lloyd, went on to a career as a correspondent for NBC network news. Calbom himself was soon filling in as news anchor and wound up winning four Emmy Awards with KING-TV.

When Calbom arrived, he found a newsroom that had not changed much technically or managerially since the last year of Stimson Bullitt's presidency. The news was still being shot on film, which meant there was an inevitable delay while the film was developed. A reporter could use that time to write and revise a coherent script, then the script could be and was actually edited. Although people spent time at the station polishing stories before they went on the air, many day-to-day reporters felt somewhat isolated from Norm Heffron, who sat in his office in a neatly pressed suit reading the *Wall Street Journal*. And Heffron wasn't really calling the shots. Don McGaffin and Bob and Charles Royer still did largely as they pleased. The other power center was still Phil Sturholm, who trained the station's cameramen and remained the dominant personality in news.

The company's need for capital remained, too, as King Broadcasting looked forward to buying more cable systems and perhaps more broadcasting stations. "With the potential for profits flat locally, it is widely expected that KING will go public in a few years in order to raise capital to buy into a major West Coast market,"

David Brewster wrote at the end of 1973. "That would probably end the Bullitt family dominance."

Capital wasn't the only possible reason for going public. Dorothy Bullitt turned eighty in 1972. Under the federal tax laws then in effect, if she died, inheritance taxes on her very large block of stock would have to be paid at once. Since her family didn't have the cash to pay them and couldn't sell the stock on the open market to raise cash, the whole company might have to be sold. Going public would raise enough money to pay the taxes and would create an active market in King Broadcasting stock.

Private investors could bring cash into the company, too. Shortly after King split off its real estate holdings, local business families offered to do just that. But they evidently figured that Dorothy Bullitt and her daughters were so hard up they'd take anything they could get. The local investors offered to buy 51 percent of the company if the Bullitts would guarantee them a profit. The investors would get control without risk. This struck Dorothy Bullitt and her daughters as not only a bad deal but a condescending offer. They declined. They didn't think they were in such desperate straits. When Patsy Collins encountered one of their would-be saviors at a cocktail party, he said, "You need help." She replied, "Not from you."

With company assets no longer tied up in downtown Seattle real estate—or in shaky Far Eastern ventures—King Broadcasting had become a much more attractive investment. Ancil Payne, Payson Hall, and the Bullitt family started talking seriously about selling stock to the public.

With company assets no longer tied up in downtown Seattle real estate—or in shaky Far Eastern ventures—King Broadcasting had become a much more attractive investment. Ancil Payne, Payson Hall, and the Bullitt family started talking seriously about selling stock to the public. In the spring of 1976, the board heard presentations by five underwriting firms. Four of the five recommended going public. They thought King would have a window of opportunity through the middle of 1977. King's board of directors resolved that it was "in the best interests of the corporation to effect a public issue of common stock" and that King's corporate "officers are authorized to take the necessary steps to effect a public issue." The board decided to move toward a $5 million to $6 million stock sale, and to look at three possible investment bankers. Board members were particularly impressed by the head of Kidder Peabody's West Coast operations, Robert Smelick, and they asked Kidder Peabody to develop the idea further.

The company's managers, including Payne, Jay Wright, and Payson Hall, all wanted a public stock offering. The family thought it might want one, too—but for different reasons, and not without reservations. "Harriet and Mother and I thought we needed to go public to avoid a fire sale when Mother died," Collins recalled. "I think the officers wanted to go public to bring more capital into the company." Payne and the company's other managers assumed the company had made a firm decision to go public. But the family assumed no such thing—or, if it had made such an assumption at some point, it quickly reconsidered. Certainly the family viewed a public stock offering as a momentous step. Before the January board meeting, Dorothy Bullitt talked in her office with both her daughters, Payne, Hall, and Willoughby about the idea of a sale. King "has reached the point for which we have striven," she wrote in her journal. "We are in position financially to make a public offering—*if* we want to. We have a decision to make—probably the biggest we have ever made."

The family could make that decision whether management liked it or not: Dorothy Bullitt, Harriet Bullitt, and Patsy Collins still owned virtually all the stock, and if they didn't want King Broadcasting to go public, that would be that.

At more or less the last minute—when Payne and the other managers thought the stock offering was all but a fait accompli—the family dug in its heels. Dorothy Bullitt and her daughters decided they weren't ready to take the company public and give up their ability to choose King's other shareholders. They would have retained a controlling interest in the public company, but they would not have been able to decide who else could own stock. In addition, federal tax laws had changed, allowing inheritance taxes to be paid over a period of years, so there would no longer be a tax problem if Dorothy Bullitt died. The family's main reason for considering a public stock offering had disappeared. The deal was off. (Although, as a result of the discussions, investment banker Bob Smelick joined the King Broadcasting board.) From then on, it was clear that the company would have to raise additional capital by borrowing.

King Broadcasting's ownership stayed the same, but a lot of the company's old, familiar figures were about to disappear. In August 1976, within a week of each other, Henry Owen and Gloria Chandler both died. Owen had officially retired in 1967, but as the administrator who had made King work for its first fifteen years, he was a key figure in company history and he was still important to Dorothy Bullitt. Chandler had been even more important to Dorothy Bullitt as a friend and companion. She had been her ally in the Portland hearing and the company's early source of children's programming; her death hit Dorothy Bullitt hard.

That same year, Bullitt's cousin, Fred Stimson, finally retired. Cousin Fred, who had been the night man at the transmitter, had been receiving one-year exemptions from the company's mandatory retirement policy since the mid-1960s, but now it was finally time for him to stop. Jay Wright formally retired, too, although he continued to work for King as a consultant. The retirement that probably affected more people than any other was that of Peggy Zachary, who had run the coffee shop since the 1950s and had been a central figure at King. The old gang really had gone.

The news staff changed, too. There was always a good deal of turnover, but the key personalities had remained relatively constant for years. Jim Harriott had already left and had been replaced as evening anchor by Mike James. (Don McGaffin and Charles Royer had urged Payne to hire James for the job.) In 1977, Charles Royer decided to run for mayor of Seattle, and the Royer brothers left to launch his political campaign. After winning a difficult battle in the primary, Charles Royer was elected to the first of his three terms as mayor of Seattle.

Near the end of 1977, reporter Julie Blacklow quit, telling *Seattle Post-Intelligencer* television columnist Susan Paynter that "the place is a hassle" and that her reasons for quitting included "the inhuman working hours" and "the time limitations on stories." Paynter reported that "the people who mattered, in her mind, to the creative spirit of the news staff have gone." This did not endear the abrasive Blacklow to King Broadcasting management—a fact that would later have some significance.

Despite the turnover, the place was not exactly going to the dogs. When Royer told McGaffin that he was going to quit, McGaffin asked Payne to hire Bob Simmons, who was then working a couple of days a week for station KABC in Los Angeles. Around three o'clock one afternoon, Simmons was sitting at a typewriter in the KABC newsroom, writing a story for that evening's news, when the telephone rang. It was McGaffin. Would he like to work for KING-TV?

Simmons had been intrigued by KING ever since he had first seen it in 1968, and he knew that it had a reputation as perhaps the best station to work for in the United States. He said yes.

King Broadcasting was sending people and cameras all over. At the beginning of 1977, it opened a Washington, D.C., bureau for all three King stations. In 1979 KING-TV would send Phil Sturholm and Jean Enersen to China. That same year, the station sent reporters to Miami for the start of serial killer Ted Bundy's murder trial. Closer to home, KING-TV covered the *Treasures of Tutankhamen*, an exhibit of ancient Egyptian art that drew more than a million viewers to the Seattle Center in 1978, as well as total eclipse of the sun that could be seen from Washington and Oregon in February 1979. When the Seattle Supersonics won the 1979 National Basketball Association championship, Northwest Mobile TV carried for CBS all the final games played in Seattle.

When Mount St. Helens erupted in 1980, KGW-TV was the first television station in the country to broadcast pictures of the eruption; KING-TV was the first station in Seattle. Volcanic ash descended like drifting snow over much of Eastern Washington. In Spokane, broadcasting equipment was fouled by the ash, and KREM-TV employees had to work in dust masks. The mountain erupted on a Sunday morning, but KING-TV employees converged on the station. Crews from KING and KREM set up shop at Amboy Peak, fifteen miles from the still-erupting mountain. They used remotes from that location and took shots from helicopters. Both stations produced news broadcasts and documentaries, and less than a week after the eruption, KING-TV's weatherman, Jeff Renner, broadcast a Mount St. Helens special. KING-TV's evening news show on the night the mountain erupted was Seattle's highest-rated news show of the spring. Nearly two weeks after the explosion, a TV memo noted that the news department was "just trying to keep up with the mountain" but that "staff morale is very high."

KING-TV had continued hiring people who had never worked in television before. In 1975, independent news and talk radio station KTW-FM went out of business, leaving its employees looking for work. Several wound up at KING-TV. One was Aaron Brown, who joined KING as an assistant assignment editor. Brown wanted to be on the air, but KING management wouldn't let him until he got his college degree. When Brown arrived at KING, he was universally known as "Skip." That didn't sound very authoritative, and before he could become an on-the-air personality, he had to transform himself into "Aaron." The name change must have worked: he became an anchor at KING-TV, switched to KIRO-TV, and wound up in New York as a network anchor with ABC.

Another radio refugee was Greg Palmer, who did not go directly to KING but started an advertising agency in Seattle. Norm Heffron called him out of the blue in 1977 and asked if he'd be interested in the about-to-be-created position of movie critic. He said no. Heffron told him the critic would only have to be on the air for two minutes a day. Not caring much one way or the other, Palmer auditioned and got the job. No one else covered the arts regularly on local television news at that time, so he could make up the job as he went along. Palmer couldn't bring cameras into a scheduled performance of the plays he reviewed, but he got actors onstage during the day and filmed them for the evening news. This obviously took a good deal of the actors' time and effort, so Palmer never asked people to perform part of a play that he was going to pan.

In the late 1970s, King also hired a thirty-five-year-old vice president of the New York–based Bankers Trust Company, Steve Clifford. Clifford was a deputy controller of New York City during its financial crisis of the mid-1970s, and had helped renegotiate and restructure the city's debt. At King, Clifford became vice president for finance and planning.

The nature of news production was changing. In the late 1970s, KING started shooting news footage on tape. The first local station in the country to have a videotape machine in its studio, it was the last station in Seattle to videotape its news.

King provided opportunities for new people to do all kinds of things. In the late 1970s, the company hired a twenty-six-year-old man who had just been freed on a work-release program from the state penitentiary at Walla Walla, where he had served time for burglary. He had learned a trade in the prison print shop, and he worked as a printer at KING. He was not a troublesome employee, although people sometimes remarked on how late he worked and what a flashy car he drove. In late April 1978, the Secret Service arrested him and an accomplice in a parking lot outside a restaurant not far from the station. It turned out he had been working late at KING printing $20 bills. The Secret Service said he had printed more than $15,000 in counterfeit $20 bills and had plans to produce a half million dollars' worth of counterfeit $10 bills. With hindsight, someone should have been curious when he ordered a lot of ink in "currency green."

The 1970s may have represented a high point for television news in general. The entire broadcasting industry was making money.

Although cable TV had started making inroads, the networks still captured virtually all of the national audience. News budgets were fat.

The nature of news production was changing. New "electronic news gathering" technology enabled the image picked up by a camera to be beamed directly to the station, where it could be broadcast live, or recorded directly on tape. In the late 1970s, KING started shooting news footage on tape. The first local station in the country to have a videotape machine in its studio, it was the last station in Seattle to videotape its news. KING-TV news producers had dragged their feet for a number of reasons. They felt that by using up to four projectors at once, they could get effects with film that were impossible with tape. They felt that the edited and scripted stories they did on film were superior to the stand-up on-the-spot reporting to which tape was best adapted.

They also figured that they could use the new technology whenever it was appropriate. But since videotape was used only occasionally, they didn't learn to use it very well. As videotape took over at KING-TV and everywhere else, there was no longer built-in time to write and edit scripts. Reporters started routinely doing ad-libbed stand-up reports from sites at which things might be happening or, more frequently, sites at which things had already or not yet happened. Eventually, people organizing planned events learned to time them so that they could be covered live on regularly scheduled news broadcasts. At first, the events and the news shows were generally out of sync, but KING-TV started doing live reports just like everyone else. Reporter Hal Calbom, who was terrified by the prospect—and the reality—of being on camera live, transferred to public affairs in 1978. (The final straw for Calbom was having to do a live stand-up report while eating piroshki at a Fat Tuesday celebration in Pioneer Square.)

While changes in technology and approach were making news reporting less structured in the 1970s, changes in the competitive environment began to erode broadcast television's position as the only game in town. Cable TV (CATV) wouldn't become an equal competitor until the 1980s, but cable was clearly gaining ground. In 1972, the president of the National Cable Television Association, David H.

Forster, who was in Spokane for a conference at the Ridpath Hotel, told the *Spokesman-Review* that there were already "indications that cable television is moving out of the traditional role of bringing television signals that can't otherwise be received into homes and into total communications." Two years before that, when an NBC executive called Ancil Payne to ask him to serve on the network's affiliate committee, the executive said, "I won't tell them that you own cable."

Even earlier, ambitious cable companies outbid broadcast TV for the right to show old movies. In February 1969, Eric Bremner wrote Jay Wright that a man from Warner Brothers had visited KING-TV and said that "they are receiving innumerable inquiries concerning feature films from CATV systems. Company policy so far has been to sell none. . . . [But the Warner Brothers man] notes the CATVs are offering about three times what they would normally expect to get from a [broadcast] station."

Some broadcasters already saw the new medium as a rival. It was just a matter of time: once enough homes were hooked up to cable, the cable audience would be an irresistible target for independent programming and advertisement. That day was clearly coming. In 1975, an estimated 15 percent of American homes already had cable; a year later, NBC predicted that 30 percent of all American homes would have cable by 1985. For years, King had focused on cable systems only in places called "shadow areas," where the lay of the land interfered with broadcasting signals and cable provided a clearer picture. But any lingering notions that cable was primarily a tool for improving picture quality must have been dispelled no later than 1974, when the Showtime and HBO cable networks both made presentations to King.

The company was still buying up relatively small cable systems. Payne was sometimes frustrated by the slow pace of acquisitions— King Videocable general manager Ed Hewson would not be rushed—but in part, the slow growth reflected the company owners' financial conservatism. Dorothy Bullitt always wanted to avoid debt. She would remind people, "Father used to say that one didn't buy anything until one went to the bank and made sure one had the money to pay for it." Once, when she was asked if being in debt bothered her, she replied, "Oh yes! I can't sleep at night." And King's financial conservatism went beyond a distaste for borrowing: if the company didn't think a property would be worth a lot more money in a relatively few years, it wouldn't invest. Hewson wanted to acquire some larger cable systems, but the company considered them beyond its means.

King started buying up new broadcasting properties, as well as cable. In November 1977, for the first time, it bought broadcast stations outside the Northwest, picking up—in a package deal—radio stations KYA-AM and FM in San Francisco and WRTH-AM in St. Louis. (Actually, the station was located in Wood River, Illinois, just across the Mississippi River from St. Louis.) The St. Louis adventure did not work out well. It took a lot of time to ride herd on an operation in the Midwest. With the two-hour time difference, a King executive who wanted to visit the company's new possession had to blow a whole day getting there. The time difference also made phone communication more difficult than it was on the West Coast. King executives tried to avoid trips to St. Louis. The operation never made money. King unloaded its St. Louis station six years later. And it drew a lesson from the experience: don't buy a broadcasting station that far afield. King's owners passed up opportunities in other parts of the country—including one in Orlando, Florida, that would almost certainly have been very profitable— because the company was not organized to manage a station long-distance and they didn't want to try.

Idaho was a different story. In 1980, Payne got a call from Bob Krueger, who ran the family-owned KTVB-TV in Boise, and who had met Payne while King's president chaired the NBC affiliates committee. Krueger was staying in Seattle at the Olympic Hotel. He wanted to have lunch with Payne. Payne said he wasn't free for lunch, but he could pick up Krueger at the hotel and they could drive around for a while and talk. Krueger said they'd only have to drive around one block; it wouldn't take long. Payne pulled into the hotel's drive-through entrance and picked up Krueger at the curb, and the two men talked as they drove through downtown Seattle. Krueger got right to the point: his mother-in-law, Georgia Davidson, who owned the station, wanted to sell, and since she admired Dorothy Bullitt—for years, they had been the only two women who attended National Association of Broadcasters conventions as station owners—she wanted to sell to King. Payne flew to Boise, pretending that he had to go there on NBC affiliate business, and met secretly with Davidson. It really did seem like a secret meeting: she talked with him in a room with all the drapes pulled. Payne said he was sure she had a price below which she wouldn't go, and it was a fair price; why didn't she just tell him what it was, and King would pay it. She asked for a minute to confer with her financial people. Payne left the room. When he came back, she said $14 million. King's board approved and, more or less overnight, the company owned a network station in Boise. Krueger stayed on as general manager.

By 1980, the national and regional economies had slid into a deep recession, and advertising revenues were down. In August 1980, a KING-TV memo told managers, "Business is lousy. Don't spend unless it is absolutely necessary." The following June, another memo reported that "we have been asked to hold off on capital budget projects until January 1982 because of cash flow."

In fiscal 1979, just before the economy went bad, King committed itself to building programs in Portland and San Francisco and to construction of a new corporate headquarters right behind the old Aurora Avenue building in Seattle.

The old King Broadcasting headquarters were threadbare and cramped. In the spring of 1980, a television memo complained, "[w]e have mice problems in the studios." The former furniture store was an ill-planned warren of hallways and offices. The only available public meeting space except the hallways, where plenty of conversations took place, was the coffee shop. Small and windowless, without any noticeable "decor," the coffee shop formed the social heart of the building.

The newsroom was the building's center of energy. Stuck at the north end of the warehouse-like blue structure, several steps below the floors on which executives worked, the newsroom seemed somehow immune to the technological progress that was transforming the industry. It was jammed full of desks and people, its floor covered with tacky carpeting that had absorbed countless cups of spilled coffee, its air filled with the sound of manual typewriters. There was never enough room. A person would stand up, walk to the videotape machine, walk back, and find some one else sitting at his desk. Late in the day, as deadlines approached, tension rose, and reporters fought over vacant desks. Perhaps as an alternative to physical violence, people swore constantly. One day, with deadlines approaching, Simmons looked up and saw Sturholm and the other "shooters" rushing around to get film ready. Newspapers were piled here and there. Dust lay thick on unused surfaces. In the midst of the chaos someone was practicing putting. Tennis rackets in hand, Don McGaffin and Aaron Brown were batting a shuttlecock back and forth across the newsroom. Simmons thought, "I *love* this place."

In 1979 and 1980, first KING-TV and then KGW-TV was named News Photography Station of the Year. For three straight years, beginning in 1979, KING-TV garnered prestigious awards for journalism and public affairs.

But it couldn't last. The building had long since become an anachronism. Here was a high-profile company with $70 million in annual operating revenues bursting the seams of a drab, grim structure that had outlived its usefulness as a discount furniture store in the 1950s. So King built itself a new corporate headquarters—roomier, airier, and more presentable—a monument to the company's own growing prosperity.

King now owned broadcasting stations in Seattle, Portland, Spokane, Boise, and San Francisco, the largest mobile television production company in the West, and cable systems serving 62,800 customers. Between 1970 and 1980, its assets had tripled in value, from $25 million to $75 million. In fiscal 1981, despite the deep recession, King earned profits of $4.8 million.

And it was winning awards. In 1979 and 1980, first KING-TV and then KGW-TV was named News Photography Station of the Year. For three straight years, beginning in 1979, KING-TV garnered prestigious awards for journalism and public affairs, including a Gabriel Award as the best local television station in the United States. In 1981, Emory Bundy won the Abraham Lincoln Award as the best public affairs director in the country.

The next year, when the respected broadcast journalist and journalism professor Fred W. Friendly delivered the annual Chet Huntley Memorial Lecture at New York University, he said that most "local [television] news ranges from awful to not-so-awful," but that there were "some notable exceptions." One of the notable exceptions he mentioned by name—the only one on the West Coast—was KING-TV.

Dorothy Bullitt herself was very much a presence, perceived as both the gracious hostess who gave King the feel of a family business and the patrician of iron conscience who made reporters feel free to write and say whatever struck them as true. The stories about "Mrs. B" still proliferated.

In the mid-1960s, Dorothy Bullitt had discovered her father's old tugboat, the *Stimson*, rotting at a dock in Lake Union, where it soon sank. She bought the fifty-seven-foot wooden boat and had it raised and completely renovated. Shortly after work on the old tug was complete, a tall-masted sailing ship entered Puget Sound. Phil Sturholm and reporter Al Wallace wanted to go out first thing in the morning to photograph it. Dorothy Bullitt told Wallace they could use the *Stimson*, which was moored in Lake Union. Wallace and Sturholm arrived at the dock before daylight. When they stepped onto the boat in the early morning darkness they found Dorothy Bullitt already on board, waiting to serve them doughnuts and coffee.

When Bob Simmons was new at KING-TV, he satirized the arguments of the people who opposed an initiative that would have required a deposit on every bottle of beer or soft drink sold in the state. (Oregon passed a bottle bill in the mid-1970s, but Washington didn't.) Shortly after Simmons's commentary on the bottle bill, Dorothy Bullitt approached him in the coffee shop and asked him if he knew that her friend, Ned Skinner, was very upset about it. Simmons, panicking, stammered an apology; he hadn't dreamed that the commentary would offend a friend of hers. But Simmons misunderstood. She wasn't angry. She was delighted. "I thought you might like to hit him again," she suggested, and walked away.

Dorothy Bullitt had an easier time with new developments in politics than she did with new developments in popular music. When the chronically troubled KING-AM radio station switched to a Top 40 pop music format, Payne warned all the board members not to listen, but Dorothy Bullitt didn't mind the switch because her grandchildren liked the music. KGW's switch to Top 40—which no one had warned her about—was a different story. One day, she flew to Portland to visit the station. In the taxi she took from the airport, the radio was tuned to raucous popular music. She asked the driver to switch his dial to KGW. He told her that *was* KGW. She was horrified. When she arrived at KGW she demanded a change. The man in charge of radio did as she said. Advertisers, who had bought time on what they assumed would be a Top 40 station, were furious, and many pulled their ads. The change didn't last.

King's new headquarters, with its five-story atrium, its windows, its spaces for different departments, its expanded coffee shop, and its separate executive floor, was more grandiose than anything Dorothy Bullitt had envisioned. At the building's grand opening, she told Charles Royer, by then campaigning for a second term as mayor, and her old friend Frances Owen, still a King board member, "Henry [Owen] and I would *never* have built anything like this!"

She probably wouldn't have. And maybe the current management of King shouldn't have. The new building was arguably a cause and certainly a handy symbol of changes that the company went through around that time.

Departments were separated from each other in a way they never had been before. Management was segregated on the fifth floor. Payne and Bremner kept walking around and talking with people in the halls, but for the first time since Dorothy Bullitt and Henry Owen moved their offices out of the Smith Tower, managers were physically separated from everyone else. Inevitably, there was less casual contact than there had been for most of the previous thirty-five years. The old direct appeals to corporate executives were harder to make. People who ten years or even two years before might have reported to colleagues that "Ancil says" something or other were now likely to report that "management says" or "the fifth floor says." The company had grown less personal.

> *Management was segregated on the fifth floor. Payne and Bremner kept walking around and talking with people in the halls, but for the first time since Dorothy Bullitt and Henry Owen moved their offices out of the Smith Tower, managers were physically separated from everyone else.*

Widening the new gap between employees and managers, Payne started providing all the top managers with company cars. Dorothy Bullitt had been notorious for arriving at work in her old blue Ford, albeit—in her last years—with a chauffeur. Now, King managers drove new Mercedes as a company-paid perk. Steve Clifford, who got one of the new cars, thought it was a terribly divisive step for the company to take—but he didn't refuse his own Mercedes. There was a growing sense that the company was being run for the benefit of its managers.

No one was supposed to smoke in the new building. Ten years later, when it was common to see exiled smokers huddled in doorways outside their places of employment, that would have been expected. At the time, employees who had smoked all their working lives grumbled bitterly. Dorothy Bullitt didn't complain; she simply ignored the new policy. She and her friend John Leffler (who by then had retired as Dean of St. Mark's Episcopal Cathedral and had moved into an office next to hers in the owners' compound that occupied a

In the early 1980s, King Broadcasting moved from the cramped, drab space it had occupied for thirty years. Its sleek new headquarters reflected the corporation's growing prosperity.

corner of the fifth floor) kept the air opaque with their cigarette smoke. The air got so smoky that Patsy Collins, who also had an office in the owners' compound, would step out onto the roof to breathe.

The new building's rather grand entrance opened into a five-story atrium, where a major water sculpture by George Tsutakawa filled a corner opposite the door. King employees gathered in the atrium for the sculpture's grand unveiling. People expected a great gush of water. Instead, a thin, almost imperceptible stream trickled down. Some employees took that as a symbol of the gap between their expectations and their actual experience of the new building. A leak developed in the new roof. Some photographers satirized the sculpture by erecting a column of film cans under the leak and letting the water trickle down. They were told they'd better get rid of that thing. Management seemed to have lost its sense of humor.

Programming had changed, too. After two generations of televising the Seafair hydroplane races, the station simply stopped. Seafair officials decided to give one station exclusive permission to cover the races and to charge for the privilege. KING-TV let someone else do it. On a more substantive level, sales considerations started driving programming decisions.

The company was inevitably growing larger and more institutional and would have continued to do so whether or not it built itself a fancy new headquarters. Payne, who had been active for years in network policymaking and had served as chairman of the network's affiliates committee, seemed to withdraw somewhat from KING-TV. This shouldn't have surprised anyone; Payne was, after all, president of a large and growing company with broadcasting operations in five states. There was no reason why he should focus on KING-TV's day-to-day operations. That employees had come to expect his attention, to assume that he would try to guide every sparrow's fall in Seattle, illustrated how much the company's owners and top management had invested their efforts and emotions in the part, rather than the whole. Nevertheless, people tended to feel that without Payne's everyday presence, management suffered, and the company became less personal.

(By the mid-eighties, key people were gone. Al Wallace died. Phil Sturholm left to become assistant news director of a station in Sacramento. Don McGaffin later left to become a media critic for a station in San Francisco. Within the next couple of years, Emory Bundy and Don LaCombe left, too.)

As Payne stepped back from day-to-day management, the influence of other managers increased. During the 1980s, some of these managers did not treat employees with the kind of respect that had always characterized King. In Dorothy Bullitt's world, everyone, even the lowliest of the help, was treated with respect. Now, some managers would be nice to people above them in the pecking order, nasty to people below. Bremner, who tended to see the best in everyone, had trouble believing that some of these managers really weren't very nice. Payne didn't seem to see it, either.

There were some unfortunate firings. In the spring of 1980, when sportscaster Ray McMackin read about his firing in the newspaper—and then was officially fired by phone—Harriet Bullitt wrote to Payne that "[t]he way Ray McMackin's termination was handled . . . makes me wonder whether this company has gotten so big that all these layers of management have gotten isolated from the top. If we grow so big that managers anywhere down the line can neither learn nor teach the basic principles of how to treat people, especially those who have been with the company for a long time . . . then I want a smaller company. . . . I would rather shrink some of our enterprises than risk getting like the federal government, where people don't care." In another example, sports reporter Elaine Perkins learned she had been fired when she called the company credit union one day and was asked how she expected to pay for her new car, now that she no longer had a job. Her firing became a bitter joke. After that, people would tell each other, "You'd better call the credit union."

———

In the spring of 1981, Don McGaffin and cameraman Randy Partin flew to El Salvador and covered the then-little-noticed civil war between left-wing guerrillas and right-wing armies nominally controlled by the U.S.-aided central government. They were captured by a guerrilla group and held for thirty-six hours. After they convinced the guerrillas that the "Washington" on their driver's licenses and credit cards referred not to the site of CIA headquarters but to the location of Mount St. Helens—which even peasants fighting in the jungle had heard about—their captors grew friendly. The guerrillas even offered to attack government troops so that McGaffin and Partin could get action footage. The KING newsmen declined. Their series, "Poor El Salvador," ran for five straight nights.

During the economic trauma of the early 1980s, the Washington Public Power Supply System (WPPSS, pronounced "whoops"), a consortium of public utilities aided and abetted by the federal Bonneville Power Administration, was failing spectacularly in its attempt to build five nuclear power plants. The WPPSS nuclear scheme didn't take into account the huge drop in demand that followed the energy price increases of the 1970s or the tremendous rise in nuclear plant construction costs, to say nothing of the astounding mismanagement, bungling, and dishonesty that plagued the WPPSS construction effort. In 1982, Plants 4 and 5 were "terminated." The next year, WPPSS defaulted on $2.3 billion worth of municipal bonds, creating the largest municipal default in American history. In the meantime, Congress had passed the Pacific Northwest Electric Power Planning and Conservation Act of 1980, which established a regional power council with the authority to create power plans for the entire Northwest. When WPPSS terminated Plants 4 and 5, the council was putting together its first regional plan. What to do about electricity was perhaps the largest question facing the region.

In 1982, Bundy and the public affairs staff, with Hal Calbom as co-writer and co-host and Don LaCombe as executive producer, put together a special entitled "Electrical Storm." Using a combination of scripted narrative, stand-up interviews, and live audience participation in Seattle, Portland, Boise, and Spokane, the program looked at the WPPSS debacle itself, at the prices of and prospects for other sources of energy, including conservation, and at the ways in which the Columbia River dam system affected salmon. The special won the 1982 Champion Media Award for Economic Understanding in the broadcast category. The judges said it was the best entry received in any category during the entire six-year history of the award.

In 1984, Payne wrote in a memo to KING-TV's station manager that to "a greater degree than most television news organizations, KING feels a responsibility to improve its community and people through news service."

People still felt free to try things that were a little out of the mainstream. Greg Palmer, who stopped reviewing plays in 1983, took a camera crew to Elma, Washington, between Grays Harbor and Olympia, and made a half-hour special on a "Small-Town Saturday Night."

In contrast, television stations around the country cut back on specials, documentaries, and public affairs. Some people have suggested that by the late 1980s, the old, sustained, single-topic network documentary was dead. It was a form that suited King Broadcasting perfectly: serious, informative, good for you. It assumed a duty to inform the public about subjects of consequence and also assumed that the public would have few alternatives to watching. By the mid-1980s, those assumptions had largely disappeared from American television. New York University journalism professor Edwin Diamond has observed in *The Media Show* that the old-school documentary could still be found on public broadcasting channels, but had been replaced on the networks by shorter segments with flashier technique and a focus on scandal and personal concerns, rather than political issues.

Payne kept King doing traditional documentaries—partly, he said, because they were among the things television did best, the things that gave a station its distinctive character. News was still important, too. In 1984, Payne wrote in a memo to KING-TV's station manager that to "a greater degree than most television news organizations, KING feels a responsibility to improve its community and people through news service." Payne wasn't convinced that KING-TV was doing all it could. "While we still focus inordinate attention on free-way accidents, roof fires, barn burnings, and fender bending," he wrote, "we direct neither time nor effort to adequately cover matters of greater importance to our communities." It was even worse on weekends. "[W]e put an overwhelming percentage of our time and attention—I would propose no less than 85 percent—into five days of our production," Payne wrote, "leaving the Saturday and Sunday news broadcasts virtually orphaned. The crew is skeletal, few telephones are manned, one can fire a sixteen-inch cannon through the newsroom at any one time and not strike more than one person. As a consequence, the Saturday and Sunday news reporting is highly predictable: death, fire, destruction, and sports." The weekend news—every bit as bad as Payne suggested—was the wave of the future. Soon—by choice, rather than as a result of short staffing—virtually all local newscasts, including KING-TV's, would be devoted largely to crime, natural disaster, sports, and weather. But for the time being, King was trying—albeit perhaps not as hard as it once did—to be something more. Its news staffs were larger than ever.

The company was still growing. Cable revenues were catching up with radio revenues. Not that King was getting out of radio: in 1983, the company sold its St. Louis radio station, but the board authorized the purchase of a new San Francisco AM radio station, KSFO, the following year (as soon as King could unload its old San Francisco AM station, KYA, which had an inferior signal). In 1986, King bought television station KHNL in Honolulu. The Honolulu station, which had no network affiliation and broadcast in Japanese, was seen strictly as an opportunity to make money. King changed it to an English-language station, tried to build it up as an independent broadcaster, and finally affiliated it with Rupert Murdoch's new Fox network.

The company plunged briefly into cellular phone technology, too. In 1986, King's Washington, D.C., cable lawyer asked if the company would be interested in getting involved with a cable acquisition program. Another client of his, an entrepreneur named George Lindeman, who had already invested in cable television, was starting to buy up cellular phone franchises. Lindeman wanted to hook up with a communications company that was known and respected. King had already made a stab at entering the booming cellular phone business and had concluded that there was no place in it for a small investor; here, dropped in its lap, was a chance to be part of something big. Payne got the board of directors to authorize an investment of $5 million. He and investment banker Robert Smelick worked out a strategy, then Payne flew to New York, talked with Lindeman, and committed King to the cellular phone venture. George Willoughby, by then King Broadcasting's vice president, corporate and legal, became King's representative on the cellular company's board. When Lindeman later wanted to invest in public utilities, King bailed out, pocketing a profit of some $60 million.

In the mid- and late 1980s, KING-TV did more than perhaps any other American television station to cover the final decade of the U.S.S.R. One can find historical roots for this not-obviously logical pairing of a Seattle television station and the Soviet empire: Scott Bullitt's cousin, William C. Bullitt, was the United States' first ambassador to the Soviet Union, opening the nation's embassy in Moscow after Franklin D. Roosevelt recognized the Marxist government in 1933. But in fact, while that historical connection gave a certain resonance to KING's coverage of the U.S.S.R. a half century later, there was no connection.

In 1982, the United States and the Soviet Union were still building foreign policies around their rivalry, President Ronald Reagan was calling the U.S.S.R. "the Evil Empire," Soviet troops were fighting a frustrating war in Afghanistan, and both sides were busily engaged in an arms buildup. "Target Seattle" sponsored a week of educational events about nuclear war. As part of the Target Seattle events, a group of people in Seattle wrote a letter to the people of Tashkent, in Soviet central Asia, about the desirability of not blowing each other up. A Seattle delegation planned to deliver the letter personally. Anne Stadler, who had helped draft the letter and had by that time succeeded Emory Bundy as KING-TV's director of public affairs, wanted to send along a camera crew. Everything seemed all ready to go, but the day before the delegation was to leave, Gosteleradio, the Soviet television agency, sent a telex demanding to see all the film KING-TV shot before the camera crew left the Soviet Union. Soviet officials with whom Stadler later became close told her afterward that the telex was just a negotiating ploy, not an absolute demand. But it seemed absolute at the time. Stadler and KING-TV general manager Sturges Dorrance agreed that under those circumstances, KING-TV couldn't go. The delegation left for Tashkent without a KING-TV camera along.

The next opportunity for KING-TV to visit the Soviet Union arose in 1983 when Mayor Charles Royer scheduled a trip. Jean Enersen was to accompany the mayor's delegation. Stadler planned to try a space bridge, a satellite connection that would enable Enersen to broadcast live from the U.S.S.R. Before the delegation left, however, a Soviet fighter plane shot down unarmed Korean Airlines Flight 007, triggering an international incident. Royer cancelled his trip.

KING's interest in a space bridge came to the attention of the people who produced Phil Donohue's network talk show. In December 1985, KING-TV and Soviet Gosteleradio produced "A Citizens' Summit," in which Donohue and a Soviet television commentator fluent in English, Vladimir Pozner, moderated a two-hour discussion between members of studio audiences in Seattle and Leningrad.

That was followed in May 1986 by three shows in which Pozner came to the KING studios: a discussion with anchors Mike James and Lori Matsukawa, another with Jim Compton and Jean Enersen, and a third with members of the Seattle audience for "A Citizens' Summit."

Stadler felt frustrated by the brevity of discussion on "A Citizens' Summit." No one had time to really develop an idea. She subsequently thought of flying a member of the Seattle audience to Leningrad to visit the family of a Russian audience member, then flying the Russian to America for a reciprocal visit, while KING cameras recorded their conversations and captured details of their daily lives. She set it up with the help of two Gosteleradio producers. An American high school teacher, Ron Morrow, and his wife flew to Leningrad to visit the family of Russian artist Andrei Yakovlev. Seven KING-TV people went along. They tried to capture not only the Russian family's life but also the experience of shooting a film in the U.S.S.R. One wide shot showed Yakovlev and his family at the dinner table in their very small home with a crowd of American and Soviet television people standing behind them.

In February 1987, KING-TV broadcast "Face to Face: U.S./U.S.S.R.," a ninety-minute documentary about the visits of Morrow and Yakovlev and their families. In July, the station broadcast a studio discussion between American and Soviet athletes competing in Seattle.

While the company was doing some of its groundbreaking U.S.S.R. coverage, it was also doing things that suggested—to some of its veteran employees—that it had started changing for the worse.

In October 1985, KING-TV became bitterly divided over a story that the station didn't hesitate to cover. A convicted murderer on work-release from state prison kidnapped ten-year-old Leah Dawn Mauceri in Bellingham, a town ninety miles north of Seattle, and held her for ransom. The Bellingham police launched an investigation and called in the FBI.

FBI agents were talking to each other over clear channels that could be picked up on a police scanner, and a radio reporter who had heard them told KING's night TV assignment editor, Bill Baker, that something was going on. Baker turned on his own police scanners and heard conversations that indicated something was happening in Olympia. He sent a reporter and cameraman to the Olympia area. He also called the FBI. An agent at FBI headquarters told him to stay out of the area in which the FBI was operating. But where was the FBI operating? The agent wouldn't say.

Later, when the voices Baker picked up on the scanner made it clear that something was happening north of Seattle, he sent Julie Blacklow and a cameraman to Mount Vernon. (Blacklow had returned to the station on a part-time basis and had then worked her way back into a full-time reporter's job. Payne and other top managers were less than delighted to see her back. Some co-workers theorized that management appreciated Blacklow's aggressive, cynical attitude when it was directed toward her news sources, but didn't much care for the same attitude when it was directed toward her bosses. But the top managers didn't meddle in hiring at that level, and they were stuck with Blacklow again.)

With Blacklow and her cameraman heading north, Baker heard on his scanner that some people were heading for Stanwood, south of Mount Vernon. He told Blacklow and the cameraman to turn off the freeway at the Stanwood exit. There, they found a parked station wagon bristling with antennas. Blacklow pulled up next to it and asked the men in the front seat if they were from the FBI. They denied it, but not convincingly, and she kept after them. The FBI called Baker and told him to get her out of there. He did. No one at KING had known—nor had any way of knowing—that the Stanwood exit was the meeting place at which the kidnapper had agreed to drop the kidnapped girl. But it was. The moment the KING-TV van disappeared, the kidnapper's car came over the hill.

If the kidnapper had seen a television camera waiting with the FBI, there was no telling what he might have done. As it happened, he didn't see the KING-TV van. While Blacklow's—and other KING-TV reporters'—presence *might* have led to the girl's death, it didn't.

The child wasn't handed over to the FBI at Stanwood. After her stepfather delivered $250,000 in ransom money, she eventually was dropped at St. Peter Hospital in Olympia. The kidnapper was later shot and killed by a Bellingham SWAT team member.

The Bellingham police chief criticized KING-TV for getting in the way. The Whatcom County prosecutor said, "They could have compromised the life of this child to get a scoop." The girl's parents sued KING. The high-minded, community-spirited company of Dorothy Bullitt and Stimson Bullitt and Ancil Payne was suddenly being portrayed as a bunch of irresponsible bottom-feeders, willing to jeopardize a young girl's life to get a tabloid story. Other television stations had stayed away. KING-TV's news director, Don Varyu, initially called the accusations "reprehensible," but later, KING-TV's general manager, Sturges Dorrance, held a news conference at which he and Varyu apologized publicly.

Blacklow, already low on management's list, had been at the center of it all. When management tried to investigate, she allegedly said things she did not say later to the lawyers. Payne thought she should be suspended until the company could figure out what really happened. But in April 1986, Dorrance fired her. Baker, the assignment editor was fired, too.

KING-TV had a perfect right to fire Blacklow, but her union contract specified a firing procedure; Dorrance hadn't followed the process. Blacklow filed a union grievance and, under the contract, the dispute was submitted to arbitration. Essentially everyone in the newsroom rallied around her and was more than willing to testify on her behalf. Not everyone believed that she was right. Not everyone liked her. But the issue seemed bigger than who Blacklow was or what she had or hadn't done. Outsiders had criticized the way KING reporters had covered a story. Management should have pulled the wagons into a circle and stuck up for its own people. Instead, it had apologized publicly for their actions and then turned on them, offering them up as scapegoats to appease the outside critics. At least, that was the way the KING news staff saw it.

Feelings ran high. There were meetings at which people shouted at each other. Some employees were called in individually to hear managers talk about dishonesty.

Blacklow won her arbitration and she was reinstated, continuing at KING until 1992. She also sued the company for damages. (After Payne retired in 1987, the suit was settled out of court. The newsroom threw a victory party.)

The Blacklow incident marked a watershed for KING-TV. For the first time, the station's news staff and management developed an us-versus-them relationship. People did not quit over the incident. Complaints about newsroom morale were nothing new, but this new relationship seemed different. News people felt that perhaps the company's managers and owners no longer trusted them fully.

It was too bad that Payne's tenure at King ended on such a sour note. By any standard, he had been extraordinarily successful. Coming in at a financial nadir and turning the company around was perhaps the least of his accomplishments. The company's slim

> *The Blacklow incident marked a watershed for KING-TV. For the first time, the station's news staff and management developed an us-versus-them relationship.*

profits and actual losses in the late 1960s and early 1970s had, after all, been blamed on Stimson Bullitt's plunges into non-broadcasting fields and his lack of interest in commercial TV. King Broadcasting would probably have turned around under anyone willing to dump the money-losing ventures of the 1960s.

But the company had done more than recover—it had prospered immoderately. To the basic Northwestern triangle of Seattle, Portland, and Spokane, it had added stations in Boise, Honolulu, and San Francisco. The cable operation had more than 90,000 subscribers.

If the company was no longer shaping a new medium as it had been when Dorothy Bullitt, Henry Owen, Otto Brandt, and Lee Schulman were running things, or striking out in daring if unprofitable new directions as it had under Stimson Bullitt, it had attained a remarkably high level of quality. The three Gabriel Awards, the 1974 Peabody, the bushels of other national awards and local Emmies had all been won on Payne's watch. While King had not been immune to the general drift of television news toward shallow sensationalism, it had kept producing local documentaries and pumping money into public affairs after most other companies had decided those were luxuries they no longer cared to afford. Don McGaffin, who spent two decades in television and was never reticent about telling what he considered the truth, thought that Payne was the best broadcasting executive he had ever known.

CHAPTER SEVEN

END GAME
1987–1992

NCIL PAYNE WAS A tough act to follow. The company's man on a white horse for more than a decade, personally larger than life, he would be impossible to replace with someone of equal stature.

By the middle of 1986, knowing that Payne was about to retire, the board started looking for a successor. First the selection committee, which included Patsy Collins, Harriet Bullitt, and Dick Riddell, had to decide whether it wanted to promote someone already working for the company or conduct a national search for someone else. Payne put together a list of outside candidates, but the search committee decided that it made more sense to stick with someone who already knew the company and the region. As Dorothy Bullitt said, "Better the devil you know than the devil you don't."

Many people assumed that there wasn't much to decide. Eric Bremner was the heir apparent. His resume could hardly have been better: honors graduate of the University of Washington, experienced in personnel and promotion, general manager of the stations in

King executives at the time of Ancil Payne's retirement in 1987. LEFT TO RIGHT: James Kime, Steve Clifford, George Willoughby, Ancil Payne, Joe Duffy, Eric Bremner, Ed Hewson, Suzanne Sorkness

Spokane and Seattle, head of KING-TV during its resurgence in the 1970s, vice president in charge of television, chairman of the NBC network affiliates' news committee. He was one of the candidates. Another was George Willoughby, who had been the company counsel since 1974. The third was Steve Clifford, who had been vice president for finance and planning since 1978.

The committee chose Clifford. But it tried to hedge its bets. Committee members knew that he had no experience in broadcasting and was not considered good with people. In fact, he rubbed a lot of people the wrong way. He was a New Yorker, and a lot of people in the Northwest—with its culture of Scandinavian reticence—were put off by his brash style.

He had little patience with some of the social niceties. After he became president, a couple of NBC executives arrived at King Broadcasting headquarters to see him. Ellen Neel, at the reception desk, phoned Clifford to tell him they were there. Tell them how to find his office, Clifford said, and send them up to the fifth floor. Neel was appalled that he wouldn't even meet them at the elevator. She asked him, pointedly, if that wasn't inappropriate. She didn't know how he'd take her assertiveness. He didn't mind at all; after that, their relationship grew closer.

No one on the selection committee was optimistic about Clifford's bedside manner, so when the committee and board chose him as corporate president and CEO, they also chose Bremner—who was terrific with people and had worked in television for almost thirty years—as co-president in charge of broadcasting.

People who had considered Bremner the heir apparent were shocked when the committee picked Clifford. Committee members realized that Clifford would be condemned by some critics as a mere "bean counter." A lot of people also considered him a philistine—this was ironic, since he loved opera and had majored in art history at Columbia. It reflected the fact that he was a bottom-line guy with a less-than-reverent attitude toward KING's news coverage and tradition.

After Payne retired on June 30, 1987, Clifford did not try to emulate him. Payne read the station's on-air editorials; Clifford didn't. Payne's management style was extremely personal; Clifford installed a much more formal—and, necessarily, more bureaucratic, turf-conscious—management structure.

Some people later assumed that Clifford had been hired because the family had already decided to sell the company in 1987 and wanted him to make the balance sheet look good for prospective buyers. Eventually that was what he wound up doing, but it wasn't the original idea. The selection committee asked each candidate a list of questions that included: "What areas of company growth should be given priority?" "Should editorial policy be decided by each station manager?" "To what extent should money be used for personnel motivation?" Committee members were particularly impressed by Clifford's clear sense of where the company should go. No candidate advocated major changes. But Clifford proposed concrete goals and ways of achieving them. That was a major reason why the committee chose him.

For the next couple of years, despite subsequent complaints about corporate penny-pinching, King continued doing some expansive projects. At a time during which television stations across the country were cutting back money for documentaries, Bob Simmons was allowed to make one about the effects of urbanization on the Snoqualmie Valley, east of Seattle—an important local subject but not one calculated to draw a large audience. And KING-TV's public affairs department expanded its coverage of the U.S.S.R. In January 1988, KING-TV broadcast a space bridge discussion between groups of Russian and American teenagers, and in March, KING provided studios and crew for five new discussions conceived by Gosteleradio between Vladimir Pozner and American audiences. The discussions ran on Soviet television that May, right before the Moscow summit meeting between U.S. President Ronald Reagan and Soviet leader Mikhail Gorbachev. Earlier, in April, Jean Enersen had appeared for a full week on the Soviet morning news program "120 Minutes," where she was not allowed to broadcast a story about Soviet soldiers returning from the unpopular war in Afghanistan. All of Enersen's programs also ran on KING-TV news. In December, the hosts of "120 Minutes" visited Seattle, where they did stories for KING news as well as for their own program. Many of the American images that Russians saw during the period of Gorbachev's *glasnost* and *perestroika*, right before the Soviet empire broke up, were images of Seattle.

At around the same time, the company more than doubled its number of cable subscribers. King Videocable was looking for systems in high-income suburbs. It was willing to go outside the West to find them. The system in the Minneapolis suburb of Brooklyn Park looked too attractive to pass up. King acquired its 46,000 subscribers. A company just trying to make its books look good to potential buyers wouldn't have taken on the necessary debt.

Despite the documentaries and the U.S.S.R. coverage and the investments, some people subsequently insisted that King Broadcasting took a turn for the worse as soon as Clifford replaced Payne. Others felt that King had already taken a turn for the worse; people just hadn't been willing to acknowledge it until Payne retired.

Certainly, the financial pressure on American television stations to find the lowest common denominator had increased and showed no sign of abating. Cable had become a serious competitor for audience and for advertising dollars, and a new network was starting to compete for the broadcast audience. By 1986, "cable TV . . . had blossomed into a Goliath," writes Ken Auletta in his book *Three Blind Mice: How the TV Networks Lost Their Way.* "A decade before, cable television reached a paltry 15 percent of American households. By 1985, almost forty million Americans were cable subscribers, and 46.2 percent of all American homes could have a cable hookup if they wished. A viewer at home could choose from as many as fifty-five cable channels, ten pay-cable services, or a variety of independent television stations. . . . In the fall of 1986, Rupert Murdoch would launch the Fox network. . . . That the networks would lose viewers was, no doubt, inevitable."

Network television faced new competition from home movies, too. Auletta writes, "By 1985, VCRs would be in 20 percent of all American homes. Six years later, seven out of ten homes would have one.

"With this variety of viewing choices, network TV viewership had plunged. By 1984, 75 percent of all homes were tuned on a typical evening to one of three networks, down from 92 percent in 1976; over the next seven years this number would slip to 62 percent, and dip below 50 percent on some nights. The networks would lose one of every three viewers."

The networks didn't know what to do. They reacted rather as the complacent Big Three American auto makers had reacted years earlier to Japanese competition.

When the networks did respond to their new environment, they put pressure on their affiliates, and played down the importance of serious news. At an NBC affiliate board meeting in late 1986, affiliate representatives heard NBC chairman Bob Wright refer to news as "a very, very expensive product," writes Auletta. "They heard him say that network news was considered 'a dinosaur.' The fixed costs of the worldwide NBC News operation were $200 million, Wright said, and 'we shouldn't be out there as your partners spending $200 million on something that you think is nice, but not something that we really think is a high priority. . . .' After Wright spoke, Eric Bremner, chairman of the affiliates news committee, rose and urged Wright 'not to take too seriously the publicity that says network news is a dinosaur.' News is what differentiates NBC from cable or Fox. It's 'what makes us what we are,' and 'if you feel we don't recognize that, then I think you need to know how we feel.'"

———

At King Broadcasting, the dual presidency didn't work out as the board had hoped. People still came face-to-face with Clifford's sometimes abrasive manner. Before long, some people felt that Bremner withdrew. Less assertive than Clifford, Bremner approached decision-making very differently—he tended to mull things over; Clifford made snap decisions. As a result, Clifford had often decided to act while Bremner was still thinking about it. Over time, Clifford wound up deciding more and more things, leaving Bremner with less and less. Bremner didn't see his role that way but, like Payne before him, he had become chairman of the NBC affiliates board, spending less time in Seattle.

Payne's retirement had clearly been a watershed for King, but as a symbol, it paled beside Dorothy Bullitt's death on June 27, 1989. There had never been a King Broadcasting Company without her, and her death signaled the end of the old King.

Payne's retirement had clearly been a watershed for King, but as a symbol, it paled beside Dorothy Bullitt's death on June 27, 1989. There had never been a King Broadcasting Company without her, and her death signaled the end of the old King. Or perhaps her passing just put the final seal on the changes that had already transformed the company.

From Dorothy Bullitt's own point of view, the good times had ended nearly thirty years before, when she left the presidency. Although she could only be pleased by her company's success, she had watched King—and television—grow into something she didn't quite recognize. She had always been interested in the future, but in her later years she had not wholeheartedly embraced the advances in communications technology. She never learned how to program a VCR. (This may not have distinguished her from most other Americans, much less most other Americans in their nineties.) She never bought music on CDs. For that matter, she had never bought music on long-playing records—all her records were 78s.

If she wasn't entirely comfortable with the new consumer technologies, she was decidedly uncomfortable with contemporary grammar and usage. Since at least the 1970s, she had criticized the grammar and pronunciation she heard on the air and had recorded the offending language in her journals.

No one should have been surprised to find that Dorothy Bullitt had some reservations about the world of the late-twentieth century. She had, after all, spent her early childhood in the world of the late nineteenth. Once, in the 1980s, a group of people was talking in the King lunchroom about the impact of television on political campaigns. Someone said that the old Rough Rider, Theodore Roosevelt, probably wouldn't have been electable in the modern world because he had a high, squeaky voice. "I don't remember his voice as high and squeaky," said Dorothy Bullitt in her own gravelly tones. Greg Palmer, who was there, was stunned. Here was a woman who had actually *heard* Teddy Roosevelt make a campaign speech from the back of a railroad car in 1904.

Her appearance and manner always reflected the standards of a different time. "She wore good tweed suits and addressed people formally," David Brewster wrote in the *Seattle Weekly* after she died. "When she and Ancil Payne . . . went to lunch, it was always 'Mr. Payne' and 'Mrs. Bullitt.'"

And yet, in the last years of her life, when she talked about King's shortcomings, she didn't complain about the modern lack of formality. The trouble with King, she told Payne, was that "not enough people are having enough fun."

When Dorothy Bullitt died, people tended to remember her less as a businesswoman than as a slightly anachronistic business owner who cared about people and about doing something for her community. "Not so long ago, the board of King Broadcasting discussed the purchase of yet another television station," Charles Royer wrote in the *Seattle Post-Intelligencer*. "The bean counters said, 'this place is a cash register. Low overhead, no news, and just enough public affairs to get by. We run some movies, sell some spots, and count the money.' As they went around the big table, most talked about how nice it would be to have some more cash flow.

"Then it came to Mrs. Bullitt, who said, 'Is that why we are in the business? Cash flow?' The subject was dropped." Royer's story was fiction, but it fit the Dorothy Bullitt legend.

"She said she would prefer these stations to be more like the *New York Times* than the [defunct tabloid] *New York Mirror*," Payne told the *Seattle Times*. "I repeated it a thousand times, I suppose. That was a kind of guiding light that all of us tried to follow."

Dorothy Bullitt really had stood for something. As with all symbols, her significance depended not merely on what she actually did and said but also on how her character and actions were perceived. Nevertheless, she personified for many people both inside and outside the company the best of King Broadcasting. Bremner likened her to the Queen of England.

———

Harriet Bullitt and Patsy Collins never considered a sale when their mother died. They said nothing would change. Payne, for one, didn't believe them and he wasn't the only one who expected them to sell. They clearly weren't having fun. Deciding whether or not to, say, buy another California cable system wasn't their idea of a good time.

If the sisters had been able to influence what went on the air, they might have felt differently, but they had no such influence. They sometimes suggested subjects, but that was about as far as it went. They disapproved of three station managers and pressed Payne and Clifford to fire them, but neither chief executive ever did.

As majority owners, they might, of course, have gone further—except for the contracts they had signed in order to get Payne and

Clifford as CEOs. Phil Sturholm, who had a lot of affection for both of them, said later that "when [Collins] and her sister were on the board at King, she told me they were always being outvoted. If you have 51 percent of the stock you're never outvoted. However, I think she and Harriet tired of the infighting." Beyond that, they could not undermine the authority of the managers they had hired.

Collins's frustration reached a peak in February 1990, when the cast and crew of a KING-TV show called "Evening" flew down to Rio and broadcast for a week from the beach at Copacabana. Collins thought she could figure out better ways to spend $100,000. She called her sister Harriet and asked, wouldn't it be nice if we could spend our own money? Harriet said yes, but how? Patsy replied, sell the company. Harriet asked, do you think we could? They talked about it for half an hour. They were both enthusiastic about the idea.

The first person they told was Steve Clifford. Although people later assumed that they had hired Clifford to sell the company, when they told him that they wanted to sell it, he turned pale.

The decision to sell King wasn't simply an impulse, of course. People had always speculated about how much the company was worth. Clifford had told the sisters a couple of years before that the market was as high as it was likely to get, and that if they wanted to sell, this was the time. They knew that network television faced increasing competition. Cable had started cutting sharply into its advertising revenue in the late 1980s. A lot of people were pessimistic about the future of broadcast TV.

Harriet Bullitt and Patsy Collins also faced the question of Dorothy Bullitt's estate. Most of her King stock had been left to the Bullitt Foundation. Federal tax laws require a nonprofit foundation to give away 5 percent of its assets every year. The Bullitt Foundation's assets included a great deal of stock but relatively little cash. The foundation couldn't sell the stock on the open market. To get cash, it would have to sell stock back to the company. King Broadcasting had enough cash flow to buy the stock, but not the stock of every other shareholder who might want to sell, as it would be legally required to do. In addition, Collins and Bullitt knew the company had to invest in new broadcasting technology, and they didn't want to create a major drain on its resources.

A sale made sense to both the sisters. It would make them very rich, and they felt they could accomplish more by giving money directly to causes they chose personally than by owning a broadcasting company in the economic environment of the 1990s. It would make the Bullitt Foundation very rich, too; once their mother's stock was sold, the foundation would become far and away the largest funder of environmental causes in the Pacific Northwest.

They didn't think Dorothy Bullitt would turn over in her grave. She had not been a sentimental woman. She hadn't hesitated to sell the house in which her first two children had been born. (She did express regrets about parting with the Coliseum Theater, which Stimson Bullitt sold in 1967. When he proposed selling the 1411 Fourth Avenue Building she had inherited from her father, she silently shed a tear, and that was enough to stop the sale. Otherwise, she never spoke a word of regret about selling anything else.)

They knew, of course, that she had wanted them to *want* the company. She had never abandoned her dream of a dynastic corporation. Her daughters, Collins and Bullitt, could conceivably have passed management of the company down to the next generation, but they felt that was out of the question. For one thing, neither they nor their families owned all the stock; they knew that anointing any member of the third generation as the new corporate leader would generate shareholder lawsuits. For another, no one in the next generation had any interest in broadcasting. The sisters never seriously considered handing King over to someone in their children's generation. Family management had ended nineteen years before.

How could it have been otherwise? None of Dorothy Bullitt's grandchildren had been groomed to take over the business; none had acquired even the ad hoc experience that had been thrust upon their parents. The company had never given much serious thought to succession at any level, to preparing a Steve Clifford, for example, by giving him some broadcasting experience before plunging him into the presidency. Nor had the company ever made a serious effort to institutionalize its ideals. Even at the height of King's sometimes-quixotic idealism during the 1960s, managers seldom if ever talked about the content or quality of what went on the air.

After the idea was proposed, Clifford called board member Ancil Payne, who was in London, and asked him to help sell the company. Payne got on a plane to Seattle. Patsy called Bob Smelick, the investment banker, and Dick Riddell, who were also members of King's board.

Smelick flew to Seattle, too. He, Payne, Clifford, Riddell, Collins, and Bullitt sat down to figure out what they should do. That first meeting, Smelick later recalled, was on the level of "gee, maybe we oughta consider selling the company." They all decided to go ahead.

Collins and Bullitt didn't want to sell King Broadcasting Company to just anyone. They wanted a buyer who would maintain high standards. And they

Collins and Bullitt didn't want to sell King Broadcasting Company to just anyone. They wanted a buyer who would maintain high standards. And they wanted someone who would buy the whole company, not just the cable systems or just KING-TV or any other single part.

wanted someone who would buy the whole company, not just the cable systems or just KING-TV or any other single part. There were practical reasons to keep the company together: every time part of the company sold, the proceeds would be treated as taxable income to what remained of the company. The market value of the rest would decline, as would the amount of money that the owners ultimately received.

The sisters had a horror of selling King to an entertainment company such as Disney or Paramount. But they had a legal responsibility to the other shareholders to take the highest offer. They therefore didn't want to publicize the fact that the company was for sale. They kept it a secret.

They didn't think they'd have trouble finding a buyer. They thought it would be as easy as picking up the phone. Payne figured the process would take only around six weeks. And why not? People had always been interested in buying King. Not long before, over lunch with Payne and Clifford, Tom Murphy, head of the huge Capital Cities/ABC media company, had said, "If you ever decide to sell. . . ." Payne had no trouble assembling a list of people who had said similar things. This was a list of *acceptable* buyers; if he had included people to whom Collins and Bullitt wouldn't want to sell, the list would have been longer. Collins, Bullitt, Payne, Smelick, and Riddell all liked the idea of selling King to any of five companies, including the Gannett newspaper chain, the Los Angeles–based Times-Mirror Company—whose president Collins knew—and the Washington Post Company—whose chairman Bullitt knew—all of which had expressed interest.

In the hot market for broadcasting companies that peaked a couple of years before, Smelick figured, they could have essentially auctioned off the company and received around ten serious bids. By the time they made their move, that hot market for broadcasting companies had cooled. Pessimism about the future of network TV was only part of the story. The economic boom of the 1980s had faded. Pressured by the Federal Reserve, banks were no longer lending money for the highly leveraged buyouts of media corporations that had driven prices up a couple of years before. Companies that a few years before had been looking for ways to expand were now looking for ways to cut costs.

The companies at the top of King Broadcasting's list all thought better of it. The Times-Mirror Company had seen its flagship *Los Angeles Times* come under increasing pressure from suburban dailies and had seen the *Times*'s classified advertising revenue drop 12 percent. It wasn't looking for new investments. At the Washington Post Company, chairman Katherine Graham seemed enthusiastic, but she subsequently brought into the negotiations a New York group associated with the billionaire investor Warren Buffett—who was a board member and shareholder of her company, as well as of Capital

Cities/ABC. Buffett's people were skeptical about broadcast television at that particular time, and they weren't about to pay much for King. So it went. Finding a buyer wasn't going to be as easy as Collins and Bullitt had assumed. Broadcasting companies had passed their peak of value.

It wasn't going to be as private, either. After the potential buyers on King's short list said no, there seemed no point in trying to keep the process secret any longer, and there was a real point in letting other potential buyers know the company was for sale. So in August 1990, the sisters held their press conference in the Stimson-Green mansion and announced to the world that King Broadcasting Company was on the market.

Experts quoted in the press sounded skeptical about the company's chances of finding a buyer. "Everyone has rounded up the usual suspects for consideration [as buyers], like NBC and Capital Cities/ABC," an analyst named Bishop Cheen told the *Post Intelligencer*. "But when you start looking closely, they don't really fit. . . . You'd be asking companies to tie up debt at a time when that's a no-no on Wall Street. So when you ask me which company would be a potential buyer . . . I just don't know."

Several companies, including Dorothy Bullitt's old rival for the Portland channel, Westinghouse, were interested. After a lot of preliminary conversation, Smelick announced that anyone who was serious about buying King should fax an offer to his San Francisco office by the following night. He would fly to Seattle with the faxes and meet Collins, Payne, Riddell, and Bullitt at the Rainier Club for dinner, over which they could decide which offer looked best. A snowstorm kept Smelick's plane from landing in Seattle, and the flight was diverted to Spokane. From a pay phone, Smelick called the Rainier Club and described the offers. The formal bids made clear what the group at the Rainier Club already realized: only the Rhode Island–based Providence Journal Company was willing to straightforwardly buy both television and cable and to pay cash.

A family-owned corporation that published the daily *Providence Journal*, King's suitor also owned broadcasting properties. *Forbes* had estimated King's break-up value at $1.5 billion. The Journal Company had made more than half a billion dollars when it sold its cellular telephone systems in the Southeast, and it was looking for places to invest. But the Journal Company wasn't eager to plow all its cash into buying King. It brought in an investment firm, Kelso, as a 50-percent partner. And it was reluctant to offer anything approaching the $110 to $120 a share that the sisters wanted.

In its fax to Smelick, the Journal Company made what he considered a "ridiculous" lowball offer. The East Coast company's negotiators evidently figured that in a bad market for broadcasting properties, King's owners might be willing to take whatever they could get. "My objective was to convince them that wasn't the case," Smelick later explained. The months of negotiation "got down to convincing them we weren't going to sell to them at a stupid price."

King Broadcasting also tried to convince the Providence Journal and Kelso that it was worth the money Smelick and Payne were asking. Although Clifford had not been hired to sell the company, he wound up running a company that was for sale. And once King went on the market, its goals and its sense of the possible really did change.

Even Clifford thought things went downhill. It was inevitable. King had always been a commercial broadcasting company. It did some things better than most of its competitors only because its owners weren't determined to squeeze every last dollar from the operation. The company made lots of money, but the Bullitt family was willing to spend more on public affairs, documentaries, and other commercial nonessentials than most other owners were, so King tended to earn slightly less outrageous profits than many other companies with network affiliates in Top 30 markets.

That was fine for the Bullitts. But a potential buyer wouldn't be looking for a company that kept its costs high and made less money than the competition. To enhance King Broadcasting Company's sales appeal, Clifford would have to keep ratings up and costs down.

Negotiations with the Providence Journal left no doubt that this was true. The company had a good reputation, but it was looking for investments, not opportunities to do good works, and Kelso never pretended to care about anything but profit. At the second meeting, held at the Four Seasons Olympic Hotel, Clifford said frankly that King's cash flow might not meet expectations. Smelick and Payne were surprised. The Providence Journal's negotiators seemed shocked. Clifford's announcement, Smelick thought, "really spooked them." The Journal's negotiators soon announced that if cash flow failed to meet certain targets, the deal was off. Neither Bullitt and Collins nor Clifford wanted the deal to fall through. Smelick and Payne didn't believe the Providence Journal would really walk away, but low cash flows might have driven the price down. From then on, Clifford did whatever it took to hit those cash flow targets. For the first time, making money became King Broadcasting Company's main goal.

KING-TV news became ratings-driven as it had never been before. The new pressure to save money, Clifford felt, provided a good excuse for everyone who had never really wanted to do public affairs to cut back on it. Money for special projects dried up.

The specials on Soviet culture were over. In 1990, athletes from the Soviet Union, the United States, and other nations were scheduled to converge on Seattle for the first American staging of the Goodwill Games. KING-TV was to provide the official coverage. Anne Stadler had planned to take a camera crew to Russia to make programs about Soviet life and culture that could be used as background for the games. She had everything arranged, but the programs were never made. KING-TV's management was no longer interested in making specials.

Hiring an experienced news director named Bob Jordan turned out to be the most divisive move KING-TV made. Jordan was hired from Sacramento in March 1990 by KING-TV general manager Rick Blangiardi, who had come from King's Honolulu station the year before. KING's latest news director soon told the *Post-Intelligencer* that "the ratings are how we make our money in this business—and this is a business."

Everyone who had come in and tried to take control of the newsroom had made enemies. Always somewhat anarchic, after the Julie Blacklow incident, when the news director had sided with management against his reporters and cameramen, the newsroom became almost totally unmanaged. People assigned themselves to stories. The least senior people had to cover the least interesting stories. If no one was interested, something might not be covered. Jordan got the newsroom under control. But he did a lot more than that.

Jordan wrote people such nasty notes that some reporters complained to Mike James, their union representative, who got management to make him stop.

The morning news was accompanied by a woman signing for viewers who couldn't hear. According to one widely repeated story, Jordan saw her on the screen and demanded, "What's *that*?" He was told (inaccurately) that Dorothy Bullitt had started the practice long ago. "Can't you people get it through your heads?" he shouted. "Mrs. Bullitt is *dead*."

Jordan's input went beyond personal style. The whole tone of the news operation changed. For the first time, sales and promotion people sat in on the daily editorial meetings at which news stories were chosen.

Jordan told Simmons that the station would stop developing its own stories and just cover the same things everyone else did because "the viewers don't want to see stories they haven't seen before."

In 1992, a federal judge ruled that Metro, the quasi-governmental agency that managed sewage disposal and transportation in the Seattle area, had violated the Supreme Court's "one-man-one-vote" rule. The second-largest governmental body in the state would have to be combined with King County government. Simmons was assigned to the story. At midmorning, the executive producer told him to drop it because the marketing and sales people didn't think it would attract viewers. Simmons protested that it was an important story. He was told that no one cared.

Collins and Bullitt didn't like what was happening to the station's news coverage and general management. Clifford didn't like it either. But selling the company was now everyone's top priority. Firing a news director or a station manager might send the wrong signal to prospective buyers.

Actually, after a while, the only attractive buyer was the Providence Journal Company. Other potential buyers wanted to cut deals that the Bullitt sisters wouldn't accept. Some were interested in buying the cable systems, but not the broadcasting properties. Others would take KING and KGW but not the stations in Boise or Honolulu. A Hollywood producer wanted an exclusive right to buy the company before he had lined up the financing. A Minneapolis insurance company wanted to exchange stock. Within the company, Jim Compton was approached a couple of times by employees who wanted to buy King through the employee stock ownership plan. Payne urged him not to get involved with any employee buyout. Compton didn't. The public got the impression—and the sisters were glad enough to give the impression—that the owners had sorted through a list of possible purchasers and had chosen the people from Providence. The fact was that they had little choice.

The Journal Company was interested primarily in King's cable systems. It wasn't enthusiastic about the broadcasting stations, although KING-TV was obviously valuable and KGW-TV a solid investment.

When the chairman and the president of the Providence Journal Company flew to Seattle, they met Bullitt and Collins at the Stimson-Green mansion—a site chosen to emphasize the Northwest's history. Smelick and Payne followed up by stressing the company's place in its communities. Smelick kept reminding the people from Providence that KING-TV and KGW-TV were "trophy properties."

The Bullitt sisters and their negotiators tried to sell the people from Providence on the Pacific Northwest. They weren't just marketing a company; they were marketing a region. Unlike Rhode Island, the Northwest was a growth area. On an excursion to the top of the Columbia Center building in Seattle, Smelick gestured to the panorama of city, mountains, and Puget Sound, and told the Providence Journal's president tongue-in-cheek, "All this can be yours."

A number of negotiating sessions ended at drop-dead impasses. The Journal wanted to analyze possible scenarios endlessly. The Kelso negotiator tried to move things along, but Smelick antagonized the

Journal people by urging them to get moving. Payne added some tactical melodramatics: once he stood up, scooped his papers off the desk, stuffed them into his briefcase, and got ready to walk out.

By the end of the negotiations, there was no love lost between Payne and Smelick and the people from Providence. And there was some real anxiety about the Journal's willingness to pay an acceptable price. At one point, after what Smelick described as "one of the many get-lost meetings," Payne, Smelick, Collins, and Bullitt got together at McCormick's Fish House in downtown Seattle and talked about what they'd do if the deal fell through. They might wind up hiring a caretaker management and selling parts of the company—possibly the cable and radio operations—after all.

Eventually, there was a showdown. Would the Providence Journal pay $110 a share or wouldn't it? Would King hold fast to its price? As Smelick explained, "We had to not blink." They didn't.

The final negotiating points were hammered out on a conference call one night when Smelick was in Sun Valley and the Kelso negotiator was at a bridge tournament in Canada.

The deal was on. The market had stabilized somewhat, and in the end, the Journal and Kelso offered $110 a share for everything except the radio stations, which would be sold separately, and Northwest Mobile TV, which would be bought by Clifford and Bremner and run by Clifford. Collins and Bullitt bought the radio stations. They subsequently sold KING-AM. KING-FM over the years had become a profitable classical music station with a format that appealed to a broad classical-music audience, netting about three-quarters of a million dollars each year. The station won a national Marconi Award for broadcasting excellence. Collins and Bullitt eventually donated KING-FM to a coalition of Seattle arts groups. After subtracting King's liabilities, the shareholders would get about $350 million.

On March 1, 1991, in the King Broadcasting headquarters atrium, Collins and Bullitt told the company's Seattle employees that King would be sold to the Providence Journal Company. The negotiations had been a well-kept secret. No one outside an inner circle had known how they were progressing—or with whom. When the

LEFT TO RIGHT: Patsy Bullitt Collins, Harriet Bullitt, and Stimson Bullitt in 1992.

announcement was made, the Journal people were there, sitting on a couch at the back of the podium. They were expecting a hostile reaction. When Collins said that the Journal had bought King, they were pleasantly surprised to hear some King employees cheer and clap. They didn't realize that there had been an office betting pool about the buyer, and the people who were clapping and cheering had just won. Later, Collins, Bullitt, and top Providence Journal executives announced the letter of intent at a press conference in the Stimson-Green mansion.

Several of the sale terms remained to be worked out. The negotiations continued for nearly a year, growing more and more acrimonious. When everything seemed to be settled, the Journal's president called Payne with some afterthoughts. Exasperated, Payne told him not to call again.

Finally, in February 1992, Collins gave a dinner for both companies' top executives and the King board at the Stimson-Green mansion to celebrate closing the sale. A professional clown was on hand to keep the atmosphere light. A full-length portrait of Dorothy

Bullitt, which until that morning had hung in the King headquarters atrium, looked down from a wall.

———

The Providence Journal Company quickly fired general manager Rick Blangiardi. KING-TV's public affairs department was scrapped, a move that put KING-TV squarely in the national mainstream. Virtually no station bothered maintaining a public affairs staff in the 1990s. But for the company Dorothy Bullitt had founded in 1946, the change was significant. Now King Broadcasting Company was going to be managed for the bottom line.

One employee, who had worked for the company on and off since 1966 and took a rather cynical view of its idealistic reputation, felt another difference. The company's old spirit was gone. Without the moral force of family ownership, without knowing that people like Ancil Payne were still up there on the fifth floor, working at King now felt rather like working at Wendy's. When the company was sold, he said, "the life went out of this place."

———

Inevitably, a lot of myths and misconceptions had grown up around King Broadcasting Company. Outsiders tended to believe, virtually to the end, that Dorothy Bullitt was still calling the shots, although she had given up the company's presidency in 1961. They tended to think of King Broadcasting as a crusading liberal company, although they were usually thinking only of its flagship Seattle station, and even there, a lot of the crusading reputation had carried over from Stimson Bullitt's tenure in the 1960s. They tended to identify the company with the family, which was logical enough, but to forget that nonfamily members such as Otto Brandt and Lee Schulman were the ones who had actually made King Broadcasting work.

The company had seen television evolve from a novelty to the nation's main source of information and entertainment. It had helped create a mass national television audience in the 1950s and 1960s and had seen that audience increasingly fragmented by cable channels and new networks in the 1970s and 1980s. Dorothy Bullitt's life had spanned almost the entire period. It had in fact spanned a much longer sweep of history than that: she had lived through not only the arrival of the transcontinental television cable in 1952 but also the arrival of the transcontinental railroad sixty years earlier. She had seen not only the World's Fair of 1962 but also the Alaska-Yukon-Pacific Exposition of 1909. She did not even enter the broadcasting business until she was fifty-four years old.

The company she founded couldn't help being special in some respects. King Broadcasting ran the first television station north of Los Angeles and west of Kansas City, and the people who worked for her in those early years were "inventing television." Experimentation and a feeling of camaraderie were inevitable; Dorothy Bullitt's principles and aspirations were not. There was no reason why her radio and television stations had to do award-winning children's programs or let the "Father of the Hydrogen Bomb" debate an advocate of nuclear disarmament on the air.

It was true that King could afford its bold experiments and high-mindedness and controversial stands because for much of its history, as a broadcasting company that owned a network television affiliate in a major market, it had the proverbial license to print money. Nevertheless, many other companies owned network affiliates in major markets without ever being tempted into bold experiments or high-mindedness or controversial stands. They simply made as much money as they could. King's willingness to try things that antagonized advertisers or wound up losing money reflected the fact that it was a family business, not responsible only to anonymous shareholders, and that the family wanted to accomplish some things that couldn't be measured in dollars and cents. Although Dorothy Bullitt cared deeply about money—even in the early days, her award-winning children's shows and earnest debates on the hydrogen bomb didn't crowd out network schlock or minor-league baseball or professional wrestling— she and her children never insisted on making every possible dime. That made all the difference.

Now, television had grown even less hospitable to serious coverage of news and public affairs. Some people dated that change to the introduction of the remote channel changer. You could no longer afford to tax the viewer's attention span for even a moment. If you did, he or she would just press a button and you'd be gone. Other people dated the change to the introduction of overnight ratings in 1986. Advertisers could see how well you had done last night. Therefore you had to pitch every day's programming to the lowest common denominator.

Less regulation and more competition also contributed to the change. With the easing of FCC control in Ronald Reagan's first term, the growing competition from new networks and cable channels, and the fragmentation of the mass audience, even network television started gearing itself toward short attention spans and tabloid sensibilities. "[I]n the early 1980s," Jonathan Alter wrote in *Newsweek*, Rupert "Murdoch and others discovered tabloid TV, and the loosening of the old network system led to syndicated talk shows. . . . These programs invaded the turf of the supermarket tabloids and made their fare more vivid and central to mass culture. The shows became so pervasive that mainstream news organizations like ABC News . . . began to play catch-up, though with higher standards. . . . Until the 1980s, network news divisions were largely insulated from moneymaking pressures. They were ornaments of respectability useful for status and license renewal. But now the ratings pressure is unrelenting, and the emphasis is on the hot story or interview."

If the Bullitt family was truly committed to running a certain kind of television station, a certain kind of broadcasting empire, then by 1992 it was high time—perhaps a little past time—to get out.

Ironically, the decline of mainstream TV news into a tabloid sensibility coincided with its live broadcasting of major historical events. When the Communist empire collapsed in Eastern Europe, people could sit in their living rooms and watch Germans tearing down the Berlin Wall, watch crowds and tanks in Red Square as a right-wing coup attempt failed just months before the U.S.S.R. broke up. When the United States attacked targets in Iraq during the 1991 Gulf War, they could watch the tapes taken by the jets' gun cameras as rockets and smart bombs homed in on their targets.

That was great television, and people were mesmerized. But more often, viewers were mesmerized by gossip and scandal and routine violence. Before, regulators had insisted on a certain level of public service and certain standards of taste. Broadcast television stations, enjoying their oligopoly, had been under relatively little pressure to push those standards down. By the late 1980s, all that had changed. There was less regulation and more competition—both of which were admirable in the abstract but meant in practice that television stations and networks had both the incentive and the freedom to wallow in sensationalism. People can watch televised congressional debates, but they can also watch TV all day without ever seeing anything that has serious content. They can inhabit separate realities. If the old KING-TV monopoly and the decades of network oligopoly had, in a sense, created a community of information, the new, fragmented medium is creating distinct subcommunities that see and therefore know different kinds of things. "It is as if two societies . . . have come into being in the country," Edwin Diamond has written in the *Media Show*. "Elites tune to an information-rich world; others have an information-poor diet. When that happens in a democratic society, a lot more than a program form becomes endangered."

The traditional networks and stations, still trying to cultivate a mass audience, have been caught in the middle. They have, in many cases, retained their old veneer of staid, serious reporting while dwelling on murders, sex crimes, and natural disasters. "Dressing up sensationalism in respectable clothes . . . sets in motion a media version of Gresham's Law with bad journalism driving good journalism out of circulation," Steve Salerno wrote in the *Wall Street Journal*. "[T]his tactic legitimizes the trivial, sanctifies the obscene, and, via constant repetition, significantly raises the 'cringe threshold,' deadening the impact of things that ought to be abhorrent to us all."

By 1992, it was by no means clear that a broadcaster could afford many ideals. It had been a different time, a different world, in which Dorothy Bullitt, the lumber baron's daughter, had first felt an obligation to raise the cultural level of her community. But she had felt one. In 1962, when KING-TV won a DuPont Award, *Newsweek* reported that the King Broadcasting company's "[c]osts are so high that at least one [King] station each year loses money. 'With a smaller staff, buying films instead of making them ourselves, we could pay the stockholders,' Mrs. Bullitt says. 'But our stockholders would rather have good programming.'" At that time, "the stockholders" largely meant Dorothy Bullitt herself; she still owned some 85 percent of the shares.

Two decades later, when Anne Stadler was KING-TV's director of public affairs, Dorothy Bullitt would periodically call her and invite her upstairs to talk. During one of Stadler's visits, King Broadcasting's founder told this story. David Sarnoff—the man who developed commercial television in this country, who built RCA and NBC, whom she pursued so diligently to get an NBC affiliation—asked her what she wanted out of television.

She told him, "To do community service and to make money."

Sarnoff replied, "You can't do both."

"Well," Dorothy Bullitt told Stadler with shining eyes, "I guess I showed him, didn't I?"

ACKNOWLEDGMENTS

M OST OF MY RESEARCH was based on correspondence, notes and memos, board meeting minutes, financial statements, personnel files, annual reports, and newspaper clipping notebooks from the privately held King Broadcasting Company archives. Thelma Palmer's taped interviews with a number of key people about the company's early days were also particularly helpful.

Much of King Broadcasting Company history resides in people's memories. I am grateful to the following people for their time and knowledge: Bill Baker, Stan Boreson, Eric Bremner, David Brewster, Harriet Bullitt, Stimson Bullitt, Emory Bundy, Peter Bunzel, Steve Clifford, Patsy Collins, Hal Calbom, Enrique Cerna, Jim Compton, Bob Faw, Roger Hagan, Delphine Haley, James Heacock, Ken Hermanson, Alan Honick, David Ishii, Mike James, Al Kaul, John Komen, Don LaCombe, Linda LaCombe, Lana Rae Lenz, Don McGaffin, Ellen Neel, Greg Palmer, Ancil Payne, Dick Riddell,

Bob Royer, Lee Schulman, Bob Simmons, Robert Smelick, Al Smith,
Anne Stadler, Phil Sturholm, Jonathan Whetzel, George Willoughby,
Jay Wright, and Frank Yanigamachi.

INDEX

ABOUT THE AUTHOR

D ANIEL JACK CHASAN is a writer whose articles have appeared in *The New Yorker, Smithsonian,* and *Audubon.* He is the author of ten books, including *The Smithsonian Guides to Natural America: The Pacific Northwest.* He lives with his wife on Vashon Island, Washington.